T0360429

INNOVATIVE INSTITUTIONS, PUBLIC POLICIES AND PRIVATE STRATEGIES FOR AGRO-ENTERPRISE DEVELOPMENT

INNOVATIVE INSTITUTIONS, PUBLIC POLICIES AND PRIVATE STRATEGIES FOR AGRO-ENTERPRISE DEVELOPMENT

Edited by

Ralph D Christy (Cornell University, USA)

Carlos A da Silva (UN Food and Agriculture Organization, Italy)

Nomathemba Mhlanga (UN Food and Agriculture Organization, Italy)

Edward Mabaya (Cornell University, USA)

Krisztina Tihanyi (Market Matters Inc., USA)

Published by

Food and Agriculture Organization of the United Nations and Market Matters Inc. with World Scientific Publishing Co. Pte. Ltd.

 **World Scientific**

Published by

The Food and Agriculture Organization of the United Nations
Viale delle Terme di Caracalla, 00153 Rome, Italy

and

World Scientific Publishing Co. Pte. Ltd.
5 Toh Tuck Link, Singapore 596224
USA office: 27 Warren Street, Suite 401-402, Hackensack, NJ 07601
UK office: 57 Shelton Street, Covent Garden, London WC2H 9HE

Library of Congress Cataloging-in-Publication Data
Christy, Ralph D.
    Innovative institutions, public policies and private strategies for agro-enterprise development / by
Ralph D Christy (Cornell University, USA), Carlos A da Silva (Food and Agriculture Organization,
Italy), Nomathemba Mhlanga (Food and Agriculture Organization, Italy), Krisztina Tihanyi (Market
Matters Inc., USA) & Edward Mabaya (Cornell University, USA).
        pages cm
    Includes bibliographical references.
    ISBN 978-9814596602
    1. Agricultural industries--Developing countries. 2. Produce trade--Developing countries. I. Title.
    HD9018.D44C473 2015
    338.109172'4--dc23

                                                    2014009133

British Library Cataloguing-in-Publication Data
A catalogue record for this book is available from the British Library.

Front Cover image: ©FAO/J. Koelen
Back Cover images: ©FAO/Bay Ismoyo; ©FAO/Alessia Pierdomenico; ©FAO/G. Bizzarri

© FAO, 2015

Printed in Singapore

CONTENTS

PREFACE

In collaboration with the International Association of Agricultural Economists (IAAE), the Food and Agriculture Organization of the United Nations (FAO) and the Cornell International Institute for Food, Agriculture and Development (CIIFAD), Cornell University, organized an international symposium on the topic "Innovative Institutions, Public Policies, and Private Strategies for Inclusive Agro-Enterprise Development," as part of the Triennial Meetings of the IAAE held in Foz do Iguaçu, Brazil, in August 2012.

Agro-enterprises, broadly defined as the businesses related to the agricultural sector, are an important source of employment and income generation in developing countries. Often small in scale, they offer market access to smallholder producers and enhance incomes in both farm and non-farm sectors. Spanning both rural and urban areas, agro-enterprises can be an important element for reducing overall poverty within developing countries, thus contributing to inclusive development.

This book of readings includes the major papers presented at the joint FAO/CIIFAD/Cornell University symposium. They were selected competitively from 180 proposals submitted by scholars, researchers and development practitioners from around the world. The presentations highlighted innovative institutional arrangements, novel analytical methods for analyzing them, and key policy prescriptions for bringing these innovations to scale. The papers examined the influence of markets and the transfer of technology to agro-enterprises on food security, poverty, and economic growth and identified alternative market access strategies for sustainable economic development. It is hoped that the contributions hereby presented will add new knowledge to the consideration of agro-enterprises as a channel to promote inclusive development and economic growth.

The Editors
Ithaca and Rome, November 2013

ABOUT THE EDITORS

Ralph D. Christy, Director, Cornell International Institute for Food, Agriculture, and Development, and Professor, The Dyson School of Applied Economics and Management, Cornell University, Ithaca, New York, USA.

Carlos A. da Silva, Senior Agribusiness Economist, Rural Infrastructure and Agro-Industries Division, Food and Agriculture Organization of the United Nations (FAO), Rome, Italy.

Edward Mabaya, Research Associate, The Dyson School of Applied Economics and Management, and Assistant Director, Cornell International Institute for Food, Agriculture, and Development, Cornell University, Ithaca, New York, USA.

Nomathemba Mhlanga, Agribusiness Economist, Rural Infrastructure and Agro-Industries Division, Food and Agriculture Organization of the United Nations (FAO), Rome, Italy.

Krisztina Tihanyi, Chief Operating Officer, Market Matters, Inc., Ithaca, New York, USA and Visiting Scholar, Institute for African Development and Cornell International Institute for Food, Agriculture, and Development, Cornell University, Ithaca, New York, USA.

ABOUT THE CONTRIBUTORS

Aradhna Aggarwal, Senior Fellow, National Council of Applied Economic Research, Parisila Bhawan, 11 Indraprastha Estate, New Delhi, 110002, India.

Are Ashok Kumar, Senior Scientist, Sorghum Breeding, International Crops Research Institute for the Semi-Arid Tropics (ICRISAT), Patancheru 502324, Andhra Pradesh, India.

Gali Basavaraj, Special Project Scientist (Economics), RP-MIP/DC, International Crops Research Institute for the Semi-Arid Tropics (ICRISAT), Patancheru 502324, Andhra Pradesh, India.

Theresa C. Bushman, Director of Development at Montana Conservation Corps, Bozeman, Montana, USA.

Joyce M. Chitja, Lecturer, African Centre for Food Security, School of Agricultural Sciences and Agribusiness, University of KwaZulu-Natal, Pietermaritzburg, South Africa.

Saikat Datta Mazumdar, Chief Operating Officer, NutriPlus Knowledge Program, International Crops Research Institute for the Semi-Arid Tropics (ICRISAT), Patancheru 502324, Andhra Pradesh, India.

Lithzy Flores, Independent Consultant, Sucre, Bolivia.

Berhanu Gebremedhin, Scientist-Agricultural Economist, International Livestock Research Institute, Addis Ababa, Ethiopia.

Bram Govaerts, Agronomist, International Maize and Wheat Improvement Center (CIMMYT), and Head of CIMMYT's conservation agriculture (CA) Program, Mexico.

Dirk Hoekstra, Project Manager, Improving Productivity and Market Success (IPMS) Project, International Livestock Research Institute, Addis Ababa, Ethiopia.

Sarah Holzapfel, Research Associate and PhD Candidate, Department of Agricultural Economics and Rural Development, Georg-August-Universtät Göttingen, Platz der Göttinger Sieben 5, 37073 Göttingen, Germany.

S.M. Karuppan Chetty, Senior Manager, Agri-Business Incubator Program, International Crops Research Institute for the Semi-Arid Tropics (ICRISAT), Patancheru 502324, Andhra Pradesh, India.

Edward Mabaya, Research Associate, The Dyson School of Applied Economics and Management, and Assistant Director, Cornell International Institute for Food, Agriculture, and Development, Cornell University, Ithaca, New York, USA.

Bart Minten, Senior Research Fellow, International Food Policy Research Institute (IFPRI) and Program Leader of the Ethiopian Strategy Support Program, Addis Ababa, Ethiopia.

Rubén Monasterios, Independent Consultant, La Paz, Bolivia.

Gabriela Monsalvo-Velázquez, Doctoral Student, Centre for Economic, Social, Agricultural Techniques and Global Agro-Industry Research (CIESTAAM), Chapingo University, Mexico.

Artemisa Montes Sylvan, Executive Director of Observatorio Mexicano de la Crisis (Mexican Observatory on Crisis), Mexico.

Sudha Narayanan, Assistant Professor, Indira Gandhi Institute of Development Research (IGIDR), Mumbai, India.

Lulama Ndibongo-Traub, Value-chain and Policy Analyst, Bureau of Food and Agricultural Policy, University of Stellenbosch, Cape Town, South Africa.

Pingali Parthasarathy Rao, Principal Scientist, International Crops Research Institute for the Semi-Arid Tropics (ICRISAT), Patancheru 502324, Andhra Pradesh, India.

Thomas Reardon, Professor at Michigan State University, East Lansing, Michigan, USA; 1000 Talents Program Scholar at Renmin University of China and Honorary Visiting Research Fellow at the International Food Policy Research Institute (IFPRI).

Chintalapani Ravinder Reddy, Senior Scientist — Technology Exchange, International Crops Research Institute for the Semi-Arid Tropics (ICRISAT), Patancheru 502324, Andhra Pradesh, India.

Yerradoddi Ramana Reddy, Visiting Scientist, International Livestock Research Institute (ILRI), Patancheru 502324, Andhra Pradesh, India.

Roberto Rendón-Medel, Centre for Economic, Social, Agricultural Techniques and Global Agro-Industry Research (CIESTAAM) of Autonomous University of Chapingo (UACh), Mexico.

Ricardo Romero-Perezgrovas, Katholieke Universiteit Leuven, Department of Earth and Environmental Sciences, Belgium.

K.M. Singh, Principal Scientist and Head of Division, Indian Council of Agricultural Research (ICAR), Patna, India.

Pinnamaneni Srinivasa Rao, Scientist, Sorghum Breeding, International Crops Research Institute for the Semi-Arid Tropics (ICRISAT), Patancheru 502324, Andhra Pradesh, India.

Rajib Sutradhar, Researcher, Jawaharlal Nehru University, New Delhi, India.

Azage Tegegne, Senior Scientist, International Livestock Research Institute, Addis Ababa, Ethiopia.

Giel Ton, Senior Researcher, Agricultural Economics Research Institute (LEI Wageningen UR), Wageningen University, the Netherlands.

Belum Venkata Subba Reddy, Principal Scientist, Sorghum Breeding, International Crops Research Institute for the Semi-Arid Tropics (ICRISAT), Patancheru 502324, Andhra Pradesh, India.

Meike Wollni, Assistant Professor, Department of Agricultural Economics and Rural Development, Georg-August-Universtät Göttingen, Platz der Göttinger Sieben 5, 37073 Göttingen, Germany.

Evaristo Yana, Independent Consultant, La Paz, Bolivia.

Linda M. Young, Department Head and Associate Professor of the Political Science, Department of Montana State University, USA.

ACKNOWLEDGMENTS

The editors wish to express their great appreciation to the authors who prepared the contributions to this book. We are thankful for their prompt responses to our editorial suggestions and for their commitment to this project.

We also acknowledge the support of the International Association of Agricultural Economists, which assisted in the dissemination of the call for chapter proposals and for including the joint FAO–CIIFAD/ Cornell Symposium in the program of their Triennial International Conference in Brazil. Walt Armbruster, from the IAAE board, is specially thanked for his collaboration with this initiative. We are also grateful to Ronald Ramabulana from the National Agricultural Marketing Council, South Africa, for moderating the presentations and discussions on policy aspects of inclusive agro-enterprise development during the Symposium.

Financial support for the symposium and for this book was provided by the Rural Infrastructure and Agro-Industries Division of the Food and Agriculture Organization of the United Nations (FAO–AGS). We are thankful to Doyle Baker, former Chief, FAO–AGS, for his technical guidance and support in both planning and executing this activity.

Our appreciation is extended to the professionals who facilitated the publication process. We thank Rachel Tucker and Lisa Pace, from FAO's publication unit, for their overall guidance, Henning Pape-Santos, for his editing work and Larissa D'Aquilio, from FAO–AGS, for her assistance and oversight. Last but not least, a thank-you to Dylan Johnson, who has provided important background research on this project.

INTRODUCTION: INNOVATIVE INSTITUTIONS, PUBLIC POLICIES AND PRIVATE STRATEGIES FOR INCLUSIVE AGRO-ENTERPRISE DEVELOPMENT

Ralph D. Christy, Carlos A. da Silva, Nomathemba Mhlanga, Krisztina Tihanyi and Edward Mabaya

The quest for sustainable development has challenged development practitioners and policymakers to shift their thinking from simple pursuit of economic growth to inclusive growth and development, whereby an increase in income and more broadly, improvement in well-being, is accompanied by reduced inequality. Similar thinking has also taken root in business strategy in what has become known as "Creating Shared Value." First coined by Michael Porter and Michael Kramer, shared value is a principle that involves creating economic value in a way that also creates value for society by addressing its needs and challenges (Porter and Kramer, 2006). The approach is thought to bring business and society closer together by enhancing the competitiveness of a company while simultaneously advancing the economic and social conditions in the communities in which the business operates,[1] thus contributing to sustainable development (Porter and Kramer, 2011).

The agricultural sector and its related businesses (agro-enterprises) due to their engagement with the majority of the world's poor, offer a significant opportunity for contributing to inclusive economic development and creating shared value. Indeed, the 2008 World

---

[1] The concept entails more than Corporate Social Responsibility.

Development Report found empirical evidence that GDP growth originating from agriculture is more effective at reducing poverty than growth coming from other economic sectors (World Bank, 2007). Agro-enterprises make important contributions to employment and income generation in developing countries. They have key roles in the production, processing and distribution of food and fiber and are central actors in developing sustainable value chains. Moreover, small-to-medium enterprises, a salient market characteristic of agro-industries in low-income countries, account for a large and growing share of the agricultural sector's value-addition and employment.

The economic performance of agro-enterprises — firm growth, profits, market share, and employment — in no small measure depends on the environment in which they operate. In most developing countries, agro-enterprises, and in particular small-and-medium agro-enterprises (SMAEs), face critical "institutional voids" in terms of capacities, soft infrastructure, finance, market services, access to appropriate technologies, and other requirements — both public and private — that need to be met for those enterprises to be viable and reliable chain partners and to have a positive impact on society overall. To address these challenges, many countries have experimented, tested and implemented innovative approaches and policies aimed at engendering the development of agro-enterprises at all levels and linking them to small-scale producers.

It is against such a background that the Food and Agriculture Organization of the United Nations (FAO) and the Cornell International Institute for Food, Agriculture and Development (CIIFAD) at Cornell University, in collaboration with the International Association of Agricultural Economists (IAAE), organized an international symposium on the topic "Innovative Institutions, Public Policies, and Private Strategies for Inclusive Agro-Enterprise Development." The meeting was organized as part of the technical program of the Triennial Meetings of the IAAE held in Foz do Iguaçu, Brazil, in August 2012. The presentations in the joint FAO–Cornell symposium highlighted innovative institutional arrangements, novel analytical methods for analyzing them, and key policy prescriptions for facilitating inclusive development and bringing these innovations to scale. This book of readings includes the major papers presented at the symposium in the form of chapters.

Through the work of leading scholars, government officials, and development practitioners this book presents innovative approaches and fundamentals that promote inclusive agro-enterprise development by offering a common platform to review and draw lessons from novel international experiences in agro-enterprise development, policies, and support institutions. The papers presented in this volume center on the following topics:

- Business models linking producers and buyers
- Agro-industry clusters, agribusiness incubators, and agro-food parks
- Technical support for small and medium enterprises
- Collective action and producer associations/cooperatives
- Risk management approaches and tools for small-holders
- Incentives for micro and missing-middle investors
- Infrastructure investments to enhance market integration

In search of a conceptual framework — the evolution of economic theory

Over the last half century, economic development theory has evolved steadily, as captured in Figure 1. Further, our understanding of economic development theory has been shaped by economic problems of low-income countries and the policies aimed at altering conditions within those economies. This constant interaction among theory, problems, and policies has offered new insights on the nature and causes of economic problems and policy options for improving them. Over time it has become clear, too, that the very goal of development has changed from increasing GDP to achieving sustainable development. Likewise, the nature of capital once expressed exclusively is physical terms, then later in human capital terms, is now thought to have a social dimension (so-called "social capital").

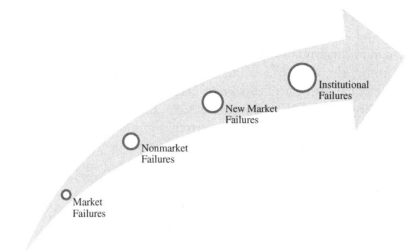

Figure 1.   Evolution of development thought: state and market
Source: Meier and Stiglitz (2001)

Market-led strategies emerged as a central feature of policy-making in developing countries in the 1950s. In the 1950s and 1960s, development problems were thought to be caused by "market failures"; by the 1980's, nonmarket failures (*e.g.*, inefficient government policies) were seen as the problem. Today, institutional failures have been identified as a critical problem to solve if economic development goals are to be attained (Figure 1).

The evolution of economic development theory notwithstanding, many social scientists view economic theories as too limited for analyzing institutional failures in poor countries because these theoretical frameworks purport to seek equilibrium as opposed to explain social change, and the assumptions made by these modes of thought do not always correspond to the realities observed in poor countries. Such people feel that policy analysis of social and economic problems requires knowledge from multiple disciplines besides economics and should include law, sociology, management, and biological sciences. Following this idea, this volume contains contributions from a variety of disciplinary backgrounds, ranging from economics to sociology, agronomy to political science.

Inclusive economic growth: Relevant concepts and theories[2]

A frequently-used concept relevant to this discussion is *pro-poor growth*. The basic definition of pro-poor growth is simply growth that benefits the poor. However, pro-poor growth may be defined in an absolute or a relative sense. In the former, the measurements take into account only the incomes of poor people and measure whether and how fast they are rising. On the other hand, using the relative definition of pro-poor growth means that one measures the rise in poor people's income along with — and against — the income trends of people with higher incomes; here growth is seen as pro-poor if the rate of increase is higher for poor people than it is for those with higher incomes (DFID, 2004). Clearly, a significant difference between the two definitions is that the absolute definition has no way of measuring the level of inequality. In other words, if we are interested in creating a more equitable society it is not enough to increase the incomes of the poor; one must also pay attention to the level of inequality in the society.

Many scholars have attempted to define inclusive economic growth and differentiate it from other measures of well-being. According to Kanbur and Rauniyar (2010), *inclusive economic growth* is generally understood to mean "growth coupled with equal opportunities." Importantly, inclusive growth means that all members of society have equal opportunities (not just the poor) and "all members of a society participate in and contribute to the growth process equally, regardless of their individual circumstances (Kanbur and Rauniyar, 2010, p. 3)."

---

[2] The authors would like to acknowledge the contributions of Dylan Johnson, an undergraduate research assistant at Cornell University, for the original drafting of this section.

The concept of inclusive growth includes economic, social and institutional dimensions. The key drivers of the economic component of are high quality infrastructure and a strong agricultural sector (Kanbur and Rauniyar, 2010). The social dimension addresses the concept of security, with a focus on health as a measure of human welfare, while the institutional dimension deals with political structure and broadening the base of participation in political processes. For example, the measurement of inclusive growth would include assessing literacy rates, and inclusive growth would strive to improve average literacy levels, along with other aspects of development. In this sense, the often-used Human Development Index (HDI) is inadequate for measuring inclusive development since it only uses per capita income and average life expectancy and gives no mention to distributional effects. On the other hand, Kanbur and Rauniyar suggest that the Millenium Development Goals (MDGs) come closer to measuring inclusive growth because they consider both non-income indicators and the distributional aspects (Kanbur and Rauniyar, 2009).

Clearly, as we move from the definitions of pro-poor growth towards inclusive growth, the concepts become more complex, multifaceted, and difficult to measure. At the same time, they reflect a recognition that the quality of human life has multiple components and determinants and a more holistic consideration may be necessary to assess development and progress. Although the chapters in this book do not have quite as lofty goals as this, they approach development challenges from a number of different disciplinary lenses in the process contributing to a growing understanding of development and growth.

Scope and organization of the book

As mentioned earlier, the goal of the symposium — and the resulting book — has been to offer a common platform to review and identify lessons from novel international experiences in agro-enterprise development to inform the agro-enterprise promotion activities of governments and development organizations. Notable in the selection of papers presented at the FAO–Cornell symposium was the growing influence of theoretical contributions from other fields other than economics, such as social psychology, to the understanding of economic decisions and relationships among value chain actors.

This book of readings is organized in four parts — Innovative Institutions; Evaluating the Impacts of Institutions; Scaling Up Innovative Institutions; and Public Policy Implications. Focusing on Innovative Institutions, Part 1 consists of three chapters. In Chapter 1, Chitja and Mabaya analyze institutional models for linking smallholder horticultural farmers to lucrative markets in South Africa using three case studies. In evaluating the alternative approaches, the paper classifies institutional innovations that improve market access for smallholder farmers into two distinct categories — push versus pull strategies — and concludes that success requires a combination of both strategies. Also focusing on the horticultural sector, Kersting and Wollni's study in Chapter 2 reveals differential effects of GlobalGAP certification on net household income and producer prices among small-scale farmers in Thailand depending on their organizational aspects. The authors find that producer-managed groups have realized significantly higher prices and to significantly higher net household incomes from GlobalGAP certification compared to exporter-managed certification groups. Monsalvo-Velazquez and her co-authors review the case of innovation networks applied to conservation agriculture in Bajio-Hub, Mexico and highlights the importance of integrating needs, actions and results through fostering the cooperation of all actors and institutions (public and private) in the network.

In Part 2, which looks at evaluating the impacts of institutions, Narayanan takes a critical view at the different ways in which exclusion can occur in the context of contract farming, an approach often lauded for offering tremendous opportunities to enhance the well-being of resource-poor smallholders in developing countries. Specifically, the study calls attention to spatial factors such as crop characteristics, agro-climatic factors or locational advantages as determinants of farmer participation contract farming schemes. The findings of the study expose shortcomings in public policy interventions that are often designed to address exclusion based on individual famer characteristics over excluded zones due to geographic comparative advantage arising from locational or agro-climatic attributes. In the subsequent chapter, Ton *et al.* revisit the challenges of collective action examining the institutional arrangements or regulations that determine survival of market-oriented farmer groups. The case of social innovation and the move towards a green economy coupled with job creation at the local level in Mexico is presented by the chapter by Montes-Sylvan.

The chapters in Part 3 look at the challenges and opportunities involved in scaling up innovative institutions through the examples of projects. Basavaraj *et al.* highlight the opportunities for agro-enterprise development from sweet sorghum in India. Through the ICRISAT crop improvement and its Agri-business Innovation Platform (AIP) Programs small-scale farmers are experimenting with adding value to sweet sorghum to produce ethanol for fuel, edible syrup for use in the food industry and bagasse for livestock feed. Their preliminary analysis shows potential for economic viability and income diversification. The chapter by Aggarwal evaluates the performance of a food park scheme and two special economic zones in India and identifies challenges in their capacity to generate employment and foster backward and forward linkages with the rest of the economy. Self-determination theory is applied by Young and Bushman to identify and examine success factors for small agricultural producers in meeting the challenges of exporting high value products, focusing on their relationship with intermediaries.

Part 4 considers the equally important dimension of policy. Gebremedhin *et al.* offer insights on how improved institutional support services are used to promote agro-enterprises in Ethiopia, while Ndibongo Traub talks about the role of government in ensuring a level playing field in South Africa's maize milling industry. Finally, Minten *et al.* give an example of the role of government in developing agrifood value chains in India. Using the case of Bihar, Minten and his co-authors document the catalytic effects of market reforms, investment subsidies, and better overall public service provision and governance in increasing and up-scaling the use of modern cold storages for reducing losses in potato value chains.

Inclusive agro-enterprise development is increasingly a theme of relevance within the broader discourse on sustainability issues, in particular with respect to the efforts to mainstream inclusion and to improve policies and institutional frameworks for responsible agricultural development. The experiences and conceptual approaches highlighted in this book add to the growing literature on these themes and should represent a contribution to improve policy and strategy design aiming at agro-based enterprise creation and sustainable growth.

References

Department For International Development (DFID) (2004). What is pro-poor and why do we need to know? *Pro-Poor Growth Briefing Note* 1 (February 2004).

Kanbur R and Rauniyar G (2009) Conceptualizing inclusive development: with applications to rural infrastructure and development assistance. *Journal of the Asia Pacific Economy* 15(4): 437–454.

Kanbur R and Rauniyar G (2010) Inclusive growth and inclusive development: a review and synthesis of Asian Development Bank literature. *Journal of the Asia Pacific Economy* 15(4): 455–469.

Meier GM and Stiglitz JE (2001) *Frontiers of Development Economics; The Future in Perspective*. New York: Oxford University Press.

Porter ME and Kramer MR (2006) Strategy and society. *Harvard Business Review* 84(12): 78–92.

Porter ME and Kramer MR (2011) Creating shared value. *Harvard Business Review* 89(1): 2.

World Bank (2007) World development report 2008: Agriculture for development. Washington DC: The World Bank.

Chapter 1

INSTITUTIONAL INNOVATIONS LINKING SMALL-SCALE FARMERS TO PRODUCE MARKETS IN SOUTH AFRICA

Joyce M. Chitja* and Edward Mabaya[†]

*African Centre for Food Security, School of Agricultural Sciences &
Agribusiness University of Kwazulu-Natal, Pietermaritzburg, South Africa
[†]Charles H. Dyson School of Applied Economics and Management
Cornell University, B75 Mann Library, Ithaca, NY 14853, USA

The importance of linking small-scale farmers to lucrative markets to improve livelihoods and food security in developing countries is well established (Singla *et al.*, 2011). Increased agricultural productivity by small-scale farmers contributes to household food security while marketed surplus sustains livelihoods and contributes to food security in both rural and urban areas. Market access, however, remains a major impediment for most small-scale farmers in developing countries (Chamberlin and Jayne, 2011). Promoting horticultural production and marketing is widely seen as an effective strategy for improving income and nutrition for smallholder farmers with relatively modest investments. The objective of this chapter is to analyze alternative institutional mechanisms that strengthen smallholder horticultural farmers' access to lucrative markets in South Africa.

First, the chapter provides a rationale for intervention within South Africa's food security and development objectives. Against this background, the chapter discusses the socioeconomic, structural and historic challenges faced by small-scale farmers trying to access lucrative markets. Not unique to South Africa, the challenges include low volumes, poor quality, seasonality in supply, poor food safety and traceability, high transportation costs, limited value addition, lack of business culture, poor market information and limited track record. Evaluating solutions, the chapter classifies institutional innovations that improve market access for smallholder farmers into two distinct categories: push versus pull strategies. Focusing primarily on the farmer, push strategies (such as micro finance institutions, collective action, training and extension) primarily seek to address the challenges faced by smallholder farmers at farm-gate level while taking the market as given. By contrast, pull strategies (such as market information systems, contract farming, alternative food networks, fresh produce markets and preferential procurement) focus on creating lucrative opportunities in the market. The chapter maps the market access challenges against the institutional innovation in the South African context.

To illustrate the above, the chapter employs three case studies of institutional innovations — Abalimi Bezekhaya (Western Cape), Umbumbulu Agri-Hub (KwaZulu-Natal) and Westfalia Estate (Limpopo) — each offering alternative business models that link farmers to markets. Using two criteria, rural–urban linkages and uniqueness of mechanism, the cases were chosen to demonstrate different market access strategies that were recently implemented in South Africa. Successful mechanism to sustain smallholder's market access in South Africa requires a combination of both push and pull strategies. This chapter closes with a look at these three peripheral issues that are important to smallholder market access in South Africa.

Introduction

In many developing countries, smallholder fruit and vegetable production has been underestimated and/or not officially recorded because most sales are performed in local markets given the infrastructural, economic and logistical barriers that inhibit its commercialization to larger markets. Promoting horticultural production and marketing is widely seen as an effective strategy for improving the quality of life for smallholder farmers, as it improves both their income and their nutrition with minimal investment. As the increase in production and productivity results in a marketed surplus in some households, government and non-governmental institutions (NGOs) shifted their focus from subsistence to market-oriented production. By increasing access to markets for smallholder farmers, horticultural activities can substantially increase incomes of smallholder farmers.

Like in most developing countries, small-scale farmers in Africa play a key role in national food security. Increased agricultural productivity at the small-scale farmer level contributes to household food security while marketed surplus sustains livelihoods and contributes to food security in both rural and urban areas. Several studies indicate that support for the small-scale farmer should be taken more seriously. The small farmer is poised to play a key role in food production and food security for future populations (IFAD, 2011; Sere, 2010; Wegner and Zwart, 2011). The importance of linking small-scale farmers to lucrative urban markets as a way to improve livelihoods and food security in developing countries is well established (Singla *et al.*, 2011). Several studies show empirical evidence to justify supporting small-scale farmers in value chains under certain conditions including limiting transaction costs and capitalizing on collective action, trust between buyers and sellers (Blandon *et al.*, 2009a; Makhura, 2001; Mkhabela, undated).

Increasingly food sales in developing countries are being delivered by supermarkets to almost 60% of food sales and South Africa has seen a spectacular rise in this trend since 1994, led by Shoprite Supermarkets (Reardon *et al.*, 2003; Traill, 2006). This rise of supermarkets as fresh produce retailers had adverse effects on the traditional fresh produce supply chains and consequently income for small-scale farmers. The rising middle class in South Africa and the almost 60% urbanization of the country positions supermarkets as important stakeholders in the agro-food industry (Louw *et al.*, 2006). On the one hand, the demand for quality and readily accessible fresh produce by the growing urbanized middle class is informed by raised concerns about healthy food fresh produce. Further, there is evidence that among the ultra poor in South Africa food production contributes significantly to household nutrition and food security (Van Averbeke and Khosa, 2009).

Perhaps as testimony to the importance of the topic, much has been published on smallholder market access in South Africa.

Louw *et al.* (2007) use a case study method to explore the options for "Securing small farmer participation in supermarket supply chains in South Africa." Vermeulen *et al.* (2008a), present an overview of "Contracting arrangements in agribusiness procurement practices in South Africa." Magingxa and Kamara (2003) also explored the "Institutional perspectives of enhancing smallholder market access in South Africa." Ortmann and King (2010) provide a comprehensive literature review of the "Research on agri-food supply chains in Southern Africa," which will not be repeated here for brevity. These and other publications have explored the issue of smallholder farmer access to supermarkets from both a public and a private strategy perspective. A key distinction of this chapter is that it looks beyond supermarkets by redefining the goal not as 'access to supermarket chains' but 'access to lucrative markets.' Another distinction of the paper is its deliberate effort to delineate both the problems and solutions for this issue, as opposed to an aggregated approach used in most papers on the topic. Much of the research is anchored on the exploration of the challenge or institutional arrangements relating to smallholder market access. Thus, a key marginal contribution of this paper is to take a broad look at all the challenges and juxtapose them to the available institutional innovations.

The objective of this chapter is to unpack the challenges and institutional innovations relating to smallholder produce farmers' access to markets in South Africa. The chapter is structured as follows. First, a rationale for intervention is provided. Second, the chapter classifies the myriad of challenges facing small-scale farmers followed by the tools or institutional innovations available to address them. These mechanisms are mirrored on three cases of small-scale market access models operating in South Africa.

The Challenge

An underlying premise of this chapter is that small-scale farmers growing fresh produce are interested in maximizing their income by fetching higher prices, both in the short and long run, for their produce. The increasing population in urban areas, coupled with higher penetration of supermarkets and other formal retail outlets in

South Africa presents an opportunity for year round market outlet for fresh produce. To date, however, the participation of small-scale farmers and emerging back farmers in these lucrative value chains has been limited. The rise of supermarkets favors the growth of formal markets at the expense of traditional or informal markets. For example, the increasing demand for convenience foods, fueled by increased female employment and new cooking technologies such as the microwave, can lock out smallholder farmers who lack the capacity to process, package and label their produce. Similarly, the increasing demand for traceability and food safety concerns increase the share of food marketed through formal channels.

Policy imperatives that seek to improve market access for small-scale farmers are important. In South Africa, the Agricultural Black Economic Empowerment (AgriBEE) policy was formulated to guide black economic empowerment within the agricultural sector toward equitable access and inclusive participation in line with the broad based black economic empowerment across all sectors in the country (NDA, 2004). The policy incentivizes preferential procurement from historically disadvantaged groups black farmers. According to Mukumbi (2008), AgriBEE may have a positive effect on some players in the supply chain, but Mukumbi warns that incentives for preferential procurement from small-scale farmers need to be strengthened. Work by Blandon *et al.* (2009a) on farmer's preferences in types of markets further indicated the need for flexibility of new market entrant farmers. This is critical for small-scale farmers due to the dynamic interaction between the household and the farming enterprise in Africa.

In South Africa, the focus on the small-scale farmer is underpinned by a stark reality of very high poverty levels (both rural and urban) despite the growth experienced by the country. South Africa remains one of the most unequal societies in the world (World Bank, 2010). The largely jobless growth experienced by South Africa has yielded very little for the poor, especially those in rural areas (Bhorat and Westhuizen, 2005). With good support, agriculture promises to avail an opportunity for the poor to drive themselves out of deep poverty by providing food for their households and selling their surplus. Markets are important to farmers because they afford them an income for their produce. Markets also encourage investment in the farming enterprises when they are clear about future income and are assured an ability to pay off debt. There is evidence that investment in agriculture is also good in increasing the speed of land reform by consolidating land reform. It is therefore critical that there be focused interventions by government and other stakeholders to ensure that growth in this sector is pro-poor to bridge the income disparities in South African.

This chapter is premised on the need for small-scale farmers to achieve sustained access to markets to break out of poverty and achieve food security. Small-scale farmer constraints to market access have been well documented and they include those of a technical (including agronomic and agro-ecological), institutional and economical nature. Solving these challenges should therefore improve market access for small-scale farmers.

On the consumption end, fruits and vegetables are a necessary component of any balanced diet supplying, among other nutrients, vitamins A and C. South Africa's staple food is *pup*, a thick porridge made from maize meal. This mainly carbohydrate food is usually taken with stewed meat, boiled leafy vegetables, milk or beans. Because of the high price of meat, milk and beans in urban areas, most low-to-middle income families are heavy consumers of vegetables. In addition, the high incidence of HIV and AIDS in South Africa is an important reason for poor households to access fresh and nutritious food (du Plessis and Lekganyane, 2010). Stable supply of vegetables and fruits at affordable prices is thus crucial for food security especially in low-income urban households. However, because of the inherent characteristics of horticultural crops — high perishability, quality variability and seasonality in production — coordination of production and consumption is essential for improving economic performance of produce markets in South Africa.

Challenges in Accessing Markets

From the perspective of small-scale farmers growing fruits and vegetables in rural and peri-urban areas, this section discusses the socioeconomic, structural and historic challenges faced in trying to access lucrative markets. These challenges are widely recognized in South Africa and other developing countries, but they are often lumped together such that symptoms are not separate from the underlying economic problems.

Low volumes: To minimize transaction costs, most formal retail outlets prefer to source their produce from a small number of suppliers. The use of centralized procurement and distribution warehouse, a model used by most retail chain stores, favors producers that can deliver large volumes. Containerization, a system of freight transport based on steel intermodal containers, also favors shipments of at least 20 metric tons. Those volumes are much higher than the amounts produced by individual smallholder farmers whose consignments are often less than 1 ton. By implication, the low volumes of produce from smallholder farmers result in high transaction costs in the consolidation mechanisms that are necessary in commercializing sales into most formal markets (Anseeuw *et al.*, 2000; Randela *et al.*, 2008).

Inferior and inconsistent quality: As long as urban consumers are willing to pay high premium for near-perfect produce, retailers will continue to demand grade A produce from their suppliers. This quality pressure favors commercial farmers, which usually have a higher percentage of grade A produce due to better husbandry techniques and higher use of purchased inputs. Lack of knowledge about grades and standards also results in sub-optimal harvesting techniques by small-scale farmers. For example, a ready-to-eat ripe and red tomato would be considered top grade in rural areas, whereas the same tomato would be rated as grade B in supermarkets where firmer and slightly ripe tomatoes are preferred. Similarly for avocadoes, large fruit size, which fetches premium in rural markets, often leads to downgrading in supermarkets. Louw *et al.* (2008) conclude that stringent requirements on product quality, safety and volume by South Africa supermarkets are a key barrier to entry for smallholder farmers.

Seasonal supply: Retailers and processors prefer to work with suppliers that can guarantee year round supply of a fresh produce. As with high volumes, year round supply reduces transaction costs throughout the supply chain. For most small-scale farmers who rely on rainfed agriculture, produce supply is highly seasonal and susceptible to adverse weather conditions. Commercial growers on the other hand have made investments in technologies such as irrigation systems and greenhouses that ensure year round supply if needed. Most of such technologies are scale biased for intensive production systems.

Costly transportation: Due to the high perishability and high volume, low value nature of fruits and vegetables, transportation is critical to linking fresh produce producers to markets. For highly perishable products such as leafy greens and strawberries, refrigerated trucks (cold supply chain) may be required to minimize postharvest losses. While South Africa has a relatively well-developed road infrastructure, the vehicles serving remote rural areas are generally suited for commuters and the options for ferrying produce are limited and costly. A study by Matungul *et al.* (2001) on market constraints faced by small-scale farmers in KwaZulu-Natal identifies costly transportation as one of several impediments.

Limited value addition: Increasingly urban consumers are looking for value added convenience when they buy fruits and vegetables. The offerings in most retail outlets now include ready-to-eat products that are washed, cut, peeled, mixed and packaged for ease of use. Consequently, the value contribution of the fruit or vegetable, as a percentage of final selling price, continues to shrink. While much of the value addition takes place in pack houses, there is significant vertical integration through market contracts, strategic alliances, and franchises among commercial producers, pack houses and retail outlets (Louw *et al.*, 2008). Suppliers with facilities to value add at farm gate have a comparative advantage when negotiating contracts with buyers. Note that much of the value adding also requires high standards of food safety and handling.

Lack of business culture: To sell produce at wholesale level often requires the producer to be legally incorporated as either a private business or cooperative. Payment systems require invoicing, bank accounts and tax compliance, which often are outside the realm of most small-scale farmers. Even in cases where farmers are organized into groups or established enough to have the requisite business infrastructure, the soft skills of business management and client engagement are often lacking. Farmers who are accustomed to spot markets in which they are paid cash upon delivery are often disappointed by the payment terms of most institutional buyers that can take up to three months to process (Louw *et al.*, 2006).

Poor market information: A study of household characteristics in two rural areas of KwaZulu-Natal conducted by Matungul *et al.* (2001) found that most households lacked market information. While modern information and communication technologies such as mobile phones have vastly improved accessibility of market information in rural areas, there are still some gaps that warrant attention. First, while small-scale farmers may be aware of the daily prices offered in the markets, they may still lack the strategic information about long-term trends and emerging opportunities. Further, specific information such as procurement strategies and requirements by each retail chain or institutional buyer is generally not available to the public. Where available, extension service personnel generally have limited market intelligence and orientation.

Limited track record: Most business linkages between commercial farmers, pack houses and retailers in South Africa have been in place for many years. As supermarkets increased their coverage, their suppliers often grew with them building on existing relationships. The social capital that has developed over the decades between large-scale buyers and sellers of fresh produce can act as a barrier to entry for emerging and small-scale farmers. Barring any malicious intentions on the part of buyers, the sunk costs related to past relationships favor continuing partnerships with historical suppliers as opposed to exploring new deals with emerging farmers. Most retailers in South Africa greatly value continuity of service, which they often secure through long-term (3 to 10 years) agreements or 'commitments to purchase' with farmers (Vermeulen *et al.*, 2008a). Trust, often earned over long periods of business partnerships, has been shown to be a requisite in successful long-term commitments along the South African value chain (Masaku *et al.*, 2004).

Institutional Innovations

Push strategies

It is useful to classify institutional innovations that improve market access by smallholder farmers into two categories, namely, push and pull strategies. By focusing primarily on the farmer, push strategies primarily seek to address the challenges faced by smallholder farmers at farm-gate level while taking the market as given. Implicit in push strategies is the assumption that if only we can get smallholder farmers to operate more like their commercial counterparts, the issues of market access would be addressed.

Microfinance institutions (MFIs): Microfinance is the provision of financial services to low-income clients who would otherwise lack access to banking and related services. Applied to rural farming communities, microfinance can alleviate some of the investment-related market access challenges. With access to finance, small-scale farmers can increase the volumes of produce, use irrigation facilities to produce year round, access a wider range of transportation options and engage in some basic value adding at farm gate. While South Africa has numerous MFIs that "straddle the country's formal and informal sectors," the pro-poor MFIs are mainly rural but their clients are not agricultural microenterprises (Baumann, 2004).

Collective action: Defined as "voluntary action taken by a group to achieve common interest" (Meinzen-Dick *et al.*, 2004), collective action is often seen as a key factor in enhancing smallholder farmers' access to lucrative markets. The establishment of farmer cooperatives as an institutional remedy for agricultural market failures has been an accepted policy alternative for most countries. Scarcely a nation in the world is without a "cooperative" organization. Socialist or capitalist, industrialized or developing, all countries claim them, and most countries nurture them. Many governments grant cooperatives special legal privileges, lines of credit, and public technical and sometimes promotional support. Within many a country's rural development policies cooperatives are the instruments of economic reform. Notwithstanding this broad support, the record of cooperative accomplishment appears to be mixed. As in other parts of the world, successful collectives among smallholder farmers in South Africa depend on good institutional arrangements and governance (Chibanda *et al.*, 2009).

Training and extension: Agricultural extension services have long been used to enhance farm productivity through the dissemination of good crop and animal husbandry and appropriate technologies. Since most smallholder farmers in South Africa cannot afford to pay for private extension services, the government, through the provincial Department of Agriculture, Forestry and Fisheries, is the main provider of public extension support services. In addition to traditional topics of crop husbandry that can address poor produce quality and out of season production, extension and training services can address market access-related issues such a product traceability, food safety, value addition and business training. These market driven extension services may take a while to develop in South Africa as most of the provinces are still struggling to cope with the challenges of reorienting their systems to meet the needs of smallholder farmers (Ngomane *et al.*, 2002). NGOs and private sector (agribusiness) are stepping in to fill some of the shortcomings in quality and effectiveness of public extension services.

Pull strategies

By contrast, pull strategies for smallholder market access focus on creating a pull in the marketplace for smallholder produce using demand driven tactics. By creating lucrative opportunities in the market, pull strategies are premised on the assumption that smallholder farmers can respond to market incentives. In other words, the problem has to be addressed in the market beyond the farm-gate.

Alternative food networks (AFNs): Instead of focusing on the barriers to entry and exit in mainstream outlets such as big name food processors and retailers, small-scale farmers can explore ways to bypass the intermediaries by establishing direct linkages to consumers. AFNs are loosely defined as systems of food production, distribution and consumption that are based on a close connection between producers and consumers to enhance value for both (Whatmore and Thorne, 1997). Also known as short food supply chains, such networks are often framed as a departure from the industrialized food value chain with 'food quality,' value chain transparency and 'locality' as key areas of distinction (Sonnino and Marsden, 2006). Key examples of AFNs include farmers' markets, community supported agriculture, on farm sales, buy local movements, urban food gardens, Fair Trade, and the Slow food movement. As high-income consumers increasingly value foods with an ethical story, smallholder farmers can supply these highly lucrative niche markets. While AFNs are growing in popularity in Europe and the United States, the trend in developing countries in relatively under-researched. Ortmann and King (2010) point out that "anecdotal evidence suggests that farmers' markets have been established in many urban areas and have become popular shopping destinations for many consumers." The South African food blog "Food with a Story" (http://www.foodwithastory.co.za/) is a manifestation of this growing interest in AFNs and highlights several examples of participation by smallholder farmers. Evidence of scalability of AFNs, both in South Africa and around the world, is, however, still sketchy at best.

Market information systems: The widespread use of information and communication technologies in developing counties over the last two decades has vastly reduced market inefficiencies that were due to limited or asymmetric information. The Kenyan Agricultural Commodity Exchange (KACE), for example, uses short messaging system (SMS) to provide real-time market information on prices in different markets of different commodities on a daily basis (Karugu, 2011). KACE also links farmers to one another by acting as a clearinghouse and/or facilitator of logistical and financial implications of a sale. Smallholders in South Africa lack such a body that could improve their bargaining power.

Contract farming: Defined as farming with pre-agreed terms of the purchase, contract farming has long been used as a means of vertical coordination especially among farmers, processors and retailers.

For highly perishable fruits and vegetables, contractual agreements can significantly reduce transaction costs as well as risks throughout the value chain (Eaton and Shepherd, 2001). While most major retailers in South Africa do not openly admit to procurement through contract farming, "all of them do issue 'growing programs' to the growers as a mechanism to coordinate volume and quality of supply" (Vermeulen *et al.*, 2008a). The same study estimates that about 80% of all fruits and vegetables (volume measures) processed in South Africa is procured through contracts. For smallholder farmers, contract farming is often manifested through out-grower schemes wherein the government, a commercial farmer or a private firm provides production and/or marketing services.

Preferential procurement: The AgriBEE scorecard gives a 20% weight for preferential procurement defined as procurement from black-owned and empowered enterprises as a proportion of total procurement. Thus, the charter provides incentives to private retailers and processors to offer preferential procurement of fruit and vegetables from historically disadvantages groups including smallholder farmers. Similarly, government institutions such as schools, prisons and hospitals are encouraged to buy from black-owned farms in sourcing fruits and vegetables in their feeding programs. Smallholder farmers can therefore compensate for their associated risks (lacking a track record) and higher transaction costs by qualifying their buyers. It is important to note, however, that this policy equally favors both small-scale and large commercial farms as long as they are black owned. As the number of large-scale commercial producers of fruits and vegetables increases, benefits to smallholder farmers from the policy instrument are likely to diminish. Table 1 shows the primary and secondary functions of the different institutional innovation that seek to address market access by smallholder farmers.

Selected Cases in South Africa

To highlight institutional innovations addressing market access by smallholder farmers in South Africa, three different cases were

Table 1:   Challenges to small-scale market access and institutional innovations for fresh produce in South Africa

Challenges/Institutional Innovations	Push Strategies					Pull Strategies			
	Micro Finance Institutions	Collective Action	Training and Extension	Market Information Systems	Contract Farming	Alternative Food Networks	Fresh Produce Markets	Preferential Procurement
Small volumes	X	XX			XX			
Poor quality		XX						
Seasonality in supply	X	X	X	XX		X	X	
Food safety and traceability	X	XX	X					
Transportation costs	XX				XX	XX		
Limited value addition	XX		XX		X	XX	XX	
Lack of business culture		X			X			
Poor market information				X	X			X
Limited track record						XX	XX	XX

Keys: XX = primary function; X = secondary function.

chosen: Abalimi Bezekhaya in Western Cape, Umbumbulu Agri-Hub in KwaZulu-Natal and Westfalia Estate in Limpopo. The three cases were selected to demonstrate alternative access strategies in South Africa by small-scale farmers in accessing the markets. In the proceeding sub-sections, the three cases are described to illustrate the different challenges faced and solutions offered. Furthermore the profiles explore the organizational structures of each institutional arrangement and delve into why they have succeeded despite the longstanding challenges.

Abalimi Bezekhaya, Western Cape

Abalimi Bezekhaya, hereafter referred to simply as Abalimi, was formed in 1982. The name of this non-profit organization means

"Planters of the Home" in isiXhosa. It is located in the poor urban Townships of Cape Town in Khayelitsha and Nyanga (Kirkland, 2008). The mission of Abalimi is to improve sustainable food production and foster environmental renewal amongst the poor in Cape Town through focusing on skills development.

The organization offers technical and marketing support to the community on its home gardens, community gardens and council owned land including school land (Kirkland, 2008). The main players of Abalimi are women although it targets all poor people. In practice women, and even older women (grandmothers), are faced with the household's daily survival (Kirkland, 2008). Abalimi provides concerted support in several areas including project implementation; resource supply; training; community building; partnerships and networking; research and development, monitoring and evaluation; organizations and financial sustainability. Now that government agencies are also focused on project implementation and resource supply, Abalimi focuses its energy on training. Abalimi has been able to take the small-scale growers that it works with through the four main phases of survival, subsistence, livelihood and finally commercialization, whereby households grow the majority of their produce for the market on plots measuring at least 50 square meters (Kirkland, 2008).

The main marketing operations of Abalimi are conducted through a marketing initiative called Harvest of Hope in recognition that fragmented marketing of the urban food projects in the Cape Town townships of Khayelitsha and Nyanga that Abalimi was involved with required co-ordination (Kirkland, 2008). Harvest of Hope markets organic vegetables in boxes on a weekly basis to residents in the Cape Town metropolitan areas using primary schools as delivery points. Customers sign up to the box scheme with Abalimi and receive vegetables on a weekly basis. Abalimi is responsible for managing the income and making payments to growers on a monthly basis.

In Abalimi's system, buyers subscribe and pay for future produce to be collected weekly at specified points. Producers are trained and technically supported, which ensures consistent quality and organic standards. Abalimi's subsidiary Harvest of Hope handles the value addition, including transportation and packaging. Over the past

20 years and through the continuous technical support to producers, a business culture and commercial outlook has developed among smallholders and each grower has built a well-known track record with Harvest of Hope. The buyers of Abalimi products are upmarket clientele motivated by principles and ethos related to health, environment and social concerns rendering Abalimi an AFN. Abalimi producers have been successful in supplying this niche market without much competition from larger producers.

Abalimi focuses largely on training its growers in specific production methods that appeal to their niche market, *i.e.*, organic and locally produced food. The growers have progressed from subsistence to commercial focus despite the relatively small sizes of their land thus providing an income to their households. Abalimi is a good example of using a mix of push and pull strategies albeit at a small scale and supporting small growers along the phases from subsistence to commercial focus. From an institutional point of view Abalimi has strong and well-established operations (over 20 years). The system is open to all township dwellers but training by Abalimi is a prerequisite to ensure production principles. Furthermore, Abalimi is built on mutual trust and no formal contracts are in place, an important market entry characteristic for smallholder market participation enabler.

Umbumbulu Agri-Hub, KwaZulu-Natal

The Umbumbulu rural area is located almost 50 km from Pietermaritzburg and forms part of Durban's Ethekwini Municipality's rural metro. This rural valley is the home of rural households of low socio-economic status. Ethekwini Municipality's focus on agricultural development in its rural metro areas has contributed financially to the establishment of a fresh vegetable value chain in 2009, uniting many backyard and small-scale farmers in supplying a cold house located in the area. The project is named the Umbumbulu AgriHub (UAH).

UAH operations are grounded in encouraging own production of locally grown food using ecologically sound principles (Paula, 2011). The organization provides technical services to farmers to ensure adherence to production standards and quality of produce, ensuring that farmers join the organization when standards have been verified. The UAH subscribes to the open resourcing strategy to meet its capacity needs thus reducing costs. Currently UAH has over 150 registered farmers but only 25 to 50 are able to supply the UAH cold room with surplus produce to be sold. The rest of the farmers grow for subsistence, but the number of those selling their produce is growing as evidenced by the growing earned income of selling farmers.

Located in a rural area where producers have poor track record of market participation, UAH has been able to attract committed producers to supply its pack house with quality produce. At the pack house value addition occurs through washing and packaging before transportation to urban customers of specialized stores and a larger fresh produce market in the Durban city center. Originally the primary role of UAH was to encourage households to grow their own food to meet food security and nutritional needs, but those growing a surplus where encouraged to supply the UAH. Although relatively new (less than 3 years in operation), the UAH model showcases how rural producers can produce quality produce that meets market requirement. The open system allows ease of entry provided growers go through technical training and adhere to organic production guidelines as set by the pack house. Due to the local proximity of the UAH pack house, producers can walk there or hire local transport to deliver produce on the appointed days. There has been a high voluntary dropout rate of producers in the early stages leaving only committed producers. The pack house takes full responsibility for marketing the produce, thus allowing producers to access markets they otherwise would not. Current challenges facing UAH include the need to increase its technical support and the limited supply of water for producers without access to irrigation technology.

Westfalia Estate, Limpopo

In the northern parts of South Africa, near Tzaneen lies the well-established commercial avocado production farm of Westfalia Estate. In the 1960s, the estate used to produce citrus as its main produce but this has now changed to the estate focusing on avocado production. In this area of Limpopo, many households produce avocado alongside other fruit. Households on average tend five trees but some grow much more than the average (Mkhabela and Khumalo, 2011).

Although South Africa produces a good tonnage of avocados, there is often a shortage during certain times of the year due to the seasonality and the temperamental bearing nature of avocados (Mkhabela and Khumalo, 2011). Against this backdrop, in August 2009 Westfalia Estate recognized that its existing avocado supply contract with Woolworths could be better fulfilled if a partnership with small-scale farmers in the Venda area were in place. According to Mkhabela and Khumalo (2011) small-scale farmers in this area were seen as strategic partners who could supply the local market with the required fruit in early February before the Westfalia orchards were ready. Despite this strategic opportunity for small-scale farmers in Venda, their inherent challenges including fragmented supply, substandard phyto-sanitary practices and inappropriate post-harvest handling remained.

The Westfalia smallholder farmer project started by an analysis of the traditional value chain to gain insight into how small-scale farmers conducted their business. Based on the insight gained, small-scale farmers received appropriate classroom and field based training and a business model for the partnership with Westfalia was developed. In this developmental based business model the principles of building, operating, training and transferring of skills and assets such as running a pack house are advocated (Mkhabela and Khumalo, 2001). Avocado production is a long-term business that requires much capital input before breaking even. Westfalia is responsible for financing this approach without demands for government funds, thus exemplifying a good public–private partnership.

Westfalia Estate is using an outgrower approach to resolve the problem of low volumes in its own production by partnering with avocado smallholders in the surrounding rural communal areas. Westfalia provides technical support in production to ensure consistent quality and quantity of produce. The estate handles all marketing functions. The observed success of Westfalia and the small-scale farmer partnership lies in the developmental approach of building, operating, training and transferring of skills and assets, which affords farmers technical support from production to market. Especially disease control for blackspot has already yielded good results. Disease control is critical for the avocado market in determining quality and accessing a more lucrative formal market both immediately and in the future.

Thinking Beyond the Smallholder Farmer

The central focus of this chapter are small-scale farmers seeking to access formal markets for their fresh produce. Given the wide range of constraints small-scale farmers face, market access requires a mix of push and pull strategies as illustrated in the three case studies. Furthermore, it is important to acknowledge that each case of farmer group and market combination requires a different mix of institutional innovations to maximize market participation. Given the welfare implication of increased market participation by smallholder farmers, successful strategies require public and private partnerships.

It is important to note that market access by smallholders is a small aspect of a much bigger, more complicated system, the global food value chain. Neither public policy nor private company strategies can afford a myopic vision of achieving market access by smallholder farmers while losing sight of broader welfare considerations, changes in South Africa's farming systems, and the global nature of agricultural value chains. This chapter closes with a look at these three peripheral issues that are important to smallholder market access in South Africa.

Urban consumer *versus* small-scale farmers — welfare considerations: Any policy intervention encouraging smallholder farmer participation must seriously consider net welfare gains. South Africa boosts a large and growing urban population, most of which is very poor. The economies of scale gained from mass production by large-scale farmers and the economies of scope gained from established vertical coordination along the supply chain can be lost in the effort to include small-scale farmers.

Stepping ladder for small-scale farmers: No farmer aspires to be a small-scale farmer forever. For most smallholder farmers, this is the only opportunity available for them. At the minimum every small-holder farmer would like to expand the scale of her operation. Policy intervention should therefore be designed to create a stepping ladder that graduates farmers from subsistence farming all the way up to large-scale commercial farming. The current land reform programs are central to this trajectory.

A global perspective: Markets need to be competitive not only at domestic level but at regional and global levels too. Low transportation costs entail that small-scale farmers in South Africa are not only competing with their large-scale counterparts in South Africa but with producers from all over the whole world. Both raw commodities and value added food products coming in from China and Brazil exert significant competitive pressure on food prices to the benefit of low-income urban households (net consumers of food) and to the detriment of small-scale farmers (net producers of food). Further, the recent entry of Wal-Mart into South Africa is likely to significantly impact market access by small-scale farmers.

References

Anseeuw W, Van Rooyen CJ and D'Haese L (2000) A strategic analysis of the informal agribusiness sector: a case study of the Pretoria cut flower street-sellers. *Agrekon* 39(2): 132–141.

Baumann T (2004) Pro-poor microcredit in South Africa: cost-efficiency and productivity of South African pro-poor microfinance institutions. *Development Southern Africa* 21(5): 785–798.

Bhorat H and Westhuizen C (2005) Economic growth, poverty and inequality in South Africa: the first decade of democracy. Report Commissioned by the Presidency Development Policy Research Unit, School of Economics, University of Cape Town.

Blandon J, Henson S and Cranfield J (2009a) Small-scale farmer participation in new agri-food supply chains: case of the supermarket supply chain for fruit and vegetables in Honduras. *Journal of International Development* 21(7): 971–984. doi:10.1002/jid.1490.

Blandon J, Henson S and Islam T (2009b) Marketing preferences of small-scale farmers in the context of new agrifood systems: a stated choice model. *Agribusiness* 25(2): 251–267. doi:10.1002/agr.20195.

Chamberlin J and Jayne TS (2011) Unpacking the Meaning of "Market Access." No. 110014, Staff Papers, Michigan State University, Department of Agricultural, Food, and Resource Economics. Available at http://EconPapers.repec.org/RePEc:ags:midasp:110014.

Chibanda M, Ortmann GF and Lyne MC (2009) Institutional and governance factors influencing the performance of selected smallholder agricultural cooperatives in KwaZulu-Natal. *Agrekon* 48(3): 293–315.

du Plessis G and Lekganyane E (2010) The role of food gardens in empowering women: a study of Makotse Women's Club in Limpopo. *Journal of Social Development In Africa* 25(2): 97–120.

Eaton C and Shepherd AW (2001) Contract farming: partnership for growth. FAO Agricultural Services Bulletin 145. Rome, Italy: FAO.

IFAD (2011) Conference on new directions for smallholder farmers. Conference Proceedings, 24–25 January, Rome.

Karugu W (2011) Kenya Agricultural Commodity Exchange (KACE): linking small-scale farmers to national and regional markets. GIM Case Study No. B068. New York: United Nations Development Programme.

Kirkland DE (2008) Harvest of hope: a case study: the sustainable development of urban agriculture projects in Cape Town, South Africa. Unpublished master's thesis, Department of Environmental and Geographical Science, University of Cape Town.

Louw A, Jordaan D, Ndanga L and Kirsten JF (2008) Alternative marketing options for small-scale farmers in the wake of changing agri-food supply chains in South Africa. *Agrekon* 47(3 September): 287–308.

Louw A, Vermeulen H and Madevu H (2006) Integrating small-scale fresh produce producers into the mainstream agri-food systems in South Africa: the case of a retailer in Venda and local farmers. Regional Consultation on Linking Farmers to Markets: Lessons Learned and Successful Practices, Cairo, Egypt, 28 January–2 February.

Louw A, Vermulen H and Kirsten J (2007) Securing small farmer participation in supermarket supply chains in South Africa. *Development Southern Africa* 24(4): 539–551.

Magingxa L and Kamara AB (2003) Institutional perspectives of enhancing smallholder market access in South Africa. Contributed Paper Presented at the 41st Annual Conference of the Agricultural Economic Association of South Africa (AEASA).

Makhura TM (2001) Overcoming transaction costs barriers to market participation of smallholder farmers in the Northern Province of South Africa. Unpublished PhD thesis, Pretoria, University of Pretoria.

Masaku MB, Kirsten JF and Owen R (2004) The role of trust in the performance of supply chains: a dyad analysis of smallholder farmers and processing firms in the sugar industry in Swaziland. *Agrekon* 43(2): 147–161.

Matungul PM, Lyne MC and Ortmann GF (2001) Transaction costs and crop marketing in the communal areas of Impendle and Swayimana, KwaZulu-Natal. *Development Southern Africa* 18(3): 347–363.

Meinzen-Dick R, Pradhan R and di Gregorio M (2004) Collective action and property rights for sustainable development: understanding property rights. *2020 Focus Brief 11. International Food Policy Research Institute*, Washington, DC.

Mkhabela T (undated) Linking farmers with markets in rural South Africa: rural development and poverty alleviation through supply chain management. Available at http://www.namc.co.za/upload/per_category/Linking%20 farmers%20to%20markets%20in%20Rural%20SA.pdf.

Mkhabela T and Khumalo L (2011) Westfalia estate: linking communal avocado farmers to lucrative markets. In Mabaya E, Tihanyi K, Karaan M and Van Rooyen J (eds.), *Case studies of Emerging Farmers and Agribusinesses*. Stellenbosch: Sun Press.

Mukumbi K (2008) South Africa's agriculture broad based black economic empowerment (AgriBEE) policy: implications from a domestic content model. MSc thesis, Michigan State University.

National Department of Agriculture (NDA) (2004) Broad based black economic empowerment in agriculture: AgriBEE reference document. Available at http://www.nda.agric.za/docs/agribee/AgriBEEReference.pdf.

Ngomane T, Thomson JS and Radhakrishna RB (2002) Public sector agricultural extension system in the Northern Province of South Africa: a system undergoing transformation. *Journal of International Agricultural Extension Education* 9(3): 31–37.

Ortmann GF and King RP (2010) Research on agri-food supply chains in Southern Africa involving small-scale farmers: current status and future possibilities. *Agrekon* 49(4): 397–417.

Randela R, Alemu ZG and Groenewald JA (2008) Factors enhancing market participation by small-scale cotton farmers. *Agrekon* 47(4): 451–469.

Reardon T, Timmer CP, Barrett CB and Berdegue J (2003) The rise of supermarkets in Africa, Asia, and Latin America. *American Journal of Agricultural Economics* 85: 1140–1146.

Sere C (2010) Backing smallholder farmers today could avert food crises tomorrow. Available at http://www.guardian.co.uk/global-development/povertymatters/2010/oct/14/smallholder-farmers-agribusiness-investment.

Singla N, Singh S and Dhindsa P (2011) Linking small farmers to emerging agricultural marketing systems in India: the case study of a fresh food retail chain in Punjab. *Agricultural Economics Research Review* 24(1): 155–159.

Sonnino R and Marsden T (2006) Beyond the divide: rethinking relationships between alternative and conventional food networks in Europe. *Journal of Economic Geography* 6: 181–199.

Traill WB (2006) The rapid rise of supermarkets? *Development Policy Review* 24(2): 163–174.

Van Averbeke W and Khosa EB (2009) *The contribution of small-scale agriculture to the nutrition of rural households in a semi-arid environment in South Africa. Water SA* 33(3).

Vermeulen H, Kirsten JF and Sartorius K (2008a) Contracting arrangements in agribusiness procurement practices in South Africa. *Agrekon* 47(2).

Vermeulen S, Woodhill J, Proctor F and Delnoye R (2008b) *Chain-Wide Learning for Inclusive Agrifood Market Development: A Guide to Multistakeholder Processes for Linking Small-Scale Producers to Modern Markets.* London, UK: IIED and Wageningen, Netherlands: Wageningen International.

Wegner L and Zwart G (2011) Who will feed the world: the production challenge. Oxfam Research Report, Oxfam.

Whatmore S and Thorne L (1997) Nourishing networks: alternative geographies of food. In Goodman D and Watts M (eds.), *Globalizing Food.* New York: Routledge, pp. 287–304.

World Bank (2010) *World Development Indicators 2010.* Washington, DC: World Bank.

Chapter 2

INNOVATIVE BUSINESS MODELS IN THE THAI HORTICULTURAL SECTOR: A PANEL DATA ANALYSIS OF THE IMPACTS OF GLOBALGAP CERTIFICATION

Sarah Holzapfel* and Meike Wollni

*Department of Agricultural Economics and Rural Development, Georg-August-Universität Göttingen, Platz der Göttinger Sieben 5, 37073 Göttingen, Germany
sarah.holzapfel@die-gdi.de

In recent years, compliance with international food safety and quality standards, such as GlobalGAP, has become increasingly important for farmers in developing countries supplying high-value markets. Adoption of the GlobalGAP standard is challenging and external support by exporters, donors or other support agencies is often necessary to enable small-scale farmers to adopt. While the factors influencing GlobalGAP adoption have been analyzed in several studies, the impacts of the standard on smallholders' livelihoods remain less clear. This study for the first time presents a panel data analysis of the effects of GlobalGAP certification on net household income (NHI) and producer prices, using a sample of 214 farmers in the Thai horticultural sector. We find that the impacts of GlobalGAP certification differ depending on whether farmers are organized in producer-managed or exporter-managed certification groups. In the producer-managed groups, GlobalGAP certification has led to significantly higher prices and to significantly higher NHIs. In the exporter-managed certification groups, however, the effect of GlobalGAP certification on both prices and NHI is insignificant. Our results suggest that monetary benefits of GlobalGAP adoption do exist, but in cases where exporters finance GlobalGAP certification, those benefits are not passed on to farmers.

Introduction

In recent years, food safety and quality standards have become increasingly important in developing countries' value chains that target high-value export markets in Europe, North America and Japan, and increasingly also domestic supermarket channels (Boselie *et al.*, 2003; Henson and Loader, 2001; Henson and Reardon, 2005). Some standards, like GlobalGAP, are discussed to have become quasi-mandatory to access these high-value markets, particularly in the case of horticultural crops. The implications for small-scale farmers are controversial and debated among development experts. While evidence exists that the proliferation of standards has led to the exclusion of small-scale farmers (Dolan and Humphrey, 2000; Graffham *et al.*, 2007; Vagneron *et al.*, 2009), several studies claim that if smallholders are able to comply, standards can have positive impacts on farmers' livelihoods (Asfaw *et al.*, 2009a, 2009b, 2010; Narrod *et al.*, 2009). To successfully integrate small-scale farmers into high-value chains where standards are required, the development of new innovative business models, such as smallholder collective action, public–private partnerships and contract farming systems, is one of the key factors (Henson *et al.*, 2005; Narrod *et al.*, 2009; Okello *et al.*, 2011). The present study focuses on a public–private partnership between Thai small- and medium-scale export companies, the German International Cooperation (GIZ), Thai universities and local farmer groups. The main objective of the partnership was to increase GlobalGAP adoption among small-scale fruit and vegetable (F&V) producers. For the purpose of certification, farmers were organized in groups and a Quality Management System (QMS) was implemented at the group level. The different business models introduced by the project varied with respect to the institutional arrangement for the QMS, which was either run by exporters or by the farmers themselves with assistance by the development project.

The main aim of this research is to evaluate the impacts of GlobalGAP certification on producer prices for F&V and on farmers' net household income (NHI). While previous works have looked at the aggregate effects of GlobalGAP adoption, we will take a more differentiated look and analyze whether the effects of GlobalGAP differ between certified farmers who are organized in producer-managed groups and those who are organized in exporter-managed groups. Our analysis is based on a panel data set collected in 2010 and 2011 among 218 farm households, of which 124 are program participants and 90 are non-participants. Of the interviewed participants, 72 farmers were successfully certified in 2010. Every household was interviewed twice over a one-year interval, which corresponds to the time periods before and after certification for the GlobalGAP adopters in our sample. To assess the impact of certification we apply the fixed effects approach, which controls for unobservable differences between treatment and control group.

Most existing studies on the impacts of GlobalGAP adoption have taken a qualitative approach and findings are still inconclusive (Asfaw *et al.*, 2009a, 2009b; Graffham *et al.*, 2007; Ouma, 2010). Graffham *et al.* (2007) in a qualitative analysis of the impacts of GlobalGAP on small-scale farmers in Kenya state that the costs incurred by farmers for complying with GlobalGAP were not offset by higher prices, resulting in many smallholders dropping out of certification schemes. Similarly, Ouma (2010) concludes that out of 12 Kenyan exporters interviewed only two rewarded farmers for attaining GlobalGAP certification with higher price premiums. In contrast, Kariuki *et al.* (2012) using a sample of 249 Kenyan French bean suppliers show that GlobalGAP adoption leads to an average price increase of 9.5% and to a reduced price decline over the season. Nevertheless, they argue that the price increase is small compared with price premiums generated by supply contracts and direct procurement by exporters. Moreover, the price increase may be overestimated in their study because they are not controlling for potential selection bias among GlobalGAP adopters (Kariuki *et al.*, 2012). It is also important to look at whether exporters benefit from GlobalGAP adoption because benefits they receive might be partly passed on to producers as incentives to comply with the standard. Ouma (2010) reports that all exporters interviewed for his study shared the opinion that GlobalGAP certification has not led to higher prices although the implementation of the standard has increased costs considerably. Price premiums are only one of the potential benefits of GlobalGAP adoption, however. Exporters and farmers might also gain from certification through enhanced market access that contributes to higher revenues. Henson *et al.* (2011) find that GlobalGAP adoption has a large significant impact on export sales of exporting enterprises in sub-Saharan Africa. At farm level, Asfaw *et al.* (2009a, 2009b, 2010), using a cross-sectional sample of small-scale Kenyan vegetable producers identified a positive impact of the standard on net income from export vegetable production, farm level productivity and farmers' health. If the analysis of income effects exclusively focuses on the income from export crop production, however, this may lead to biased results, as those farmers who successfully adopted the GlobalGAP standard may allocate resources away from other activities to increase their export crop production. To control for this effect, we will look at the impacts of GlobalGAP certification on farmers' total NHI.

The chapter proceeds as follows. First, we will provide information on the background to the study, including an overview of business models that enable small-scale farmers to adopt GlobalGAP and a short description of the development project and the groups participating in it. Next, we describe the survey design of our study. In the third section, we will present the econometric model used and introduce our hypotheses. The fourth section presents descriptive statistics and discusses our model results. Finally, we conclude presenting the main findings of our study.

Background and Data

Inclusive business models and food safety standards

External support by exporting enterprises and donors has been identified as one of the major factors influencing standard adoption by small-scale farmers in developing countries (Graffham *et al.*, 2007;

Henson *et al.*, 2005; Humphrey, 2008; Kersting and Wollni, 2012; Kleinwechter and Grethe, 2006). Certification against the GlobalGAP standard not only requires high investments in farm facilities and equipment, such as pesticide and fertilizer storages, toilets and protective clothing, but it also entails high information, administration and organizational costs. Smallholders in developing countries alone are unable to overcome these challenges because they are often disadvantaged in terms of access to credit and information. They also lack the human, physical and social capital to comply with the standard (Narrod *et al.*, 2009). Different business models have been proposed, which successfully include small-scale farmers in GlobalGAP certification schemes. In most cases, such models focus on GlobalGAP group certification, Option 2,[1] which allows small-scale farmers to benefit from economies of scale and hence reduces the compliance costs for individual producers. Moreover, a group structure lowers transaction costs for exporters who support farmers in complying with the GlobalGAP standard. In particular, the costs of providing farmers with information, technical assistance and training are reduced (Will, 2010). There are two main group types under GlobalGAP group certification: producer-managed groups and exporter-managed groups (GTZ, 2010). In many cases NGOs, donors, and other support agencies offer support to GlobalGAP certification groups that include smallholders (Graffham *et al.*, 2007; Humphrey, 2008). In a previous study, Kersting and Wollni (2012) found that Thai small-scale F&V farmers are significantly more likely to adopt the GlobalGAP standard if they are supported by donors or exporters. While there is growing evidence on how smallholders can best be included in GlobalGAP certification schemes, the benefits that farmers derive from being included are less clear. In particular, there is little evidence on the heterogeneous effects of standard compliance that may result from certification through different business models.

---

[1] More recently, some smallholder farmer certification schemes have focused on GlobalGAP Option 1 (individual certification) as a multisite operation. These schemes are forms of vertical integration or contract farming where an exporter rents land from several small-scale farmers. The different production locations are managed and certified as one farm under Option 1.

We address this knowledge gap in our study by explicitly taking into account whether farmers are organized in producer-managed or exporter-managed certification groups. For the general case of farmer organizations, Markelova *et al.* (2009) show that downstream commercial agents in the value-chain, such as exporters, may support the organization of smallholders in order to maximize their own profits, which may result in conflicts over the distribution of value added between farmers and the supporting actor. They also argue, however, that public sector facilitators or NGOs can sometimes be over-supportive, potentially leading to unsustainable business models.

Certification groups in the GlobalGAP Option 2 project

The GIZ GlobalGAP Option 2 development project[2] started in 2008 with the aim to increase the access of small commercial farmers to higher food safety, environmental and social standards. Besides directly supporting farmer groups and exporters in the GlobalGAP adoption process, the program trained farm advisors to provide consulting services to farmers and exporters and to disseminate information about GlobalGAP through seminars. At the start, the program included 355 producers, who were organized in four producer-managed groups and six exporter-managed groups for certification. In the course of the program, five groups and the majority of farmers dropped out of the project, so that in the end only 28 farmers were certified in three exporter-managed groups and 54 farmers were certified in three farmer-managed groups. In the exporter-managed groups, the majority of non-recurrent and recurrent costs associated with GlobalGAP compliance was paid for by the exporters. The exporters financed new farm facilities and farm equipment for their growers, such as pesticide storage units, chemical disposal sites, plot markers, first aid kits, protective clothing and grading sheds. Moreover, they also covered the majority of recurrent costs, such as

---

[2] The project described is a scaling-up project that was preceded by a pilot project exploring the possibilities of GlobalGAP Option 2 certification for Thailand.

the costs for the external audit, pesticide residue, soil and water analyses and the management of the QMS. The implementation of a QMS, which monitors the compliance of all group members, is a requirement of GlobalGAP group certification. In the external audit not each individual farmer is inspected, but only the square root of the group members, which reduces the certification costs for the individual producer. Hence, the task of the QMS is to make sure that all group members comply with the GlobalGAP regulations and that those farmers sampled in the external audit are representative for the group as a whole. For exporters, the management of the QMS implies providing farm assistance and trainings to farmers, as well as monitoring their compliance on a weekly or monthly basis, and keeping records on the compliance of all group members.

In the producer-managed groups, the lack of support by downstream actors and the lack of secure market linkages was one of the main difficulties faced by the project. Farmers organized in these groups had to cover the major share of investment costs by themselves while the program covered the costs of the external audit and laboratory analyses. The three producer-managed groups certified differ with respect to their level of market integration. A collector with very strong connections to a variety of exporters, supermarkets, restaurants and wholesalers led the first group. The second group is equally well integrated, selling directly to a variety of domestic supermarkets. The third and largest group, however, lacked linkages to high-value markets, and prior to certification; members sold their produce separately, usually to middlemen at the farm gate. With GlobalGAP certification in reach, the development program accomplished to link the group to high-value markets as well. Farmers were contracted by a packaging house that collected, washed and packed the produce. The major share was sold as fresh produce to a domestic supermarket, a smaller share was frozen and then exported, and a very small part was sold as dried produce to various channels. At the packaging house, a team of farm advisors was employed that was paid by the development program. They took over the main responsibilities in the management of the QMS and also provided farm assistance to growers.

Sampling and survey design

In order to assess the impacts of GlobalGAP certification, we carried out a panel data survey of F&V farmers in Northern, Eastern, Southern and Central Thailand.[3] The first round of data collection took place between March and May 2010 and the second round was conducted between March and May 2011. In the surveys, covering a one-year recall period from March to the end of February, we collected quantitative and qualitative information on socio-economic and farm characteristics, agricultural production and input use, marketing decisions, compliance with standards, group membership and training participation. In the following analysis, the first survey interval will be referred to as the year 2009 and the second survey interval as the year 2010.

For the sampling frame, we divided the relevant population into four strata: (1) program participants who are likely to adopt GlobalGAP ($N = 118$), (2) program participants who are unlikely to achieve GlobalGAP certification ($N = 237$), (3) non-participants in program regions ($N =$ approx. 710), and (4) non-participants outside program regions ($N =$ approx. 415). Sampling of program participants was based on a complete list of participants provided by the development program including complete names of participants, location and adoption status.[4] To obtain a sufficiently large sample of adopters we selected all households for interviews that were categorized as prospective adopters at the time of the first survey. Of the

---

[3] Interviews were carried out in the following provinces: Ayuttayah, Kanchanaburi, Nakhon Pathom, Ratchaburi, Samut Sakhorn, Saraburi (Central Thailand); Chachoengsao, Prachin Buri, Sa Kaew (Eastern Thailand); Chumporn (Southern Thailand); Chiang Mai, Phayao, Phichit (Northern Thailand).

[4] During the preparation phase of the first survey in the beginning of 2010, 118 households were listed as prospective adopters by the development project. At this stage, farmers were classified as likely adopters if they were in the adoption process and expected to achieve certification by mid-2010, *i.e.*, within the duration of the development project. In addition, six households are included in the category of prospective adopters who were certified before the survey and took part in the development project because they needed assistance to become recertified.

118[5] households listed as prospective adopters, 97 were available for interviews in the first survey round. For the second strata, we randomly selected 49 households from the list to be included in the sample. Non-participants within and outside program regions were sampled through random walks, provided they produced at least one of the products considered for GlobalGAP certification.[6] Our internal control group, consisting of non-participant households within program regions, was sampled in villages where the development program was active. Hence, this group was exposed to the activities of the development program and is potentially affected by spillover effects. Therefore, to have a more robust control group, we additionally sampled non-participants outside program regions. Ten districts were identified as external control areas through consultations with agricultural professors in Thailand and stakeholders of the development program. The selected districts have similar agro-ecological conditions as districts within program regions and are known as major production areas of the crops considered for GlobalGAP certification by program participants. In total, 287 farmers were interviewed in 2010 of which 146 are program participants, 84 are non-participants within program regions and 57 are non-participants outside program regions.

To some extent sample attrition occurred in 2011, so that we were able to interview 218 of the 287 households a second time. Of the 218 households interviewed in the second survey, 124 are program participants, 57 are non-participants in program regions and 37 are non-participants outside program regions. There are different reasons for why some farmers were not included in the second survey. First, for some of the households the contact information given was incorrect or they had moved away, and second, some households were not available for interviews. In the following analysis, we will only use

---

[5] Only 82 of the households initially classified as prospective adopters became certified.

[6] The following products were considered for GlobalGAP certification: asparagus, cantaloupe, dragon fruit, durian, green okra, lychee, mango, mangosteen, papaya, spring onion, yard long bean, and different kinds of herbs and green leafy vegetables.

214 of the 218 households because four households stopped growing F&Vs completely.

Econometric Analysis

The main objective of our study is to analyze the impact of GlobalGAP certification on (1) producer prices for F&V and on (2) NHI. In addition to average treatment effects, we are interested in whether the effect of GlobalGAP depends on the type of business model used, namely producer-managed groups or exporter-managed groups for certification. For this purpose, we formulate different specifications of a panel data model estimating mean F&V producer prices and NHI. In a first specification for both income and price analysis, we include a dummy variable that is equal to 1 if a farmer is GlobalGAP certified in 2010[7] and 0 otherwise. In a second specification, we include two dummy variables, the first one being equal to 1 if a farmer is certified in an exporter-managed group and the second one being equal to 1 if a farmer is certified in a producer-managed group. Furthermore, since economies of scale are likely to be important in the adoption of the GlobalGAP standard, the income effect of certification may vary depending on farm size. We therefore include variables on the size of the area that is certified — the certified area in producer-managed and in exporter-managed groups — in additional specifications of our model. The adoption of the GlobalGAP standard is likely to be correlated with unobservable characteristics that also influence producer prices and NHI.[8] In particular, farmers who are more motivated and progressive are more likely to achieve certification with GlobalGAP, which is a complex and knowledge-intensive standard. These personal characteristics and attitudes, however, are also likely to positively

---

[7] For the purpose of our estimation, we define the six farmers who were certified in both survey periods as non-adopters in 2009 because we expect that not only initial certification, but also the renewal of the certificate have a positive influence on prices and NHI. If they are classified as adopters in both time periods, they are counted as non-certified farmers in the fixed effects model because there is no change in certification status between the years.

[8] This may also refer to several other variables included on the right-hand side of our model.

affect the ability of the household to obtain higher prices and incomes. As we cannot control for these unobserved variables, a simple ex-post comparison of prices and incomes between adopters and non-adopters would most likely lead to biased estimates. Given that we have data before and after certification for both adopters and non-adopters, we use a fixed effects model to control for time-invariant unobserved heterogeneity across households. The fixed effects model is specified as follows:

$$y_{it} = x_{it}\beta + v_{it},$$

where t denotes the time period, i indicates the individual, and x_{it} is a vector of observable variables that change across both time t and individuals i, variables that change across i but not t, and variables that change over time but not across individuals. The error term v_{it} is a composite error term ($v_{it} \equiv c_i + u_{it}$) that consists of the unobserved effect c_i, which captures features of individuals that do not change over time, such as ability and motivation, and u_{it} which is the idiosyncratic error that changes over t as well as across i. The unobserved effect c_i is allowed to be correlated with the explanatory variables.[9] Hence, once we include time-variant explanatory variables along with time-invariant unobserved effects in our model, the value of the time-variant variables in previous years has no effect on the outcome variable in the current year. The fixed effects estimator uses the variation over time within each cross-sectional observation and is based on time-demeaned data. Explanatory variables that are constant over time are removed by the time-demeaning and hence cannot be estimated with the fixed effects approach (Wooldridge, 2010).

We will use two weights in the estimation procedure: sampling weights[10] to account for the overrepresentation of development

---

[9] Here, we assume that the managerial ability and other unobserved effects are roughly constant over time. The shortcoming of our model is that we cannot control for unobserved effects that are time-variant and correlated with the outcome variable.

[10] Sampling weights are calculated as the inverse of the sampling fraction, *i.e.*, the total number of households in each population divided by the number of samples drawn from that population.

program participants in our sample and inverse probability weights to correct for sample attrition that is based on observable character-istics. To test whether sampling attrition is random or not, we carried out attrition probit tests (Fitzgerald *et al.*, 1998) and pooled tests (Becketti *et al.*, 1988). The results of both tests show that attrition is nonrandom in our sample. More specifically, we find that participa-tion in the development project, age of household head and location of household significantly influence attrition. Hence, we calculate inverse probability weights, which give more weight to households that are similar to households that are likely to attrite than to house-holds that are more comparable to non-attritors. Weights are calcu-lated as follows. First, the predicted probabilities of the unrestricted retention probit model are estimated using explanatory variables that are observable for both attritor and non-attritor households, and that might be correlated with the likelihood of attrition. Then the model is re-estimated as a restricted model including only those explanatory variables that are not significantly associated with attrition. The inverse probability weights are then calculated as the ratio of restricted to unrestricted probabilities (Baulch and Quisumbing, 2011).[11]

Impact of GlobalGAP certification on producer prices

To estimate the impact of GlobalGAP certification on producer prices we estimate a model with the log transformed mean weighted price per kilogram of F&V[12] as a dependent variable. To measure the effects of GlobalGAP certification, we include a dummy variable measuring GlobalGAP certification in 2010 in a first specification and two dummies for certification in exporter-managed groups and producer-managed groups in a second specification. As additional

---

[11] Results of the attrition tests and the calculation of inverse probability weights are provided by the authors on request.

[12] For each farmer, the mean weighted price per kg of products $n = 1 \ldots N$ in grades $i = 1 \ldots In$ is calculated as follows: $\bar{P} = \sum_{n=1}^{N} \sum_{in=1}^{In} \left(\frac{qnin}{Q} \right) * p_{nin}$, where Q = total quantity of F&V sold, q_{nin} = quantity of product in grade i, p_{ini} = price of product n in grade i.

explanatory variables, we include the total quantity of F&V sold, the share of F&V sold to high-value markets, the share of F&V sold that is graded, three variables related to contracts and resource provision by buyers, and a year dummy variable measuring time fixed effects. In addition, we include a range of variables capturing the share of different crops in the total quantity of F&V sold[13] to account for price differentials between different F&V products.

Regarding our first research question, *i.e.*, the impact of GlobalGAP certification on producer prices for F&Vs, we hypothesize that there are significant price premiums associated with GlobalGAP certified produce. The GlobalGAP standard adds value to the product by assuring buyers that desired but unobservable product attributes, such as adherence to maximum residue levels or the use of safe irrigation water, are fulfilled. In the absence of a certificate, product attributes unobservable to the buyer do not entail price premiums, unless there are reputation effects that enable the producer to credibly assure the customer that the product possesses the desired characteristics (Fafchamps *et al.*, 2008). Our second hypothesis, which will be tested in a second model, refers to the heterogeneous impact of GlobalGAP certification on prices, depending on the type of business model used. We expect that certified farmers in producer-managed groups benefit from higher price premiums as compared with farmers in exporter-managed groups. While in the producer-managed groups, adopters themselves and the development program covered the costs of compliance, in the exporter-managed groups mainly the exporters covered both non-recurrent and recurrent costs for GlobalGAP adoption. We therefore expect that exporters implicitly deduct the costs incurred for GlobalGAP certification from producer prices, hence resulting in significantly reduced price premiums. On the other hand, exporters may decide to pay price premiums to reward farmers for complying with the GlobalGAP standard. Exporters have undertaken large transaction-specific investments to support farmers in the GlobalGAP

---

[13] We use the share of different crops in the total quantity of F&V sold instead of crop dummies because the shares vary across the two years, whereas crop dummies are largely constant over time in our sample.

adoption process, leaving them at risk of farmers' opportunistic behavior. Therefore, they may choose to set prices high enough to discourage side-selling of farmers at times when market prices are higher than the prices agreed upon in the contract (Minten *et al.*, 2009).

With respect to the other explanatory variables included in the models, we expect a positive influence of the total quantity sold on prices because farmers selling larger amounts are expected to have a higher bargaining power. In addition, the per unit costs of price and contract negotiations for buyers are lower for larger than for smaller transactions, which may be reflected in higher prices paid to larger farmers. In line with this, Mausch *et al.* (2009) find that small-scale GlobalGAP certified farmers receive 16% lower prices than large-scale certified farmers, which they attribute to lower bargaining power and higher monitoring and enforcement costs associated with smaller farmers. The variable "share of F&V sold to high-value markets" includes the share sold to exporters and supermarkets either directly or through specialized suppliers. We expect a positive influence of the variable since high-value markets demand the consistent delivery of high-quality products, which is usually rewarded with price premiums. The share of F&V sold that is graded is also expected to have a positive influence on prices. Through grading, observable variation in product quality is accounted for by price differentials. Furthermore, we hypothesize that production under contract can have a significant influence on product prices. For the analysis, we classify contracts in two main categories: market-specification[14] contracts and production-management[15] contracts (Minot, 1986). Market-specification contracts

---

[14] We classify a contract as a market-specification contract if the farmer has a written or oral agreement with the buyer, and at least one of the following is specified in the contract: pricing of the product, product grades, timing of delivery, or amount of delivery, but no requirements are specified in terms of production methods or input use. Farm assistance is also not provided.

[15] We classify a contract as a production-management contract if the farmer has a written or oral agreement with the buyer, and at least one of the following is specified in the contract: use of only those crop protection products that are approved by the buyer, record keeping requirements, or production according to the regulations of

are negotiated prior to the harvest and usually include details on prices, quality and timing of delivery. Market-specification contracts may have a positive or negative influence on prices. On the one hand, their impact may be negative if small-scale farmers are risk averse and therefore willing to accept guaranteed future prices that are below the expected market price (Key and Runsten, 1999). On the other hand, marketing contracts may include a premium for higher quality and firms may set prices that are high enough to prevent contracted producers from side-selling to other buyers at times of high market demand (Minten *et al.*, 2009). Production-management contracts, in addition to the above-mentioned specifications, define a particular production method or input regime to be followed by the farmer. Frequently, buyers provide farmers with market information and technical assistance to overcome missing markets for information (Minot, 1986), which is especially relevant in the context of supplying high-value export markets that demand stringent food safety and quality standards (Key and Runsten, 1999). The impact of production-management contracts on producer prices is also unclear *a priori*. On the one hand, the impact may be positive if farmers' efforts to follow strict guidelines laid out in the contract are rewarded by higher prices. On the other hand, buyers may implicitly charge farmers for the services provided resulting in lower producer prices (Minot, 1986). Finally, we hypothesize that input and credit provision by buyers has a negative influence on prices. Credits and inputs are often provided to farmers at subsidized rates and the costs of these subsidies are then subtracted from product prices (Minot, 1986).

The GlobalGAP standard, however, is not only expected to influence producer prices directly, but may also influence several of the marketing-related factors that are included as explanatory variables in our models, and thus have an indirect effect on producer prices. In particular, GlobalGAP certification may be positively associated with larger shares sold to high-value markets and larger shares sold as

---

the Q-GAP standard. The contract is also classified as a production-management contract if the buyer provides farm assistance. Production-management contracts can also include details described above as classifying market-specification contracts.

graded produce. Certification can serve as a signal to buyers that producers are adhered to the strict food safety and quality rules of the
standard, thus improving their access to high-value markets. Since in
high-value markets product grades for observable attributes such as
size, color and variety are used more frequently (Jaffee *et al.*, 2011),
greater participation in such markets will also lead to an increase in
the share of produce that is graded. Furthermore, GlobalGAP certification is often associated with tighter buyer–producer relations and
increased resource provision by buyers. As a result, producers and
buyers may engage in contractual agreements that also influence the
prices received by producers. To account for these potential correlations between GlobalGAP certification and other explanatory variables, we show two specifications of the panel data model on mean
F&V producer prices. The first specification excludes the marketing-
related variables, such as participation in high-value markets, grading,
contracts and resource provision by buyers, to capture the full effect
of GlobalGAP certification on producer prices. The second specification controls for all potential factors attempting to disentangle the
effect of different marketing strategies.

Impact of GlobalGAP on NHI

Our second research objective relates to the impact of GlobalGAP
certification on NHI. We calculate NHI as follows[16]:

$$NHI = (TFR - VC) + OFE + NSE,$$

where TFR = total farm revenue, VC = variable costs, OFE = wages
and salaries from off-farm employment, and NSE = net returns from
self-employment.

Different model specifications are formulated to estimate the
average and subgroup-specific mean impact as well as the per hectare
effect of GlobalGAP certification on farmers' NHI. In a first specification, we include a dummy variable that is equal to 1 if a farmer is

---

[16] Unfortunately, we do not have information on the amount of remittances received
by households and therefore cannot account for their value in the calculation of NHI.

certified in 2010, 0 otherwise, which measures the average effect of certification. In a second specification, we include two dummies for certification in exporter-managed groups and producer-managed groups to look at heterogeneous treatment effects between subgroups of adopters. Furthermore, to measure the per hectare effect of GlobalGAP certification, we include the size of the GlobalGAP certified area in hectares, the certified area in producer-managed and exporter-managed groups as explanatory variables in further specifications.

As additional control variables, we include the area cultivated with F&V measured in hectares, the area cultivated with other crops, the number of household members working off-farm, the total number of household members as a proxy for access to family labor, a range of variables capturing the share of the area cultivated with different products separately for F&Vs and for other crops, and a dummy variable that is equal to 1 if the household has experienced a drought. One of the project regions was affected by a severe drought in 2010, which led to large harvest losses. We do not include a year dummy in the model because it is highly correlated with the dummy for drought in 2010.

Since GlobalGAP certified farmers are likely to increase their share of F&V sold to high-value markets and to receive higher product prices, we also expect a positive effect of certification on NHI. On the other hand, premium prices for GlobalGAP adoption do not necessarily imply higher net incomes because the GlobalGAP standard is associated with significant compliance and adjustment costs that might diminish the positive income effect generated by higher prices. While the recurrent costs of compliance, like certification fees, soil analyses and health checks, did not have to be paid by farmers in our sample, because during the first year of certification they were covered by the development program and by exporters, adjustment costs may still be substantial. Certified farmers may for example have to incur higher variable costs that are indirectly related to standard adoption, such as higher labor costs due to labor-intensive record keeping and weeding practices that are required under the GlobalGAP standard. Similarly, GlobalGAP regulations stipulate that only those chemicals may be used that are registered in the country of use for the target crop (FoodPLUS, 2011), which are often more expensive, and thus may result in higher pesticide costs (Asfaw *et al.*, 2009a). These effects are also likely to be heterogeneous among the different types of certification groups, given that farmers in producer-managed and exporter-managed groups received different levels of support and financial assistance. As argued in the previous section, farmers in exporter-managed groups are likely to receive lower price premiums, because exporters made substantial investments in farm-level upgrading. This may then also result in lower overall impacts of the GlobalGAP standard on the NHI of adopters in exporter-managed groups compared with adopters in producer-managed groups.

Results and Discussion

Descriptive statistics

Marketing of F&Vs

In the following section, we descriptively analyze changes in F&V product prices, market access and contracts following GlobalGAP certification. Table 1 shows an overview of the marketing performance of farmers in our sample. We first compare whether the marketing performance differed between certified and non-certified producers before GlobalGAP certification, and then look at the changes from 2009 (before certification) to 2010 (after certification). In addition, we compare the marketing performance between certified farmers organized in producer-managed certification groups and those organized in exporter-managed certification groups.

Comparing prices and marketing performance between certified and non-certified producers in 2009, we find that mean prices were not significantly different between the two groups before certification. Already in 2009, however, certified farmers sold a significantly higher share of their produce to high-value markets than non-certified farmers. Moreover, we find significant differences between the two groups with respect to the types of contractual arrangements used and the quantity of F&Vs sold. Compared with non-certified producers,

Table 1: Differences in marketing of F&V: prices, quantities, marketing channels and contracts

	Year 2009		Δ 2010–2009		Year 2009		Δ 2010–2009	
	Certified Farmers (N = 72)	Non-Certified Farmers (N = 131)	Certified Farmers (N = 72)	Non-Certified Farmers (N = 131)	Producer-Managed Groups (N = 49)	Exporter-Managed Groups (N = 23)	Producer-Managed Groups (N = 49)	Exporter-Managed Groups (N = 23)
Mean F&V price (US$)	0.81 (0.41)	0.72 (0.48)	0.48*** (0.63)	0.07 (0.61)	0.86 (0.47)	0.71 (0.18)	0.69*** (0.62)	0.03 (0.34)
Share sold to high-value markets	0.42*** (0.46)	0.26 (0.42)	0.36*** (0.55)	0.04 (0.44)	0.25*** (0.43)	0.79 (0.27)	0.55*** (0.50)	−0.04 (0.41)
Share sold that is graded	0.76 (0.40)	0.71 (0.43)	0.08 (0.48)	0.02 (0.49)	0.78 (0.42)	0.72 (0.35)	0.12 (0.43)	−0.003 (0.56)
Share sold under a market-specification contract	0.02*** (0.12)	0.27 (0.43)	0.02 (0.19)	−0.05 (0.57)	0.00 (0.01)	0.04 (0.21)	0.03 (0.15)	0.003 (0.27)
Share sold under a production-management contract	0.40 (0.46)	0.30 (0.44)	0.32*** (0.56)	0.02 (0.47)	0.27*** (0.44)	0.66 (0.37)	0.45*** (0.54)	0.06 (0.50)
Share sold for which inputs and/or credits are provided	0.32 (0.44)	0.26 (0.42)	−0.003 (0.40)	−0.05 (0.39)	0.16*** (0.36)	0.67 (0.40)	0.01 (0.37)	−0.02 (0.46)
Total quantity of F&V sold (kg)	13,496*** (24,383)	26,777 (43,179)	1069 (13,207)	2523 (52,006)	13554 (28,892)	13,373 (9870)	61 (13,389)	3217 (12,832)

Notes: Standard deviations are shown in parentheses. *, ** and *** imply the mean value in 2009 or the change from 2009 to 2010 is statistically different between certified and non-certified farmers or farmers certified in producer-managed groups and farmers certified in exporter-managed groups at the 10%, 5% and 1% level, respectively.

certified farmers sold less F&Vs and were less often engaged in market-specification contracts.

Next, we compare changes from 2009 to 2010 between certified and non-certified producers. We find that certified producers increased their mean price by US$0.48 on the average, whereas non-certified farmers experienced an average increase of only US$0.07. The difference is statistically significant suggesting that there are considerable price premiums associated with the GlobalGAP standard. Furthermore, certified producers already delivering higher shares of their produce to high-value markets before certification were able to further increase their access to these markets. While in the case of certified farmers the share of F&V sold to high-value markets increased by 36% between 2009 and 2010, it stayed almost constant in the case of non-certified farmers. Finally, certified farmers were able to expand the share of F&V sold under production-management contracts by 32%. This change is significantly different from the change experienced by non-certified farmers, whose contractual arrangements remained largely constant over the study period. This finding confirms that GlobalGAP adoption often goes hand in hand with more intensive farm assistance and closer monitoring by buyers, for which production management contracts can provide a safeguard.

Comparing the two groups of certified farmers, we find evidence for our hypothesis that there are heterogeneous effects of the GlobalGAP standard depending on whether certification is buyer-driven or producer-driven. We find that before GlobalGAP certification in 2009, farmers in producer-managed groups were less integrated into high-value supply chains than those organized in exporter-managed groups. They sold a significantly lower share of their produce to high-value markets, a lower share under production-management contracts, and less often received inputs or credits from buyers as compared with farmers in exporter-managed groups.

Following certification, however, farmers in producer-managed groups were able to catch up. The results for price changes following certification are particularly striking. For certified farmers in producer-managed groups, prices have nearly doubled, from US$0.86 in 2009 to US$1.55 in 2010. In contrast, the prices in exporter-managed groups have remained stable. Similarly, the share sold to high-value markets and the share sold under production-management contracts has increased significantly for members of the producer-managed certification groups, while there has been almost no change for farmers in exporter-managed groups. This can be attributed to the fact that farmers organized and certified in exporter-managed groups had the contracting exporter as their main buyer before and after certification, whereas farmers in producer-managed groups gained access to new markets as a result of certification.

Costs, revenues and household income

Table 2 shows differences in per hectare costs and revenue of F&V production for certified and non-certified producers in 2009, *i.e.*, before certification, and compares changes from 2009 to 2010. In 2009, there are no significant differences with respect to the gross revenue per hectare, total variable costs per hectare, and net revenue per hectare between certified and non-certified farmers. Comparing changes from 2009 to 2010, we find that notwithstanding the high price increase among certified farmers following certification, their gross revenue per hectare did not increase over the same period. This can be explained by an average decline in per hectare yields of 21% for certified farmers. Regarding production costs, certified farmers experienced an increase in seed costs and other variable costs per hectare that is significantly different from the change among non-certified farmers. The category 'other variable costs' includes amongst others the costs for irrigation, fuel, tractor rental, electricity and packaging material. Yet, the change in total variable costs is not statistically different between the two groups.

Next, we compare differences and changes in costs and revenues of certified farmers in producer-managed and exporter-managed groups. We find that before certification in 2009, farmers in producer-managed groups have both significantly lower gross revenues per hectare as well as significantly lower total variable costs per hectare than farmers in exporter-managed groups. The large differences in gross revenues can mainly be explained by yield differences since the

Table 2: Costs and revenue of F&V production per hectare (ha)

	Year 2009		Δ 2010–2009		Year 2009		Δ 2010–2009	
	Certified Farmers (N = 72)	Non-Certified Farmers (N = 142)	Certified Farmers (N = 72)	Non-Certified Farmers (N = 142)	Producer-Managed (N = 49)	Exporter-Managed (N = 23)	Producer-Managed (N = 49)	Exporter-Managed (N = 23)
Gross revenue (US$/ha)	6037 (4940)	6241 (7763)	−14 (5110)	−251 (10,799)	5368* (4314)	7462 (5918)	−17 (4906)	−8 (5635)
Yield in kg per ha (US$/ha)	7761 (5968)	10,744 (17,321)	−1658 (6524)	−653 (21,019)	6734** (5201)	9947 (6971)	−2566* (6545)	278 (6177)
Seed costs (US$/ha)	77 (177)	68 (279)	124** (588)	8 (294)	59 (146)	115 (228)	42* (212)	297 (985)
Pesticide costs including biopesticides (US$/ha)	140 (321)	194 (383)	35 (334)	25 (526)	106 (134)	213 (534)	28 (168)	48 (546)
Other input costs (biocides, plant growth regulators, others) (US$/ha)	117 (594)	51 (128)	−43 (700)	17 (250)	122 (692)	107 (303)	−47 (824)	−33 (313)
Chemical fertilizer costs (US$/ha)	711 (927)	934 (2094)	−101 (1308)	−46 (2084)	668 (938)	803 (917)	−20 (1437)	−275 (988)
Organic fertilizer costs (US$/ha)	93 (234)	142 (365)	19 (329)	−47 (374)	55** (90)	174 (387)	12 (132)	33 (558)

(*Continued*)

Table 2: (Continued)

	Year 2009		Δ 2010–2009		Year 2009		Δ 2010–2009	
	Certified Farmers (N = 72)	Non-Certified Farmers (N = 142)	Certified Farmers (N = 72)	Non-Certified Farmers (N = 142)	Producer-Managed (N = 49)	Exporter-Managed (N = 23)	Producer-Managed (N = 49)	Exporter-Managed (N = 23)
Hired labor costs (US$/ha)	805	581	–57	–195	719	986	–22	–132
	(1108)	(1122)	(1078)	(1104)	(947)	(1399)	(1037)	(1183)
Other variable costs (US$/ha)	236***	536	51**	–206	140***	441	22	115
	(346)	(951)	(415)	(988)	(141)	(527)	(216)	(668)
Total variable costs (US$/ha)	2139	2534	136	–447	1803**	2855	67	284
	(2015)	(3340)	(2309)	(3119)	(1849)	(2205)	(2283)	(2408)
Net revenue (US$/ha)	3898	3707	–150	196	3565	4607	–83	–292
	(4939)	(7045)	(5206)	(10,947)	(4397)	(5982)	(4988)	(5758)

Notes: Standard deviations are shown in parentheses. *, ** and *** imply the mean value in 2009 or the change from 2009 to 2010 is statistically different between certified and non-certified farmers or farmers certified in producer-managed groups and farmers certified in exporter-managed groups at the 10%, 5% and 1% level, respectively.

yield of members in producer-managed groups is significantly lower than that of farmers in exporter-managed groups. Moreover, yield changes from 2009 to 2010 are significantly different between the two groups. While the average yield per hectare of certified farmers in producer-managed groups decreased by more than 40%,[17] certified farmers in exporter-managed groups experienced a slight increase in per hectare yield. Despite the considerable decline in yields, the gross revenues of certified farmers in producer-managed groups decreased only slightly and the change is not significantly different from that of farmers certified in exporter-managed groups. This can be attributed to the significantly higher prices obtained by farmers certified in producer-managed groups after certification that helped compensate the negative yield effects.

Table 3 shows differences and changes in annual NHI by activity. For the year 2009, we do not find significant differences in income levels between certified and non-certified producers for all income categories indicating that their income structures are relatively similar. Comparing income changes, we find that although certified producers on the average experienced an increase in NHI and net F&V income, whereas non-certified farmers experienced a decrease, these differences are not statistically significant. Similarly, comparing the NHI between certified farmers in exporter-managed groups and certified farmers in producer-managed groups, we do not find significant differences between the income levels of the two groups in 2009, nor do we find significant differences in changes in income between 2009 and 2010.

Impact of GlobalGAP on producer prices

In this section, we present the estimation results of the fixed effects model explaining F&V producer prices[18] (see Table 4). The first and

---

[17] This decrease was largely due to unfavorable climatic conditions, which we control for in the econometric analysis.

[18] To test whether the unobserved effect is correlated with the explanatory variables in our models, we employed the Hausman test. In specifications (1) to (3), the null hypothesis of zero correlation is rejected at the 5% level, while in specification (4), the null hypothesis is rejected at the 10% level. Hence, we conclude that the fixed effects model is more appropriate than the random effects model for our data.

Table 3: Annual NHI in US dollars by activity

	Year 2009		Δ 2010–2009		Year 2009		Δ 2010–2009	
	Certified Farmers (N = 72)	Non-Certified Farmers (N = 142)	Certified Farmers (N = 72)	Non-Certified Farmers (N = 142)	Producer-Managed (N = 49)	Exporter-Managed (N = 23)	Producer-Managed (N = 49)	Exporter-Managed (N = 23)
Net F&V income	5530 (11,876)	12,942 (51,126)	4484 (19,279)	−2766 (50,672)	5608 (13,082)	5360 (9040)	1739 (10,783)	5773 (22,162)
Net crop income (except F&V)	1638 (4609)	1296 (5145)	214 (4357)	1189 (10,323)	1470 (1957)	1997 (7747)	316 (4303)	−3 (4560)
Net income livestock and fishery	−188 (1238)	982 (7747)	292 (2296)	−706 (8011)	−302 (1482)	55 (263)	451 (2772)	−45 (270)
Off-farm income	4198 (10,793)	3561 (8611)	970 (7804)	795 (6925)	4964 (12,490)	2564 (5609)	229 (7745)	2548 (7864)
Annual total NHI	11,177 (18,998)	18,776 (53,612)	5865 (20,386)	−1540 (51,881)	11,740 (21,861)	9976 (10,950)	6682 (22,742)	4125 (14,425)

Notes: Standard deviations are shown in parentheses. *, ** and *** imply the mean value in 2009 or the change from 2009 to 2010 is statistically different between certified and non-certified farmers or farmers certified in producer-managed groups and farmers certified in exporter-managed groups at the 10%, 5% and 1% level, respectively.

Table 4: Determinants of F&V producer prices

	(1)	(2)	(3)	(4)
GlobalGAP certified $(0/1)^{a}$	0.36***	0.19	—	—
	(0.12)	(0.12)		
GlobalGAP certified (exporter group) $(0/1)^{a}$	—	—	−0.02	0.00
			(0.15)	(0.13)
GlobalGAP certified (producer group) $(0/1)^{a}$	—	—	0.52***	0.28*
			(0.14)	(0.15)
Total quantity of F&V sold (1000 kg)	0.00	0.00**	0.00	0.00*
	(0.00)	(0.00)	(0.00)	(0.00)
Share of F&V sold to high-value markets	—	0.23**	—	0.22**
		(0.11)		(0.11)
Share of F&V sold that is graded	—	0.45**	—	0.45**
		(0.21)		(0.21)
Share of F&V sold under a market-specification contract	—	0.25***	—	0.25**
		(0.10)		(0.10)
Share of F&V sold under a production-management contract	—	0.15	—	0.14
		(0.11)		(0.11)
Share of F&V sold for which resources are provided	—	−0.02	—	−0.01
		(0.09)		(0.10)
Year 2010 $(0/1)^{b}$	0.27***	0.23***	0.26***	0.23***
	(0.09)	(0.07)	(0.09)	(0.07)
Constant	−1.34	1.15	−2.22	0.64
	(2.10)	(1.54)	(1.75)	(1.62)
Number of observations	406	406	406	406
R-squared	0.47	0.47	0.55	0.55

Notes: The dependent variable is log mean F&V price. Coefficient estimates are shown with cluster robust standard errors in parentheses. Statistical significance at the 1% (***), 5% (**) and 10% (*) level. Variables capturing the share of different F&V in the total quantity sold are included, but not shown due to space restrictions.
[a]The reference group is non-certified farmers.
[b]The reference year is 2009.

the second specifications estimate the aggregate effect of GlobalGAP certification on F&V producer prices and the third and fourth specifications analyze mean treatment effects for the subgroups of farmers certified in producer-managed and exporter-managed groups, respectively. Due to a potential correlation between the explanatory variables, specifications (1) and (3) include only a subset of the independent variables, while specifications (2) and (4) control for all potential explanatory factors.

The results shown in column (1) of Table 4 confirm our expectation that GlobalGAP certification has a positive impact on prices. On average, certification increases prices by 43%.[19] Hence, the price increase we find is much larger than the price premium of 9.5% identified by Kariuki *et al.* (2012) in their study on the Kenyan French bean sector. Adding further explanatory variables on the marketing relationship to the model (see column (2)), the coefficient for GlobalGAP certification decreases in size and becomes insignificant. This can be attributed to the correlation between GlobalGAP certification and several marketing-related variables. As was shown in the descriptive statistics, farmers were able to increase their sales to high-value markets as a result of GlobalGAP certification. Results in column (2) reveal that the share of F&Vs sold to high-value markets and the share of F&V sold that is graded have a large and significant positive impact on producer prices. Thus, our results indicate that much of the positive price effect from GlobalGAP certification is due to improved access to high-value segments through which higher prices can be obtained. Furthermore, the type of contractual agreement has an influence on the prices received by farmers. Our results show that a 10% increase in the share of F&V sold under a market-specification contract leads to an average price increase of 3%.

Looking at subgroup-specific average treatment effects (column (3) of Table 4), we find that the observed increase in average prices resulting from GlobalGAP certification is mainly driven by significant price increases in the producer-managed groups. GlobalGAP certification in producer-managed groups has led to an average price increase of 68%, while in exporter-managed groups there is no significant impact on prices. The coefficient for GlobalGAP certification in producer-managed groups remains marginally significant if further

---

[19] The exact percentage difference in the predicted price was calculated as follows for all explanatory variables: $100 * [\exp(\hat{\beta}\Delta x) - 1]$.

explanatory variables are added to the model (column (4) of Table 4), but the magnitude of the effect drops by more than half to 32%.

The finding that there is no significant price increase for farmers certified in exporter-managed groups is in line with observations of qualitative studies, which show that exporters are usually unwilling to pay price premiums for GlobalGAP-certified produce to farmers (Graffham et al., 2007; Ouma, 2010). This suggests that, if costs of compliance are mainly paid for by buyers, these costs are implicitly deducted from product prices. Our results are also confirmed by the information collected in qualitative interviews with exporters involved in the development project in our study area. None of the exporters claimed to offer price premiums to farmers after successful certification, but rather continued to pay the same prices to certified and non-certified suppliers. According to the exporters, the main short-term benefits farmers can derive from being included in the certification groups are knowledge gains and the advantages of being a preferred supplier.

Impact of GlobalGAP on NHI

Table 5 shows the results of the fixed effects model estimating farmers' NHI.[20] Specifications (1) and (2) measure the average total effect of GlobalGAP certification and the subgroup-specific mean effects of the standard on farmers certified in exporter-managed and producer-managed groups, respectively. In specifications (3) and (4), we additionally look at the per hectare effect of GlobalGAP certification.

Our results show that GlobalGAP certification is a promising option for Thai F&V farmers. On the average, GlobalGAP certification has increased farmers' annual NHI by US$10,039 (column (1)

---

[20] To test whether the unobserved effect is correlated with the explanatory variables in our models, we employed the Hausman test. In all specifications shown in Table 5, we cannot reject the null hypothesis of zero correlation and random effects and fixed effects estimates are very similar. However, we do believe that GlobalGAP certification as well as certification in exporter-managed and producer-managed groups might be correlated with unobservable characteristics that also affect NHI, and hence decide to use the fixed effects approach.

Table 5:   Determinants of NHI (US$)

	Total Effect of GlobalGAP Certification		Per Hectare Effect of GlobalGAP Certification	
	(1)	**(2)**	**(3)**	**(4)**
GlobalGAP certified (0/1)[a]	10,039*** (3800)	—	3762*** (1420)	—
GlobalGAP certified (exporter group) (0/1)[a]	—	373 (5071)	—	2343 (3311)
GlobalGAP certified (producer group) (0/1)[a]	—	14,678*** (5247)	—	3792*** (1460)
Cultivated area F&V (ha)	1853*** (735)	1833*** (730)	2095*** (652)	2091*** (652)
Cultivated area other products (ha)	1346 (983)	1392 (993)	1250 (951)	1254 (954)
No. of household members off-farm	8971** (4337)	9135** (4370)	9650** (4390)	9664** (4401)
No. of household members	−1086 (1757)	−1135 (1762)	−1145 (1755)	−1149 (1758)
Drought in 2010 (0/1)	−4873* (2550)	−5645** (2761)	−3917* (2344)	−3914* (2346)
Constant	20,675 (35,083)	19,275 (35,472)	20,821 (34,432)	20,788 (34,413)
Number of observations	428	428	428	428
R-squared	0.16	0.16	0.17	0.17

Notes: The dependent variable is NHI in US$. Coefficient estimates are shown with cluster robust standard errors in parentheses. Variables capturing the share of area cultivated with different products are included, but not shown due to space restrictions. Statistical significance at the 1% (***), 5% (**) and 10% (*) level.
[a] The reference group is non-certified farmers.

of Table 5). Looking at per hectare effects in column (3), we find that one additional hectare of certified land leads to an average increase in NHI of US$3762. The results of the remaining explanatory variables are as expected. Off-farm employment generates particularly high returns: one additional household member working off-farm contributes to an average annual income increase of US$8971. This reflects the status of Thailand as an emerging market, where remunerative opportunities for off-farm activities are increasingly available and represent an important income source for rural households (Rigg, 2005; Rigg and Nattapoolwat, 2001). The coefficient for the cultivated area with F&V is also positive and significant indicating that one additional hectare of land under F&V increases NHI by US$1853. Moreover, farmers affected by the drought in 2010 have experienced significant income losses of US$4873 on average.

Looking at heterogeneous impacts across certification groups (columns (2) and (4) of Table 5), we find that there are indeed differential effects for households certified in exporter-managed and producer-managed groups. While GlobalGAP certification in exporter-managed groups does not have a significant impact, GlobalGAP adoption in producer-managed groups has a positive and significant effect on farmers' NHI. On the average, GlobalGAP certification in producer-managed groups leads to US$14,678 higher NHIs and to an income increase of US$3792 per hectare of land that is certified. These results are similar to our findings that price effects are positive and significant for farmers certified in producer-managed groups, but not for farmers certified in exporter-managed groups.

The large positive impact of GlobalGAP on the household income of farmers certified in producer-managed groups suggests that GlobalGAP certification can be profitable for small-scale farmers. It needs to be kept in mind, however, that in the producer-managed groups in our sample, during the first year of adoption, the development program covered the recurrent costs of compliance, *i.e.*, the costs for the external audit, for laboratory analyses and for running the QMS. Hence, if farmers renew the GlobalGAP certificate in the following years, these recurrent costs have to be deducted from their income. Without the continued support of the development program it is questionable whether farmers organized in producer-managed groups will take the risk to incur the costs of recertification. Long-term links with downstream actors operating in high-value markets that provide a secure market outlet and premium prices are important incentives for farmers to continually comply with the GlobalGAP standard.

In the exporter-managed certification groups, the implementation of GlobalGAP certification has not induced many significant changes in outcome variables. Group members do not receive higher prices and have been unable to increase their sales to high-value markets. At the same time, variable costs per hectare have not risen significantly. In line with this, we do not find a significant effect of certification on NHIs of producers certified in exporter-managed groups.

One shortcoming of our results is that they represent short-term effects only. In exporter-managed groups, where certification is mostly driven by buyers, farmers might experience positive income effects in the long run. For example, adjustments in farm management and production methods implemented in the context of GlobalGAP adoption might have a positive effect on product quality that may only become visible after several growing periods. In addition, in the long run certified farmers might also benefit from increased and more stable demand for their products, allowing them to cultivate larger areas or to increase the number of production cycles. One of the exporter-managed groups, for example, grows green okra for export to Japan during the off-season when demand in Japan exceeds supply. With the GlobalGAP certificate, the exporter expects that okra can be sold year-round, even during the peak season when domestic production can almost satisfy consumer demand in Japan.

At the moment, while GlobalGAP is certainly an advantage, it is not an indispensable requirement to sell to lucrative markets in Thailand. Adoption of the standard is not widespread yet, so that exporters are forced to also source from non-certified producers. All the exporters involved in the survey source produce from a large number of smallholders, but only a tiny share of their suppliers is included in GlobalGAP certification schemes. As of mid-2010, all over Thailand only 776 F&V producers were certified under GlobalGAP Option 2, and 31 farms, mostly exporter-owned and large-scale, were certified individually under Option 1 (FoodPLUS, 2010). Our findings raise the question whether farmers in exporter-managed certification groups will continue to comply with GlobalGAP, if they do not receive any monetary benefits from certification in the short term. For Kenya, Graffham *et al.* (2007) report that a high share of smallholder farmers dropped out of exporter-managed certification schemes, because certification was not economically viable and external support was insufficient.

Conclusions

For the case of small-scale F&V farmers in Thailand, we have analyzed the impact of GlobalGAP certification on F&V product prices and farmers' NHI. While previous studies have only looked at the aggregate impacts of the standard, we find that the impact of GlobalGAP differs depending on whether certified farmers are organized in exporter-managed or producer-managed groups.

At the aggregate level, we can conclude that GlobalGAP has a significant impact on F&V producer prices, leading to an average price increase of 43%. Whether GlobalGAP certification is rewarded by higher prices depends, however, on the type of certification group and thus on the support received from downstream actors. Certified farmers in exporter-managed groups do not receive significant price premiums, whereas farmers in producer-managed groups were able to increase prices by 68% as a result of GlobalGAP certification. This can be explained by the fact that exporters covered the majority of compliance costs with GlobalGAP on behalf of their suppliers and hence were unwilling to additionally reward farmers with higher prices. Our quantitative findings are supported by qualitative interviews with the exporters involved in the development program, who stated that they did indeed not pay price premiums specifically for GlobalGAP certification. Moreover, our results are in line with previous qualitative studies on the impacts of GlobalGAP adoption, which show that farmers identify the lack of price premiums as one of the major hurdles to the sustainable implementation of the GlobalGAP standard (Graffham *et al.*, 2007; Ouma, 2010).

Concerning the impacts of GlobalGAP on NHI, we find that while certified farmers in producer-managed groups have realized large net income gains, adopters in exporter-managed groups have not benefited from certification in terms of higher household incomes. This raises the question whether certification of smallholders in exporter-managed groups is economically viable for small-scale farmers. Currently, incentives for obtaining or sustaining GlobalGAP certification are small, especially because up until now, non-certified producers in Thailand are also able to sell their produce to high-value market outlets. One limitation of our study is, however, that we are only able to look at short-term effects. In the long run, farmers in exporter-managed groups might be able to realize positive income gains, *e.g.*, through increased demand for their produce.

We can also conclude, however, that under certain circumstances GlobalGAP certification can be profitable for smallholder farmers. In the producer-managed groups, certified farmers sold their produce to supermarkets, which paid substantial price premiums for GlobalGAP certified produce translating into significantly higher net incomes for farmers. The large income gains, however, were possible only because the development project covered a major share of the recurrent costs of compliance. After the end of the development project, it is questionable whether farmers will take the risk of incurring the high costs of certification in the absence of a safe market outlet. In this context, it is critical also for farmer-managed groups to have long-term contracts with exporters or supermarkets that reward GlobalGAP certified produce with price premiums. Furthermore, to make GlobalGAP certification of smallholders sustainable, continued access to affordable training and advice on the changing requirements of food safety and quality standards is necessary beyond the usually limited duration of the development project.

Acknowledgments

We are grateful for funding received by the fiat panis foundation and by the German Academic Exchange Service.

References

Asfaw S, Mithöfer D and Waibel H (2009a) EU food safety standards, pesticide use and farm-level productivity: the case of high-value crops in Kenya. *Journal of Agricultural Economics* 60: 645–667.

Asfaw S, Mithöfer D and Waibel H (2009b) Investment in compliance with GlobalGAP standards: does it pay off for small-scale producers in Kenya? *Quarterly Journal of International Agriculture* 4: 337–362.

Asfaw S, Mithöfer D and Waibel H (2010) Agrifood supply chain, private-sector standards, and farmers' health: evidence from Kenya. *Agricultural Economics* 41: 251–263.

Baulch B and Quisumbing A (2011) Testing and adjusting for attrition in household panel data. Chronic Poverty Research Centre Toolkit Note.

Becketti S, Gould W, Lillard L and Welch F (1988) The panel study of income dynamics after fourteen years: an evaluation. *Journal of Labor Economics* 6: 472–492.

Boselie D, Henson S and Weatherspoon D (2003) Supermarket procurement practices in developing countries: redefining the roles of the public and private sectors. *American Journal of Agricultural Economics* 85: 1155–1161.

Dolan C and Humphrey J (2000) Governance and trade in fresh vegetables: the impact of UK supermarkets on the African horticulture industry. *Journal of Development Studies* 37: 147–176.

Fafchamps M, Hill RV and Minten B (2008) Quality control in nonstaple food markets: evidence from India. *Agricultural Economics* 38: 251–266.

Fitzgerald J, Gottschalk P and Moffitt R (1998) An analysis of sample attrition in panel data: the Michigan panel study of income dynamics. *The Journal of Human Resources* 33: 251–299.

FoodPLUS (2010) *GLOBALGAP Certified Producers in Thailand.* Cologne: FoodPLUS.

FoodPLUS (2011) *GLOBALGAP Control Points and Compliance Criteria. Integrated Farm Assurance. Crops Base.* Cologne: FoodPLUS.

Graffham A, Karehu E and Macgregor J (2007) Impact of EurepGAP on small-scale vegetable growers in Kenya. *Fresh Insights 6.* Available at http://www.agrifoodstandards.net/en/filemanager/active?fid=83 [accessed on 8 April 2014].

GTZ (2010) *GLOBALGAP Smallholder QMS Set-up Guide: How to Establish a QMS in your Group.* Eschborn: Deutsche Gesellschaft für Technische Zusammenarbeit (GTZ) mbH.

Henson S and Loader R (2001) Barriers to agricultural exports from developing countries: the role of sanitary and phytosanitary requirements. *World Development* 29: 85–102.

Henson S, Masakure O and Boselie D (2005) Private food safety and quality standards for fresh produce exporters: the case of Hortico Agrisystems, Zimbabwe. *Food Policy* 30: 371–384.

Henson S, Masakure O and Cranfield J (2011) Do fresh produce exporters in sub-Saharan Africa benefit from GlobalGAP certification? *World Development* 39: 375–386.

Henson S and Reardon T (2005) Private agri-food standards: implications for food policy and the agri-food system. *Food Policy* 30: 241–253.

Humphrey J (2008) *Private Standards, Small Farmers and Donor Policy: EUREPGAP in Kenya*. Sussex: University of Sussex.

Jaffee S, Henson S and Rios LD (2011) *Making the Grade: Smallholder Farmers, Emerging Standards, and Development Assistance Programs in Africa*. Washington, DC: International Bank for Reconstruction and Development/The World Bank/The University of Guelph.

Kariuki IM, Loy J-P and Herzfeld T (2012) Farmgate private standards and price premium: evidence from the GlobalGAP scheme in Kenya's French beans marketing. *Agribusiness* 28: 42–53.

Kersting S and Wollni M (2012) New institutional arrangements and standard adoption: evidence from small-scale fruit and vegetable farmers in Thailand. *Food Policy* 37: 452–462.

Key N and Runsten D (1999) Contract farming, smallholders, and rural development in Latin America: the organization of agroprocessing firms and the scale of outgrower production. *World Development* 27: 381–401.

Kleinwechter U and Grethe H (2006) The adoption of the Eurepgap standard by mango exporters in Piura, Peru. *26th International Conference of Agricultural Economists*, Gold Coast, Australia.

Markelova H, Meinzen-Dick R, Hellin J and Dohrn S (2009) Collective action for smallholder market access. *Food Policy* 34: 1–7.

Mausch K, Mithöfer D, Aswaf S and Waibel H (2009) Export vegetable production in Kenya under the EurepGAP standard: is large "more beautiful" than small? *Journal of Food Distribution Research* 40: 115–129.

Minot NW (1986) Contract farming and its effect on small farmers in less developed countries. Food Security International Development Working Papers.

Minten B, Randrianarison L and Swinnen JFM (2009) Global retail chains and poor farmers: evidence from Madagascar. *World Development* 37: 1728–1741.

Narrod C, Roy D, Okello J, Avendano B, Rich K and Thorat A (2009) Public–private partnerships and collective action in high value fruit and vegetable supply chains. *Food Policy* 34: 8–15.

Okello JJ, Narrod CA and Roy D (2011) Export standards, market institutions and smallholder farmer exclusion from fresh export vegetable high value chains: experiences from Ethiopia, Kenya and Zambia. *Journal of Agricultural Science* 3: 188–195.

Ouma S (2010) Global standards, local realities: private agrifood governance and the restructuring of the Kenyan horticulture industry. *Economic Geography* 86: 197–222.

Rigg J (2005) Land, farming, livelihoods, and poverty: rethinking the links in the rural South. *World Development* 34: 180–202.

Rigg J and Nattapoolwat S (2001) Embracing the global in Thailand: activism and pragmatism in era of deagrarianization. *World Development* 29: 945–960.

Vagneron I, Faure G and Loeillet D (2009) Is there a pilot in the chain? Identifying the key drivers of change in the fresh pineapple sector. *Food Policy* 34: 437–446.

Will M (2010) *Integrating Smallholders into Global Supply Chains. GLOBALGAP Option 2 Smallholder Group Certification Generic Manual: Lessons learnt in pilot projects in Kenya, Ghana, Thailand and Macedonia.* Eschborn: Deutsche Gesellschaft für Technische Zusammenheit (GTZ) mbH.

Wooldridge JM (2010) *Econometric Analysis of Cross Section and Panel Data.* Cambridge, MA: MIT.

Chapter 3

INNOVATIVE NETWORKS IN CONSERVATION AGRICULTURE: BAJIO HUB CASE STUDY, MEXICO

Gabriela Monsalvo-Velázquez,[*,†,‡,g]
Ricardo Romero-Perezgrovas,[‡,§] Bram Govaerts[‡]
and Roberto Rendón-Medel[*]

[*]Center for Economic, Social, Agricultural Techniques and Global
Agro-Industry Research (CIESTAAM), Chapingo University, km 38.5,
Mexico-Texcoco C.P. 56230, Chapingo, Edo. Mex. Post Office Box No. 90

[†]Visiting Fellow Cornell International Institute for Food, Agriculture and
Development, CIIFAD, Cornell University, Ithaca, NY

[‡]International Maize and Wheat Improvement Center (CIMMYT), Apdo.
Postal 6-641, 06600 Mexico, D.F., Mexico

[§]Katholieke Universiteit Leuven, Department of Earth and Environmental
Sciences; Celestijnenlaan 200 E, 3001 Leuven, Belgium

[g]gmonsalvo@gmail.com; mm2335@cornell.edu

Understanding the complexity and strength of innovation networks that disseminate knowledge about agriculture is important because these innovation networks allow actors to integrate needs, actions and results when public and private actors cooperate. The study shows that Conservation Agriculture (CA) farmers are central to the networks as a whole, both in terms of information seeking and information gathering. Moreover, when the study focused on a micro network, it was demonstrated that these CA farmers are key actors and play an important role for diffusion of CA. Ancient agricultural knowledge shapes the way farmers ultimately apply the principles of CA: Minimal soil disturbance (no-till) and permanent soil cover (mulch) combined with crops rotations. CA is conceived as a system developed with and for farmers. This study was conducted in West-Central Mexico. The analysis involved a two-stage stratified sampling statistical model, oversampling for CA farmers from a state census of farmers growing sorghum and maize. The findings in this study add evidence to the idea that network analysis is important as a helpful tool when there are reduced resources and time. Finally the study shows the efficiency and efficacy of network analysis as a strategic methodological tool to design, operate, follow up, evaluate and control social public policies.

Introduction

Agricultural challenges in the area of sustainable development[1] are growing due to the impact of climate change on the production systems that offer food for the year 2030 (Reynolds, 2010). Due to climate change, crop yields are expected to fall from 10% to 20%, between 2012 and 2050, and for that reason current agricultural production must be increased (Thorton, 2012). Taking into account that 40% of the world's population works in agriculture,[2] the goal is to improve how farmers adopt, adapt and use innovative technologies to increase agricultural output and maintain the environment whilst facing climate change challenges. This will require significant advances in research as well as the capacity of producers to recognize climatic tendencies and adapt appropriate robust technologies (Lobell and Burke, 2010).

In this context, the Consultative Group on International Agricultural Research (CGIAR) worked with the Research Program on Climate Change, Agriculture and Food Security (CCAFS) and its 15 research centers to launch an action plan to respond to a request from the United Nations Committee on Food Security. This work was presented in the United Nations Conference on Sustainable

---

[1] Seen as the guiding principle for long-term global development, sustainable development consists of three pillars: economic development, social development and environmental protection.

[2] Bruce Campell, CGIAR Declaration made in the framework of the Rio+20 meeting, http://www.bbc.co.uk/news/science-environment-18160089.

Development (UNCSD or Rio+20) which took place in Río de Janeiro, Brazil on 20–22 June 2012. The action plan can be summarized in seven main interrelated themes. These themes are as follows:

(i) The world's agricultural systems face an uphill struggle in feeding a projected 9 billion to 10 billion people by 2050. Climate change introduces a significant hurdle in this struggle,

(ii) Securing and maintaining necessary levels of calories, protein and nutrients for populations around the world will be an exceptional challenge,

(iii) Recalibrating agriculture in the face of climate change is more than planting crops that can tolerate warmer weather. Some commodities, for example, can grow in warm weather but cannot resist the insects and diseases whose prevalence will increase. Others can tolerate a lack of water but not the sporadic flooding that occurs with more common weather extremes,

(iv) Even as global deforestation continues, trees continue to be valued as a provider of agricultural commodities like nuts and fruit; as a mitigating resource that removes carbon dioxide from the atmosphere; and also as a staple of adaptation — trees help stabilize soil erosion, better regulate water, as well as provide shade, firewood and fodder,

(v) Production of the most common commodity staples — wheat, maize and rice — will be challenged by new weather patterns. Adjustments in production, replacement with commodities that can tolerate the new conditions in different regions and innovations in technology are key elements of adaptation,

(vi) Raising livestock and catching fish and other aquatic products — two of the more common sources of protein — will also be challenged by a new climate. In some areas, different plants, breeds and species can provide substitutions, but in others, adaptation is critical,

(vii) This recalibration of agriculture will eventually extend beyond what is grown and raised. The world's many cultures must adapt to the changing dinner menu forced upon them due to climate change (Thorton, 2012).

Those seven themes describe how agricultural research can contribute to sustainable development and food security in the future. The action plan includes the following highlights: (i) adopt an interdisciplinary approach to broadly coordinate cooperation and promote a regulatory framework with economic incentives; (ii) tackle unequal distribution of natural resources and their benefits through governance and distributing technology; (iii) support knowledge exchange systems for small farmers to improve the management of crops, livestock and natural resources, with the goal of increasing production and minimizing negative environmental impact; and (iv) strengthen and support local groups, small farmers and shepherds in food production.

Mexico has 29.9 million agricultural hectares (24.6 in rain-fed and 5.3 irrigated) all of which could benefit new technologies. In this context the Program for the Sustainable Modernization of Traditional Agriculture (MasAgro)[3] was lunched as a national effort to catalyze and boost the adaptation and adoption of new agricultural technologies, in order to increase crop yields in a sustainable way (CIMMYT, 2010). Moreover, MasAgro seeks to respond to the predicted 25.7% reduction in food production as a result of climate change (*Scientific American*, 2010). The program's main challenge is to harmonize all current federal and local programs and direct financial resources toward achieving the same goal. This effort requires coordination of resources and cooperation among institutions concerned with sustainable rural development in Mexico.

MasAgro considers Conservation Agriculture[4] (CA) to be one of the more robust sustainable agricultural systems that can help to overcome the predicted yield losses due to climatic change effects when complemented with other component technologies such as improved varieties, integrated pest management systems, site specific nutrient recommendations (organic's coming), efficient mechanization,

---

[3] The Mexican government, through the Ministry of Agriculture, Livestock, Rural Development, Fishing and Food (SAGARPA) and the International Maize and Wheat Improvement Center (CIMMYT) runs MasAgro.

[4] "… defined as minimal soil disturbance (no-till) and permanent soil cover (mulch) combined with rotations, as a more sustainable cultivation system for the future." (Hobbs, 2007)

among others. The three main goals of CA are high and stable yields, reduced environmental impact and increase producer income. To help farmers adapt and adopt CA and other complex technologies, Hobbs and Govaerts (2010) recommend combining research and participative extension, which should be concentrated in a few defined locations that represent the local production system.

MasAgro initiative calls its innovation network a hub. In selected agro-ecological areas a basic hub structure is developed that includes the establishment of research and experimental platforms, so-called farmer modules and extension areas (see figures in Results and Discussion). Experimental platforms are based in universities and research institutes or are set up with interested collaborators such as farmer organizations or the private sector. Research in the platforms integrates component technologies within a working production system that is locally adapted and improves the proposed technologies, while solving problems arising from farmer trials and experiences which are specific to the local crop systems. Additionally, the experimental platforms serve to train farmers, extension agents, researchers, and other collaborators to better disseminate agricultural technologies and practices through the innovation network. This research analyzed one of MasAgro Hubs: Bajio Hub.

Rogers' (1995) theory of dissemination argues that the most important part is the analysis of actors and agents of change. Given this approach, the first step of our study was to determine what practices, type of agriculture and modes of communication are used by each actor, agent or node. "Node" is a technical term used in networks; "agent" is a socioeconomic organization; and "actors" are all participants in agricultural processes including farmers (men and women) buyers, suppliers, and trainers, among others. These determinations in turn established whether or not a new piece of knowledge, action or tool is adopted. The results showed the producer is the central point of our analysis, and based on this we can determine the producer's connections with all other actors in the network. Sen (2010) concurs with this approach, saying that when attention is focused on the individual as an agent of change, rather than collectives of people, the individual's progress is well suited to the social environment so her/his needs will be achieved.

The analysis of innovation networks[5] allows us to identify all visible actors, as well as actors and agents that may not have been previously considered because they were absent at meetings or did not take part in public initiatives. The contributions of these actors, however, should be respected and recognized for their actions and individual achievements. This is what Granovetter (1985) refers as *weak links that make the difference.*

To understand how all actors and agents responsible for the institutional evolution effort interact in a hub, the analysis of rural social networks was applied to map real dimensions and central nodes. In this case study the data showed the farmer's effectiveness in the adaptation, adoption and diffusion of innovative CA in the Mexican Bajio Hub.

Within MasAgro regional networks are established to facilitate and foster research and extension. On-farm testing and trials are linked to the strategic science platforms operated by international centers and national research institutes to foster a global understanding of production systems and their adaptability to different environments, as well as cropping systems and farmers' circumstances (Govaerts *et al.*, 2009; Reynolds *et al.*, 2011, Spielman *et al.*, 2011). The three main questions for this research were: Are the CA farmers (also called nodes or agents or actors) central to the mapping of innovation network? What is the level of connectivity among CA farmers within the region we are studying? Is the diversity of these connections related to CA adoption?

Materials and Methods

Study location

The study took place in the central western zone of Mexico, in the states of Guanajuato and Michoacan de Ocampo. Field studies were carried out during the months of August and September 2011. Both

---

[5] An innovation network is the total set of actors or agents involved in the idea, development, dissemination, adoption, adaptation and appropriation of an innovation. For agriculture, agents and actors are as follows: producers, research centers, providers of supplies, machinery and technology, extension practitioners, the industry and more.

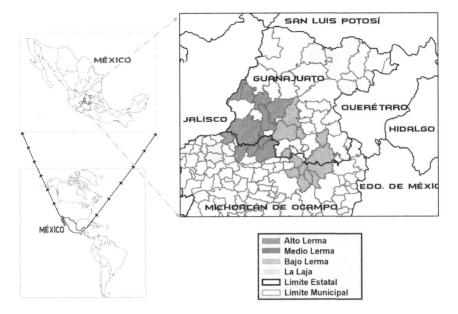

Figure 1.   Bajio hub, Mexico

Source: Prepared by the authors.

states are in the hydrological zone Lerma-Chapala, which forms the Bajio hub.[6] Four regions are found in these two states: High, Medium and Low Lerma (irrigation zone) and the rain-fed La Laja (Figure 1).

The four regions encompass a total of 32 municipalities, 128,584 rural production units (field production cells with different types of land tenure) and 741,630 hectares of production farms and forests (CEDERSA, 2011). With 42,103 production units, the municipalities in Medium Lerma alone surpasses the entire High Lerma region (Table 1), which is considered the most productive region, as it sits at the head of a human-made water distribution system from the Lerma River. The Medium Lerma region also has the greatest surface area of production forests and farms, measured in hectares. La Laja is notable

---

[6] The hub is an extension model of agricultural technologies with a holistic vision, through the catalysis and coordination of actions among all actors involved in productive changes in key agro-ecological zones.

Table 1: Sub regions and the municipalities of the Bajío Hub

Region	High Lerma		Medium Lerma		Low Lerma	La Laja	Total
	Guanajuato	Michoacan	Guanajuato	Michoacan	Michoacan	Guanajuato	
Munici-palities	Acámbaro, Jaral del Progreso, Moroleón, Salamanca, Tarimoro, Valle de Santiago	Álvaro Obregón, Cuitzéo, Charo, Indaparapeo, Queréndaro, Tarímbaro, Zinapécuaro	Abasolo, Irapuato, Pénjamo, Purísima del Rincón, Romita, San Francisco del Rincón	Angamacutiro, Penjamillo, La Piedad, Puruandiro, José Sixto Verduzco	Chavinda, Ecuandureo, Ixtlán, Zamora	San José Iturbide, Villagrán, San Diego de la Unión, San Luis de la Paz	
Total	6	7	6	5	4	4	32

Source: Prepared by the authors.

for being a temperate region, with low rainfall. This zone also has a growing number of migrants, constantly increasing remittances and higher female participation in agricultural activities. Moreover, the La Laja zone is special due to its saline soil composition and high mineral levels, which make it difficult to diversify agriculture production.

Table 1 shows the municipalities that were selected on the sample for each region. The Bajio is an extensive highland plain in Central Mexico (20° N, 101° E) which includes the states of Guanajuato and Michoacan de Ocampo. The area ranges in elevation from approximately 1600 meters to 2000 meters above sea level (Erenstein, 1999). Deep, fertile Vertisols and Phaeozems are the most common soil types found here.

The Bajio has two clear seasons: a wet season between May and October with rainfall of up to 160 mm per month, during which mainly maize (*Zea mays*) and sorghum (*Sorghum bicolor*) are grown, and a dry season between November and April with mean rainfall of 10 mm per month, in which mainly wheat (*Triticum aestivum*) and barley (*Hordeum vulgare*) are grown under irrigation (Erenstein, 1999).

Sampling and statistical analysis

From a total of 11,521 farmers derived from a census database, 305 farmers were selected with a stratified statistical sampling with 95% of confidence level. The survey (see Appendix A) included three questions to map the networks: social, technical and commercial.

The survey was distributed to 305 farmers (men and women) for a total of 1,270 nodes, actors and agents mapped. Software applications Ucinet and Key Player were used to analyze the data and perform statistical calculations, using the total count and average of in-degrees following the Wasserman and Faust (1994) methodology.

Analytical methods

In addition to the Ucinet and Key Player program for analysis, other qualitative techniques were applied to complement the statistical data shown in the quantitative results. The qualitative techniques used included participatory observation, transects, and in-depth interviews. All of these methods served to strengthen, support and better explain the numbers obtained in the analysis of networks in rural environments.

In order to correctly implement network analysis, we took into account the following operational definitions to guide us in understanding the indicators used to respond to the research questions (Scott, 2000; Wasserman and Faust, 1994). Three networks were defined: (i) social networks (closeness in terms of trust and friendship), (ii) technical networks (closeness in terms of who helps producers solve problems) and (iii) commercial networks (nodes or actors that buy or sell items necessary for agricultural activity). Based on these three dimensions, the network methodology identifies three types of actors, institutions, organizations and food producers, according to the roles they play:

Diffusers or sources: Innovative actors or nodes who convey their own experiences and manage and disseminate knowledge. These are people whose work is looked to by others when they have to make a decision, despite not always having positive results. They are known as "*crazy* people." They are usually quiet, observe the facts and do not like to be in public meetings or publicly take responsibility for others. They play a moral authority role. Their influence measured in terms of networking is called *in-degrees*. In-degrees are the sum of relationships that a node or actor has when others have referred to the node or actor. In terms of our research, it refers to the number of times that other producers refer to the same producer to consult or share information on agricultural activities (Figure 2).

Collectors: Actors characterized by constantly searching for information. Collectors know everyone and others consult them because they are frequently trying to obtain as much information as they can. They are sociable and almost always present at demonstration fairs for new technologies, equipment meetings, local producer assembly meetings, and meeting promoting governmental programs. Collectors have the reputation of knowing everything about everyone. The measure of networks for collectors is called *out-degrees*, which is the sum of relationships that a node or actor has with other nodes or actors within the network (Figure 3).

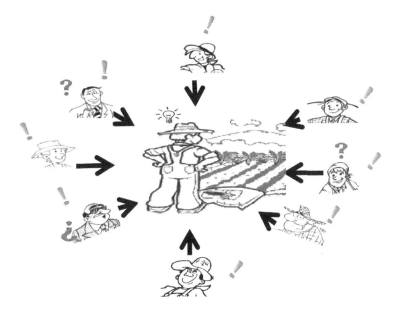

Figure 2.   Farmer who is referred by others as a source of knowledge

Figure 3.   Out-degrees

Figure 4.   Farmer, actor or organization that connects two (or more) actors, organization or institutions

Bridgers or connectors: People, organizations, consortia or institutions that bridge the gaps among actor and goods or services. The measure for connectors is called *centrality betweenness*, which describes the central actors that are the most active as they have the most links to other actors within the network. This measure is the number of nodes or actors directly related with a central node or actor within the network (Figure 4).

Another measure of network analysis is *degree of closeness*, which is the position that nodes or actors have and from which they reach all other actors within the network. A producer's position is determined by the connections he or she has with all the other producers within the network. In many cases, producers with the highest degree of closeness may not be the most popular producers, or the best-known within the network, but they are key producers for their moral weight and the respect they have earned for their performance in farming activities. Other farmers in the locale, zone or state recognize them as *experts*.

    "...How happy I felt when I saw in the magazine "link" (in Spanish: Enl**AC**) a producer like me! who sows the same crop and went through the same problem ... he was saying that it was the way were he could resolved and he obtain a good raise (tons) with Conservation Agriculture ... hard for me but I must admit that although my "*compadre*" (close friend) is very quiet and he does not like leaving, almost always shares ... He put me in touch with the trainer who helped me with my problem..." (Field Interview 03 GTO-MICH)

As shown in Figure 5, each node or actor has its own individual importance, meaning each node or producer has its own value in the network. This value is also called the *geodesic distance*, and it represents the distance between a node or actor and the rest of the nodes or actors in the network. The sum of these distances between nodes, actors and producers is called closeness. A high degree of closeness indicates an easy capacity to forge connections among actors within the network. This indicator describes the distance between nodes or producers and the degree of distance between producers within the Bajio hub network in the current study.

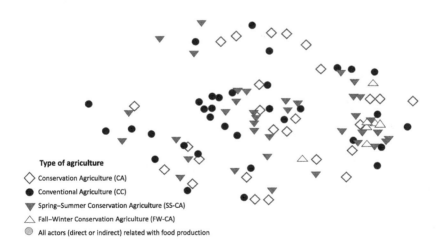

Figure 5. Network map indicating the various types of agriculture in the Medium Lerma zone, Bajio Hub

Results and Discussion

The first objective was to identify all relations among producers within the Bajio hub network. The data indicate the positions of farmers who are practicing CA, conventional agriculture (CC), only spring–summer conservation agriculture (SS-CA) and only fall–winter conservation agriculture (FW-CA), as shown in Figure 5. The grey circles represent actors involved in agriculture activities, such as trainers, technical personnel, researchers, industries, governmental institutions, *among others*.

Based on network analysis applied to rural social dynamics in the Bajio hub and calculated with Freeman's measure of centrality, an out-degree centralization of 1.77% and a normalized in-degree of 0.10% in the general network were obtained. These results indicate that there are many producers seeking information and a comparative dearth of available sources to provide the information that these producers seek.

These results clearly indicate the presence of a fertile territory to adopt CA technology. There are lots of producers looking for information, while at the same time sharing information that come from their experience and linking up to make the network more dynamic. The rest of the indicators will help us answer the questions proposed in the first section of this study.

First question: Are CA nodes, agents and actors central to the mapping of social networks?

The results show that CA nodes, agents and actors are central agricultural producers featured in the current study shared detailed information about management, practices and ways in which they understand, practice and adopt CA as a fundamental part of their agricultural practices. Thus, four ways of practicing CA were identified and abbreviated as shown in Table 2.

The 1,270 network nodes are distributed as follows: 162 CA, 118 CC, 90 SS-CA and only 11 FW-CA nodes. The above results take into account that the CA nodes–actors–producers are where

Table 2:   Types of agriculture

Type of Agriculture		Characteristics
CA	Conservation Agriculture	Soil disturbance, including leaving land fallow, sub-soiling, tilling, basins, cleaning or eliminating plant residue from previous crops and establishing a single crop on a section of or the entire agricultural surface.
CC	Conventional Agriculture	Soil disturbance, including leaving land fallow, sub-soiling, tilling, basins, cleaning or eliminating plant residue from previous crops and establishing a single crop on a section of or the entire agricultural surface.
SS-CA	Spring–Summer Conservation Agriculture	Takes advantage of crop residue from winter harvest (when not packed or sold for animal feed, in the case of barley, wheat or sorghum). During preparation stage for spring planting there is no or minimal soil disturbance and when summer harvest is over, crop residues are totally or partially used for animal feed (dairy or bovine cows or smaller barnyard animals). Crop residues are left to cover the soil. Two or three alternative crops on the same land surface.
FW-CA	Fall–Winter Conservation Agriculture	Whether they plow or not, there is no soil disturbance in winter. They leave crop residue and/or partially remove it if the producers need to take care of large animals.

Source: Prepared by the authors.

the majority of nodes and actors look for information. They teach, solve problems and provide CA information (see Tables 2, 3 and 4).

The average in-degree result (Table 3) is the intensity of consultation reported by producers that have adopted or appropriated CA practices as well as the producers that report strong closeness. Both are found in category 1, corresponding to CA practices, with an average of 0.109 in-degrees and an average of 0.149 degrees of high

Table 3:　Bajio hub: count and average total of in-degrees and reciprocity

Type of Agriculture	Count In-degrees	Average In-degrees	Average Reciprocal Closeness
CA	**162**	**0.109**	**0.149**
CC	118	0.035	0.041
SS-CA	90	0.045	**0.065**
FW-CA	11	0.007	0.007
Total	1270	0.101	0.140

Source: Prepared by the authors.

Table 4:　Bajio hub: count and average in-degrees by region of study

	Average In-degrees			
Type of Agriculture	High Lerma	Medium Lerma	Low Lerma	La Laja
CA	**0.122**	**0.091**	0.877	0.778
CC	0.049	0.048	0.235	0.123
SS-CA	**0.129**	0.078	0.627	0.188
FW-CA	0	0.05	**0.752**	**0.658**
Total	0.095	22.201	17.917	0.689

Source: Prepared by the authors.

closeness. As such, CA producers are better connected than others in the global Bajio hub network. Given these initial results, the data was disaggregated in order to establish if the behavioral patterns of the global Bajio Hub network would hold true in the sub regional analysis. In the High Lerma region, producers who practice general CA and those who practice SS-CA have a high level of consultation (0.12 and 0.129, respectively) with their producer counterparts. There were no producers that practiced FW-CA.

In the Middle Lerma region, the CA producers stood out from the rest of the categories with an average of 0.91. In the Low Lerma region, there was an average of 0.877 for CA and an average of 0.752 for FW-CA. As such, it can be said that the CA adoption process is dominant.

Finally, for the La Laja region, similarly to the previously mentioned zones, CA stands out with an average of 0.778 and FW-CA had an average of 0.658. Both averages indicate that there is strong adoption of CA innovations in this region. On both the individual and the general level for the regions, the in-degree measure, consultation or information search averages from producers is considerably higher for CA, SS-CA and FW-CA.

Second question: What is the level of connectivity among CA nodes within the study region?

The results indicate that the level of connectivity is closest for producers practicing CA (Table 5) and it is higher among farmers that use CA technologies during at least one crop cycle.

The data shown in Table 4 indicate that there are 162 nodes, actors or producers in the CA category, with an average of 0.149 in the reciprocity indicator. This indicates that the producers have a high level of connectivity in their relationships. This high level of connectivity in turn implies that they are consulted by their counterparts and the rest of the actors or nodes (input providers, marketers, relatives, neighbors, financers, *etc.*) in the network. They also present a high degree of connection with all actors that integrate the Bajio hub and are related to CA. The results for all four regions of the total Bajio hub network, considering the peculiarities of the hydro-agro-ecological region, are shown in Table 6.

Reciprocity in the first region, High Lerma, with an average of 148.8, is much stronger in SS-CA than in CA, FW-CA and CC. The Medium Lerma region shows intermediate behavior with an average

Table 5: Bajio hub: frequency and degrees of closeness by type of agriculture

Type of Agriculture	Frequency	Average Reciprocal Closeness
CA	162	0.149
CC	118	0.041
SS-CA	90	0.065
FW-CA	11	0.007
Total	1270	0.14

Source: Prepared by the authors.

Table 6:   Bajio hub: homophily by agriculture type in the entire network

Type of Agriculture	CA	CC	SS-CA	FW-CA
CA	985	186	728	0
CC	317	156	654	0
SS-CA	871	177	752	0
FW-CA	13	12	77	0

Source: Prepared by the authors.

of 0.115 and 0.102, respectively. The results are similar for the other two regions. This contrasts with the Low Lerma region, with an average of 1.003 reciprocity, and the La Laja region, with an average of 0.867. Reciprocal practices among nodes, actors and producers in CA are considerably stronger in these two regions.

Third question: Is the diversity of connections related to CA adoption?

This question contributes to the reflective analysis of our results from two sides of this research. During the fieldwork, the actors and producers were interviewed about how they felt about the people who practiced CA. The responses coincided with the behavior and profile of those who had been practicing CA for the longest time. The next paragraph shows the opinion of farmer who does not practice CA about other farmer who does:

> "... At the beginning, we all thought it was crazy. We didn't understand why we weren't leaving fields fallow or plowing like we normally did .... Even though we said he was crazy, out of his mind, and had a screw loose, he looked happy and he just smiled .... He always helps us and gives us advice, he lends us equipment ... and he even gives us a beer sometimes when he sees that our crops come up short .... We used to waste a lot more time moving soil around and spending on chemicals. Aren't we crazy?!" (Field Interview 08 GTO-MICH)

The attitude of most farmers who use CC is to resist change, and this evident from by the fact that they disqualify and criticize CA without having any concrete arguments to support what they say or to contradict CA's advances and results.

The producers, and some other nodes and actors that are transitioning to a complete adoption of CA technology, already show perceivable behavior shifts toward the rest of the nodes. They have started to identify with their counterparts, even reaching open reciprocity, which becomes even stronger in emergency situations due to climate change and water scarcity. The following quote is an example of how producers build their networks.

> "... The crazy, failed American couldn't convince me.... I just observe them.... I walk by their land plots and I realize that they left the crop residue, they don't burn it anymore! ... One day, a friend from Guanajuato came so I could explain to him how I fixed my equipment.... When he left, he took some eggs for breakfast and a few little plants that I gave to him.... No! We didn't know each other ... they say that rolling stones just find each other. He and I were among the people who produced the most tons this past year, and that's how we know we're not so crazy.... In Jalisco, I found another guy like myself, a little crazier actually, because he used pure fertilizer that he made himself with rocks, chilies and flowers." (Field Interview 10 GTO-MICH)

Many actors revived traditional knowledge, often inherited from their ancestors, and combine this with CA practices. Producers innovate and experiment, seeking to revive ancestral knowledge inherited from friends and family, as a way to recognize traditional wisdom when interacting with nature in two main areas of production: soil and water. This type of profile in key actors supports the performance of innovation champions (Klerkx and Aarts, 2013). A variety of activities arise from this juxtaposition: trying new varieties that grow faster and are more resistant to drought or excess water, adapting planting equipment to improve output, mixing vegetative materials (chilies, flowers, *etc.*) and minerals that fight crop plagues and plant diseases while enriching soil with nutrients, *etc.*

All of the above represents the reservoir of traditional knowledge. In Vincent Ostrom's (1980) analysis, this knowledge becomes practices, called *artifacts* when used by *artisan*-producers, and is shared among people until it becomes new common knowledge. Poteete *et al.* (2010) talk about the reach this common knowledge can obtain when people share it and replicate it.

This common knowledge, in combination with innovative CA technology, is well accepted among producers who are sensitive to the dynamically changing landscape of food production. The most obvious symptoms of this sensitivity is the attitudes and behavior of producers regarding the transition processes that their neighbors, family members, friends, colleagues, technicians, public servants, professional service providers, businessmen, lenders, among others. The only way to help them see what motivates their choice is to show them results as the interviews indicated: high and stable yields, low environmental impact and higher income for the producer. These are three goals that CIMMYT has promoted among farmers that have already begun or are starting to use CA practices.

In this context, another interesting concept is the conscious or unconscious tendency to associate ourselves with people similar to us. This concept is called *homophily*, literally, love for those like ourselves. Cristakis and Fowler (2010) state that beyond selecting our counterparts, we also select the structure of our innovation networks in the following three ways: We decide with how many people we are connected; we change how our families and close networks are connected and we control in what part of the social network we exist (center or periphery).

The above helps to understand why connection diversity, especially in micro or cellular networks, the closeness between farmers and family relationships is associated with adopting CA, using the homophily calculation (McPherson *et al.*, 2001). In this way, we can answer the third question we proposed. Below, the results obtained for each of the four types of agriculture practiced in the Bajio Hub are explained with descriptive statistics.

For type 1 CA, the relationship in the first column (CA) as well as the third (SS-CA) shows robust frequency for this association

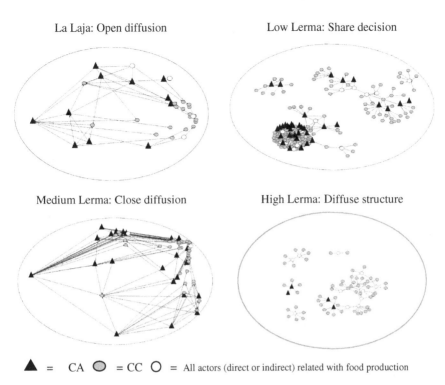

La Laja: Open diffusion   Low Lerma: Share decision

Medium Lerma: Close diffusion   High Lerma: Diffuse structure

▲ = CA ◉ = CC ◯ = All actors (direct or indirect) related with food production

Figure 6.   Study zones with four types of structural networks in the Bajio hub

(Table 6). It means the farmers with CA had strong relationships between their pairs, even in the second column, associated with CC. Producers seek association between pairs for conventional agricultural practices and others too while the CC farmers (2nd row in type of agriculture) had better connection with farmers in transition whose practice CA only in SS.

In structures with open diffusion, more nodes are atomized and access to information and to new nodes or actors becomes difficult. Therefore, there are no conditions for the kind of cooperation that is necessary for dynamic CA (Figure 6).

Diffuse structures are present in the zone La Laja, where geo-physical conditions and disperse human settlements resulted in the spread of micro-dispersed networks or cellular networks. However, despite the aforementioned conditions, the networks here are much more agile in their internal dynamics and degrees of connectivity. It is important to highlight that in this region there is increased interest in adopting technological innovations and the more proactive people performing this task are women.

Next steps for research will focus on cellular or micro networks and define how farmers are building cooperation, trust and reciprocity as basic tools for reciprocal closeness, making for strong geodesic positions. It is anticipated that information sharing in CA for adoption will be greater when some women are central nodes or actors in the network. This research will pay attention to diversity and complexity within gender relations.

Despite structural differences each region has different potential according to the objective of technological innovation applied. Knowing what determines these differences in decision-making from the attributes of each actor is an element to be developed: Are the adverse conditions and limitations — what triggers major change decisions safely and permanently?

Conclusion

Currently, network analysis is a fundamental tool for the study of the social fabric among actors, institutions and their relationships. Network analysis shows the impact of each individual within the structure of the whole network, moving beyond an individual-level focus to portray the outcomes of collective action. It is inclusive, dynamic and multiplicative. According to innovation networks theory from Rogers and Sen, it is a helpful methodological tool for policy makers and for CA innovation technology on yield. The adoption of CA in the Bajio hub is an example of how innovation networks are oriented towards the identification of nodes and actors with a higher degree of centrality, which facilitates work and dissemination as well as the adoption of complex agricultural technologies.

Farmers that currently practice CA are central to the general network map. There are specific actors and nodes that present strong in-degrees, and they are strategically selected to establish platforms and modules. With 14.9% in-degrees of closeness, we conclude that the Bajio hub's connectivity is dynamic and would facilitate faster advances thanks to the short distances between nodes. This reinforces what we have previously said about what is required for an effective strategy to encourage adoption of CA technology. This strategy increases the speed at which technology is adopted, all with a lower cost to the public policy's programs together with agriculture traditional targeting techniques.

From a network perspective, we can advance the understanding of micro social phenomena between farmers in focused, specific areas. In other words, phenomena derived from social actors that simultaneously exhibit individual, institutional and structural social interactions can be empirically observed. Regarding the micro-networks or cell networks study, it implicitly focuses on the weakest nodes and actors, which are usually omitted from consideration when thinking of medium- and long-term actions. The homophily study on relationships between pairs explains why regardless of distance or context, pairs find each other and evolve together.

This work suggests several studies relevant to the future: (i) It is important to identify small details in informal networks as well as small actors and weak nodes that could make a difference in large social structures; (ii) as such, we recommend studies that use mixed methodologies. Following these two steps would serve to highlight new issues in the rural environment, such as the role of women in rural contexts, which is fundamental to studies pertaining to the rural social dynamics. Such studies could help decision makers to design gender-sensitive interventions; and (iii) it is important to use structured methodologies that allow for comparison with other studies undertaken in other regions and provide the framework for meta-analysis. As a tool that supports the decision-making process when there are few resources and little time, network analysis is a strategic element to design, operate, follow up, evaluate and control high impact social public policies.

There are four topics for further analysis: first, individual profiles that focus on gender in micro-cellular networks; second, the evolution of deep cooperation between women in CA and women in CC, and between women and men; third, adoption by time of multiple levels of CA; and fourth, identify the interaction of multiple kinds of champions in orchestrating innovation networks as systemic local, regional and national managers.

Acknowledgments

Dr. Ralph Christy for his respectful trust and support, Danya Glabau for tracking with perfect American English writing, Dr. Peter Hobbs and Dr. David Spielman for reading and valuable comments. To Cornell (USA) and UACh (MEX) Universities (CIMMYT) and each farmer who kindly received us during fieldwork.

References

CEDERSA (2011) Centro de Estudios para el Desarrollo Rural Sustentable y la Soberanía Alimentaria (CEDRSSA) y UACh-CEDERSA.

Cristakis NA and Fowler HJ (2010) *Connected, the Surprising Power of Networks and How They Affect Us.* New York: Little, Brown.

Erenstein O (1999) The economics of soil conservation in developing countries: The case of crop residue mulching. PhD thesis. Wageningen University, the Netherlands, p. 301.

Govaerts B, Salgado JL, Chocobar AC, Flores D, Delgado F, Romero R, Rascon R, Martinez A, Verhulst N and Sayre KD (2009) Making conservation agriculture work; proof of concept of the hub approach in different agro-ecological areas in Mexico. ASA-CSSA-SSSA Annual Meeting, 1–5 November, Pittsburgh, USA.

Granovetter M (1985) Economic action and social structure: the problem of embeddedness. *American Journal of Sociology* 91: 481–510.

Hobbs PR (2007) Conservation agriculture: what is it and why is it important for future sustainable food production? *The Journal of Agricultural Science* 145: 127–137.

Hobbs PR and Govaerts B (2010) How conservation agriculture can contribute to buffering climatic change. In Reynolds MP (ed.), *Climatic Change and Crop Production.* Wallingford, UK: CABI, pp. 177–194.

International Maize and Wheat Improvement Center (CIMMYT) (2010) MAIZE — Global alliance for improving food security and the livelihoods of the resource-poor in the developing world. 1: 5–12.

Klerkx L and Aarts N (2013) The interaction of multiple champions in orchestrating innovation networks: conflicts and complementarities. *Technovation* 33(6–7): 1–18. Available at http://www.sciencedirect.com/science/article/pii/S0166497213000242 [accessed on 27 May 2013].

Lobell D and Burke M (2010) Economic impacts of climatic change on agriculture to 2030. In Reynolds MP (ed.), *Climatic Change and Crop Production*. Wallingford, UK: CABI, p. 38.

McPherson M, Smith-Lovin L and Cook JM (2001) Birds of a feather: homophily in social networks. *Annual Review of Sociology* 27: 415–444.

Ostrom V (1980) Artisanship and artifact. *Public Administration Review* 40(4): 309–317.

Poteete A, Janssen M and Ostrom E (2010) *Working Together, Collective Action, the Commons and Multiple Methods in Practice*. Princeton: Princeton University Press.

Reynolds MP (ed.) (2010) *Climatic Change and Crop Production*. Wallingford, UK: CABI.

Reynolds MP, Hellin J, Govaerts B, Kosina P, Sonder K, Hobbs P and Braun HJ (2011) Global crop improvement networks to bridge technology gaps. *Journal of Experimental Botany* 1–12. doi:10.1093/jxb/err241.

Rogers E (1995) *Diffusion of Innovations*. New York: Free Press.

Scientific American (2010) Special Issue 303(3): 60.

Scott JP (2000) *Social Networks Analysis: A Handbook*, 2nd edn. Thousand Oaks, CA: Sage.

Sen A (2010) Temas claves del siglo XXI. In Sen A and Kliksberg B (eds.), *Primero la Gente*. Barcelona: Editorial Deuso, pp. 1–79.

Spielman DJ, Davis K, Negash M and Ayele G (2011) Rural innovation systems and networks: findings from a study of Ethiopian smallholders. *Agriculture and Human Values* 28(2): 195–212.

Thorton P (2012) Recalibrating food production in the development world: global warming will change more than just the climate. Research Program on Climatic Change, Agriculture and Food Security, CCAFS Policy Brief No. 6, pp. 1–16.

Wasserman S and Faust K (1994) *Social Network Analysis, Methods and Applications*. Cambridge: Cambridge University Press.

Appendix A. Bajio Hub Survey, Administered on August–September, 2011

This survey is part of the project "Sustainable Development with Producers" and is part of the initiative "Sustainable Modernization of Traditional Agriculture" Bajio Hub Survey.

Location of land parcel (GPS):   N: _____
                                   W: _____
Altitude (masl): _____
Surveyor: _____
Supervisor: _____
*Cycles: Fall–Winter (F–W) and Spring–Summer (S–S)

I.- General
1.1.- Survey number   [   ]
1.2.- Name of farmer   _____
1.5.- Years spent in agricultural production [   ]
1.6.- Education (years)   [   ]
1.7.- Locale/Municipality/State   _____
1.8.- Name of technical advisor, if there is one   _____

XXIII.- Info-Conservation Earth-Networks

23.1 *Besides your family, whom else do you consult when planting?/Whom else do you go to in order to talk about planting? (what to plant, how to cultivate it, who has the sower...?)*

Name[/4]	Activity[/5]	ID[/6]	Observations[/7]

23.2 *When you have a problem with your plants, whom do you ask for advice on how to solve it? Who tells you how to fix it?*

Name[/4]	Activity[/5]	ID[/6]	Observations[/7]

23.3 *For planting: From whom do you buy your supplies?/ Who sells you what you need?*

Name[/4]	Activity[/5]	ID[/6]	Observations[/7]

- - End of the Survey - -

Thank you for your participation.

Chapter 4

GEOGRAPHY MATTERS: EVIDENCE AND IMPLICATIONS OF SPATIAL SELECTION IN CONTRACT FARMING SCHEMES IN SOUTHERN INDIA

Sudha Narayanan

Indira Gandhi Institute of Development Research (IGIDR),
General A. K. Vaidya Marg, Goregaon (East), Mumbai, India
sudha@igidr.ac.in

Current literature on farmer participation in dynamic agri-food supply chains focuses predominantly on one kind of inclusion based on individual farmer characteristics. Relatively less attention has been devoted to spatial selection. This chapter contends that exclusion can often be based on geographies and the precise nature of exclusion has important implications for the level at which public policy interventions should operate. This study investigates multiple sources of farmer exclusion in contract farming schemes involving agro-processors and farmers in five commodity sectors in southern India, including broiler, cotton, gherkins, marigold and papaya. Using data on 822 farmers, collected through surveys conducted between 2007 and 2010, this chapter decomposes the likelihood of inclusion into two components, spatial selection and farmer selection, to examine the pattern of exclusion across the different commodity sectors. The study finds that geography matters and that firms regularly select communities spatially over a geographic domain before choosing a portfolio of farmer–suppliers, implying that sorting across farmers is relevant only within the chosen geographies of procurement. Further the chapter discusses the implications for public policy relating to contract farming in India, especially pertaining to agro-processing clusters and agro export zones.

Introduction

The rapidly evolving agro-food sectors in developing countries are often regarded as offering rich possibilities for enhancing the well-being of resource-poor smallholders in these countries. For this to happen, these chains need to be inclusive in the first place (Barrett *et al.*, 2011; Minot, 2008; Reardon and Gulati, 2008; Swinnen, 2007). Recent scholarship has rightly focused on the drivers of smallholder inclusion in order to identify conditions under which smallholders are able to participate (Boselie *et al.*, 2003; Carter and Mesbah, 1993; Dileep *et al.*, 2002; Glover and Kusterer, 1990; Kumar, 2007; Runsten and Key, 1996a, 1996b; Von Braun *et al.*, 1989; Wang *et al.*, 2009; Zamora, 2004). However, much of the current literature on farmer participation in dynamic supply chains, whether in agro-processing or the supermarket-driven retail sector, focuses predominantly on one kind of inclusion, namely that based on individual farmer characteristics, including farm size, farmer wealth and access to resources (Dev and Rao, 2005; Glover and Ghee Lim, 1992; Miyata *et al.*, 2009; Runsten and Key, 1996a, 1996b; Warning and Key, 2002). Relatively less attention has been devoted to spatial selection of procurement sheds by firms on account of crop characteristics, agro-climatic factors or locational advantages; most studies that do address these issues do so only perfunctorily. Agribusinesses on the other hand often routinely sort over geographies, sometimes choosing to cluster procurement from specific areas.

Exclusion and inclusion can therefore occur in multiple ways and the precise nature of exclusion has important implications for the level at which public policy interventions should operate. If, for example, firms tend to sort farmers by farm or individual characteristics to source produce but do not discriminate over geographies, policy interventions are best targeted at individual farmers. If, on the other hand, inclusion/exclusion is based on some notion of geographic comparative advantage arising from locational or agro-climatic attributes, this would have important implications for public policy in the excluded zones and possibly different implications for included zones.

This study presents qualitative evidence from detailed interviews with over 40 agribusinesses in India, conducted between 2007 and 2010, on procurement strategies. In addition, this chapter synthesizes research findings from a study that investigates multiple sources of farmer exclusion, focusing on contract farming schemes involving agro-processors and farmers in five commodity sectors in southern India, including broiler, cotton, gherkins, marigold and papaya. Using data on 822 farmers collected through surveys conducted over the same time period, the chapter discusses results from decomposing the likelihood of inclusion into two components, spatial selection and farmer selection, to examine the pattern of exclusion across the different commodity sectors. The empirical evidence suggests that geography matters indeed and firms regularly select communities spatially over a geographic domain before choosing a portfolio of farmer-suppliers, implying that sorting across farmers is relevant only within the chosen geographies of procurement. The study also finds that the relative importance of selection over space and agro-climatic regions varies significantly across commodities.

Following this introduction, I conceptualize a process of selection that reflects strategies that firms employ to develop procurement sheds and identify farmer suppliers in contract farming systems. I discuss examples from interviews covering a wide range of agricultural commodities. The section that follows then zooms in on five commodities — broiler chicken, cotton, gherkins, marigold and papaya — in the southern state of Tamil Nadu. I present and synthesize results from the field study to document the nature of selection. The concluding section comments on the implications for public policy relating to contract farming in India especially those pertaining to agro-processing clusters and agro export zones.

The Structural Process of Selection

Across India, firms typically tend to first select broad agro-climatic regions where it is feasible for contract commodities to grow, often locating processing plants and procurement or collection centers accordingly. Within these regions, firms choose particular geographic tracts before choosing individual farmers as contract suppliers. Firms then pick a portfolio of contract farmers, with specific volumes

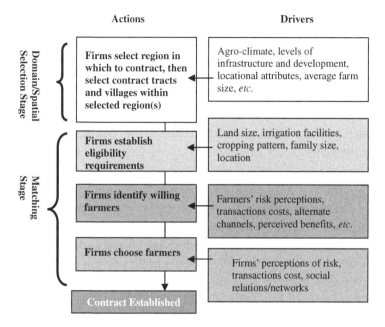

Figure 1.   The process of selection

(or acreage) to contract and have an opportunity to reassess and modify this portfolio over time, based on experience and learning and in response to changes in the external conditions. All of this is conditional on farmers being willing to contract with the firm. This selection process itself is modeled in Narayanan (2012a). The focus here is on the layered nature of selection.

Figure 1 illustrates the process where, usually, a contracting firm chooses the region (blocks) from which to source produce. I refer to this spatial selection as the 'domain layer' of selection. Firms then pick villages in these areas. Within these 'contract villages' the firm usually draws up a list of potential participants who are willing to contract, either through field officials or through intermediaries, or farmers self-identify and express a desire to participate. Subsequently, contingent on the potential participants fulfilling any eligibility criteria that the firm might establish, the firm 'chooses' farmers with whom to contract (Figure 1). At this stage, participation in contract farming schemes is a matching problem (hence called 'matching layer') of farmers willing to contract with the firm, and the firm choosing farmers with whom to contract. This is driven not just by the perceived benefits of doing so but also by mutual perceptions of reliability and trust or, inversely, riskiness. Each layer of selection is associated with a different set of covariates that influence which regions are selected and which farmers are chosen as contract suppliers.

Choosing Farmers and Choosing Geographies

Qualitative empirical evidence from interviews of agribusinesses, henceforth called Agribusiness Survey, suggests that agro-climatic conditions and seasonality are important considerations for spatial selection and hinge on the suitability of the crop to the region. Among the contract commodities studied, cotton, for instance, requires black soils and is typically less productive in other types of soils. Papaya does not do well in windy areas, where young trees may break. Similarly, given the warm temperatures in parts of India, commodities such as potatoes, marigold and some medicinal herbs are only feasible in the cooler mid-elevation regions. As a marigold processor explained, "Although earlier we procured from the plains, today we focus 90% of the procurement from the mid-elevation areas. The oleoresin content is much higher in these areas. Yield of marigold is also higher. In the plains if we get 6–7 tons/acre, in the hills it could even be as high as 15 tons/acre" (Agribusiness Survey, Karamadai, Tamil Nadu, 2007). Other characteristics, such as color and quality of the produce, may also drive a firm's spatial preference. One agribusiness executive said that the firm avoided procuring from some regions close to the plant because the gherkins that grew in that particular tract had "no color" (Agribusiness Survey, Sirumalai, Tamil Nadu, 2007).

Firms often choose areas where they can procure across many seasons, in order to run the plant throughout the year or choose a portfolio of geographic regions where they can procure in different seasons. Sometimes firms choose regions exclusively for procurement smoothing, procuring during seasons when the regular procurement shed does not grow the contract commodity. For example, the state of Jharkhand in north India was seen to be attractive for potato contracting purely because it offered the processing plant potatoes during a season when potatoes were unavailable in neighboring West Bengal, the main source of potato supplies (Agribusiness Survey, Ranchi, Jharkhand, 2008).

Often, plants are established within the agro-climatic zone where cultivation of the contract commodity is feasible. To that extent, plant location is itself a function of agro-climatic factors. Once the plant is established, perishability of produce often induces firms to procure within an acceptable radius around the plant, imposing constraints on spatial coverage. The best-known example of this is sugarcane, where the cane needs to be crushed within a few hours for optimum extraction. For papaya, once latex is extracted, it has to be used in the plant within three or four hours. So, the firms choose farmers located close to the plant. Gherkin firms in India usually procure from within a 50 kilometer radius from the plant. Gherkins are highly perishable and firms try "to get them to the processing plant as quickly as possible, within hours if possible."

Even when perishability of the crop is not a concern, firms sometimes choose a portfolio of villages in a particular tract before they match up with farmers for contracting. This may be done either to ensure yields and, hence, volumes or to obtain better contractual performance in terms of reliable deliveries. As one executive said, "We choose villages. That's what makes sense to us. We select villages where land is suitable, where there are sandy soils and good water" (Agribusiness Survey, Bangalore, Karnataka, 2008). This practice reduces the risk of not getting enough volume for processing, he pointed out. Another said, "We want to go and select villages where the farmers are very poor or tribals" to ensure better compliance (Agribusiness Survey, Hyderabad, Andhra Pradesh, 2008). Yet another executive explained, "We focused on villages that had no market access. There are many villages where farmers have no clue about the outside world, let alone about markets. Their mentality is such that they never cross the line or transgress" (Agribusiness Survey, Dindigul, Tamil Nadu, 2007).

Once villages are chosen, firms try to identify farmers with whom to contract. While firms try to sort heterogeneous farmer types based on location, reliability, size, soil quality and so forth, farmers' perceptions of the benefits and risks associated with contract farming and its spillovers drive farmers' propensity or willingness to be considered for contracting (Narayanan, 2012b). This could include a range of factors such as entry costs, family size, perceived mean, variance and correlation of the returns to the contract crop relative to alternative uses of land and labor, social learning and beliefs about impact on soil fertility and quality, health and so on. At this stage, it is not simply a matter of firms picking farmers. The identification of contract suppliers is contingent on farmers being willing to contract (Narayanan, 2012a). This is not self-evident. Many farmers choose not to contract because of their perceptions of risks and returns associated with contracting schemes.

There is often a time lag between a farmer learning of the option and actually declaring willingness to contract. In some places it is easy. An agribusiness executive said of the Punjab: "Adoption by farmers in Punjab is fairly quick. Farmers tend to watch others' fields keenly. As soon as they find something interesting, they approach you and ask: 'What is this? How does it grow? What do I have to do? Can I join?'" (Agribusiness Survey, New Delhi, 2008). In other places, it may not be so easy. An executive explained, "Farmers were skeptical and did not understand the process of ethanol making…. We undertook some demonstrations. This gave the farmers some confidence that such an option was indeed possible and real" (Agribusiness Survey, Hyderabad, Andhra Pradesh, 2007). In some cases, it is hard to persuade certain classes of farmers. For example, a firm contracting sorghum claims that it could never get the large and rich farmers interested in contracting because sorghum was considered a poor man's crop. Sometimes firms choose poor farmers, just like they choose distant villages, to ensure sustainable relationships. "We ensured that we picked some really vulnerable people who had few other alternatives. When there were enough people like that there was a critical mass that wanted to keep the contracting scheme going" (Agribusiness Survey, Vijayawada, Andhra Pradesh, 2007). At the matching stage, there is a two-sided selection process that eventually sorts farmers into contract farmers and non-participating farmers. Many firms, for crops like gherkins and papaya, only select farmers who have access to irrigation. In other crops the opposite can hold true. For jatropha for instance, an agribusiness executive explained: "We go to areas and find farmers with minimal water resources. For instance, if there is a farmer with 10 acres who is growing banana on 2 acres and leaves the 8 acres fallow for want of water, we tell him to grow jatropha on all the 10 acres. It will require the same amount of water as the two acres under banana." Sometimes, labor availability is an important criterion. A crop like gherkins, for instance, has high peak labor requirements, at the time of harvesting. In contrast, with tree crops and biofuels, firms tend to choose farmers and regions that have labor problems, and farmers are looking for crops that have low labor demand. An agribusiness executive for coconut contracting said they went to big farmers, those with 100 acres or so, since these people are looking for "low management crops." This was the case with jatropha and pongamia as well.

Farmer exclusion can thus happen due to multiple reasons working at different levels. For example, across the domain, farmers located in villages farther away from the processing plant or wholesale warehouse might be prone to exclusion, whereas within a 'contract' village, the farmer whose ethnicity is distinct from the 'lead' farmer or the dominant group might be excluded.

Decomposing the Probability of Participation

If the layered nature of selection is an appropriate way to approach the problem, we can use a simple decomposition exercise to separate the two effects following Heckman and Smith (2003). The probability that a farmer contracts $P(C)$ is given by:

$$P(C) = P(C|V)P(V|B)P(B), \qquad (1)$$

where $P(C)$ is the probability of a farmer being a contract farmer, $P(C|V)$ is the probability of a farmer contracting given that the village is selected for contracting, $P(V|B)$ is the probability that a village is selected given a block is selected, where a block is an administrative unit consisting of several villages. $P(B)$ is the probability of a block being selected as a procurement area. It is clear that the probability of a farmer contracting is equal to the conditional probability of a farmer being selected given the village is selected only when the probability of village and block being selected is one. This implies that firms do not have a geographic preference or exhibit no preference over which villages are chosen.

The empirical counterpart for this model can be expressed as

$$\rho_c = \rho_{c/v} \times \rho_{v/b} \times \rho_b, \tag{2}$$

where $\rho_{c/v}$, $\rho_{v/b}$ and ρ_b are the stage probabilities. Each stage of Figure 1, *i.e.*, the different component probabilities, can be estimated for a contract commodity using a set of stage specific covariates $X = (x_c, x_v, x_b)$. These covariates help identify the factors driving inclusiveness (or alternatively, exclusion) at different levels and enable investigation of the type of exclusion in a given contracting system (Narayanan, 2012a).

Five Cases from Southern India

This section synthesizes and reviews evidence from a field survey in the southern Indian state of Tamil Nadu. The data come from a survey of 822 farmers covering five commodity sectors — broiler chickens, cotton, gherkins, marigold and papaya — conducted between 2007 and 2010. The list of contracting farmers for the year of the survey was obtained from one contracting firm in each of the commodities studied. Based on this list, all the hamlets in the sample area were divided into contracting and non-contracting hamlets and their corresponding villages into contracting villages and on-contracting villages. A similar exercise was carried out for the larger administrative units called blocks and then districts. A stratified sampling process was followed that ensured that the samples of non-contract farmers for each commodity are drawn both from contract villages and from geographic tracts where the firm does not contract. These data were then combined with village and block level characteristics collected as part of the decennial census.[1] The survey was conducted in two phases: cotton and gherkins constitute Phase 1 and broiler, marigold, papaya and a follow-upon the same gherkins firm constitute Phase 2.

For these five commodities, the different component probabilities (namely, $\rho_{c/v}$, $\rho_{v/b}$, ρ_b) are estimated from a model that regresses current contracting status or whether the firm contracts from the region on relevant stage specific correlates, $X = (x_c, x_v, x_b)$, described in Figure 1. For details of these estimations, see Narayanan (2012a).

At the block level, the probability of a block being a contract block is estimated as a function of block characteristics constructed as the average of those characteristics across villages belonging to the block. This is estimated for all the blocks in the study area. As explanatory variables, I use proportion of land irrigated, proportion of land cultivated, average literacy, proportion of population belonging to the Scheduled Castes or Tribes, number or proportion of cultivators in the total workforce, population density, average farm size, average family size, and average household monthly income.

For the next level of spatial selection, I restrict the dataset to all villages belonging to a contract block. The dependent variable here is a binary variable on whether a village is a contract or non-contract village. This is regressed on a set of variables denoting facilities and socio-demography at the village level, from the decadal census. These include the same set of variables used for the model for block selection.

For the matching layer of selection, the estimation of farmer probability of contracting, I now restrict the data to all sample farmers in the sample villages where contracting by the subject firm takes place. At this level of selection, I use a range of farmer characteristics including socio-economic and demographic variables, asset ownership and location. I also include variables representing farmer perceptions

---

[1] The latest data available pertain to 2001, but the assumption is that these data broadly reflect the inter-village differences in infrastructure facilities in the latter part of the decade.

of the benefits and risks of contracting with the sample firm relative to the next best alternative, as indicated by the farmer.

The empirical analysis is confined to a static notion of selection, referring to the contracting status of a farmer at a particular time. Further, it also focuses on extensive participation rather than the intensity of participation. Extensive participation is a binary concept that has to do with whether or not, at a given point in time, a farmer participates in a scheme, whereas intensity of participation refers to volume or acreage that forms part of the contractual commitment. Extensive participation has dominated discussions of farmer participation in contracting schemes and is hence the focus of this work.[2] Extensive selection is relevant to the extent that firms do sort on the extensive margin, deeming some farmers to be more desirable partners than others. Detailed methods and results are presented in Narayanan (2012b). The following part reviews the findings of the regression exercise, focusing on the significant correlates and the contrasts among the different commodities.[3]

Drivers of Participation and Selection

Spatial selection

It is apparent that firms use a diversity of approaches for selection of geographies depending on the contract commodity. The broiler contracting firm chooses areas (blocks) where the average cultivated land area per household is large and where villages are tightly clustered around urban centers. Within these blocks, however, the firm appears to pick large, more sparsely populated villages where cultivation is not on a large scale, indicated both by per household availability of cultivable land and by the total number of cultivators. These villages tend to depend on agriculture, given that the majority of the workforce

---

[2] Intensive participation, or the quantity or proportion contracted, is an important dimension as well that is akin to the extent of exposure to different crops the farmer wants to have.

[3] Contact the author for datasets and results of the regression analysis.

constitutes cultivators. The average income of households in the villages selected is also lower than in villages that are not selected.

Interviews with the marigold contracting firm suggest that marigold is sourced primarily from mid-elevation regions in the northern part of the study area, where cooler temperatures are conducive to higher yields. The selection of blocks reflects this spatial preference accurately, *i.e.*, the statistically significant characteristics are those that one would associate with the hilly regions in peninsular India. Villages within these tracts are scattered around a handful of urban centers, and blocks tend to be more sparsely populated than those in the plains. The availability of cultivated land per household is low, owing to parts that are thickly forested. The contracting region is, however, also characterized by a predominance of rain-fed agriculture, represented by the higher proportion of land that is cultivated. Block selection is also positively associated with the percentage of workforce whose main occupation is agricultural labor. Within these blocks, firms choose villages where availability of cultivated land per household is higher and which are less remote in terms of distance to the nearest town. Interestingly, for marigold nearness to a town works in opposing ways at different stages of selection. While marigold contracting is prevalent in blocks where villages are scattered so that on average villages are farther away from the nearest town than in non-contract blocks, within a block firms choose villages close to urban centers. There are obvious reasons for this choice. The distance from the nearest town is a proxy for road infrastructure, and choosing villages closer to towns makes it easier for the firm to evacuate contracted volumes, just as it lowers the costs associated with delivering inputs and monitoring.

A similar pattern of block and village selection is evident with papaya contracting. The papaya firm tends to contract in blocks where villages are, on average, located farther away from towns amid sparsely populated blocks, and yet within a block tend to choose villages that are closer to towns. In the case of papaya, the collection centers for latex are located close to towns, but firm officials suggest that the location of the latex collection point is established after the identification of farmers who contract for supplying latex. The firm's selection of villages is associated positively with the irrigation facility in a village as indicated by the percentage of cultivated land that is irrigated.

The spatial selection for gherkin procurement indicates a greater preference for blocks where average cultivable land per household is small, where family sizes are large or where a relatively larger proportion of the workforce are agricultural laborers, reflecting, perhaps, the labor demands required for gherkin cultivation. Within blocks, firms seem to choose villages that are farther away from town or ones populated predominantly by people from marginalized castes. Indeed, even within the surveyed villages, during the survey, it was apparent that the hamlets where contract farmers were located tend to be remote or populated by particular social groups belonging to the Scheduled Castes and Tribes.

At the time of the survey, cotton contracting was highly concentrated in a few blocks in one district and given that this was the last season of operation it represents the vestiges of a scheme. The firm had just dropped a large number of blocks located in another district. This clustering around one urban center in one district is reflected in the selection of blocks with the average distance of villages being lower in the contracting blocks. Within the block, selection of villages is associated with lower literacy but higher average income per household. Villages where the average cultivated land per household was smaller were more likely to be contract villages. Although models estimating spatial selection do not include variables for specific agro-climatic characteristics, these models are consistent with sample firms' description of their locational preference.

Farmer selection

Across schemes, farmer level correlates of participation suggest that farmer perceptions of the risk and returns associated with contracting, relative to the next best alternative, matter. It must be emphasized that at the matching stage, farmers' participation constraint determines the pool of farmers willing to contract, and a firm's selection of farmers assumes relevance only over and above that.

In general, the higher the perceived net incremental risk associated with contracting, the less the likelihood of a farmer contracting. On average, the higher the ratio of expected mean returns to contracting over that for the next best alternative, the greater the probability of a farmer contracting. The variable representing interaction between the estimated coefficient of risk aversion and the coefficient of variation of the contract commodity's price in the alternative market is associated positively with contracting status, suggesting that on average given risk aversion, a larger variation in market prices leads farmers to contract.[4]

That different commodities make different demands on farmers is well known. Additionally, in the context of a developing country, and in the absence of strong public enforcement through the courts, firms often look for farmer characteristics that minimize their risks of contract breach and costs, which is achieved partly through picking farmers capable of getting higher yields. These attributes naturally differ depending on the nature of the commodity and the firm itself.

Of the contract commodities studied, broiler and papaya require investments upfront. Broiler growers invest in sheds, drinkers and feeders for the birds and papaya growers need to ensure that basic irrigation facilities are in place. Gherkin farmers too tend to invest in spraying machines as the crop demands high pesticide application. Consequently, for all these crops, investments by the farmer potentially increase the likelihood of being offered contracts by the firm. In the cases of cotton and marigold there is practically no investment upfront.

Papaya contracting is associated with farmers who are more literate, are among the better off in the village, are less indebted and have a greater market orientation (with a greater proportion of food being purchased rather than consumed). Given these characteristics, those

---

[4] For a detailed analysis of these aspects, see Narayanan (2012b), which incorporates measures of skewness and stochastic dominance of farmer's subjective returns distributions from contracting and not contracting. These measures are not relevant in the context of this chapter other than pointing to the phenomenon of farmers selecting out of schemes of their own accord. The results discussed here are indicative rather than comprehensive.

belonging to the disadvantaged social groups, *i.e.*, Scheduled Castes, are more likely to be selected.

The likelihood of a farmer being offered broiler contracts is higher when the farmer is literate, but also when the proportion of annual income derived from cultivation is higher. Farmers often contract for broiler owing mainly to constraints on water availability that impinges on their ability to grow field crops. Even when there is no such constraint, however, farmers often opt for poultry since, in their words, it is almost like receiving a salary, bringing in regular income throughout the year.

In the case of cotton, farmers with smaller landholdings and smaller families are associated with greater likelihood of contracting. Younger farmers appear to be more likely to contract. Interestingly, the farther away a farmer is from the nearest wholesale market the more likely the farmer contracts for cotton. Given that cotton has a spot market that makes side-selling feasible and the fact that farmers are scattered, it may well be the case that the scheme's last season hinged on those for whom costs of side-selling were relatively high. Farmers who have a higher likelihood of participating in marigold contracting appear to be illiterate, hail from marginalized social groups, have larger families and work rain-fed farms. However, the larger the land owned and the lower the proportion of annual income derived from agriculture the greater the likelihood of contracting.

For the gherkin scheme across the two phases, interestingly, there is not much consistency in the drivers of selection. For instance, while in Phase 1, farmers who had better road access are more likely to contract, the opposite holds true for the sample in Phase 2. This difference is partly on account of the seasonal differences in sources of procurement. Phase 1 was conducted in the summer, whereas Phase 2 was conducted in the winter months. Further, the sample firm had dropped areas close to the plant owing to the stiff competition from other gherkin processors in the same region. The switch in the drivers might be on account of this shift. According to the sample firm, each firm was providing cash advances to farmers in order to attract participation and matching competitors' cash advance became increasingly difficult to sustain (Agribusiness Survey, Dindigul, Tamil Nadu, November 2007).

The evidence across crops on the drivers of selection suggests that there is much heterogeneity across crops, even as there are some elements shared across schemes (risk perceptions, for example). This observation reinforces scholarly opinion that suggests there is considerable diversity and context specificity in who participates. The value of this evidence is that such heterogeneity is present even within a contiguous area with a shared political administrative structure.

Evidence on sorting

The decomposition exercise along the lines of equations (1) and (2) enables us to test for sorting more rigorously (Narayanan, 2012b). It is evident that farmers with comparable characteristics in different villages or geographic units could end up with different contracting status, not because the firm chose one farmer over the other, but because the firm chose one geographic domain over the other. At this level, there is sorting of geographic units, but not of farmers. In other words, starkly different kinds of farmers maybe equally predisposed to participate or be selected into contract farming systems purely by virtue of their shared geographic domain. Modeling this stage gets at the notion of regional specialization in particular commodities based on comparative advantage and of geographic poverty traps (Barrett and Swallow, 2006). Exclusion in the sense of which farmer is preferred, say, based on individual farmer characteristics acquires relevance only within a selected village or hamlet. The firm sorts heterogeneous cultivators in the village from among willing contractees into contract suppliers and those who are not.

Specifically, this decomposition allows one to examine if 'similar' farmers in terms of the propensity to be selected (that is, the estimated probabilities based on observable farmer characteristics at the matching level) still end up with different contracting status because of selection at the domain level. This is one kind of exclusion. The other kind of exclusion would be where the propensity of region selection is the same, but farmers could nevertheless get sorted into those who are excluded and those who are included based on individual characteristics salient in the matching stage. I use this to demonstrate the levels at which sorting by firms takes place for different contract commodities studied.

The selection decomposition exercise allows for a simple comparison of the contribution of spatial selection or the domain layer and the contribution of farmer selection at the matching stage. To do this, I use the nearest neighbor matching method, where each observation belonging to the group of farmers that contract for a commodity is matched up with an observation from the group of farmers who do not contract with the commodity, on the basis of closeness of predicted constituent probabilities. The average difference in predicted probability of the other constituent probabilities is computed.[5] For example, to estimate the difference in estimated predicted probabilities that a block or village is selected, observations are matched on the basis of closeness of estimated predicted probability of a farmer being selected, given that the block or village is selected. Thus, to examine how significant the aspect of spatial selection or the domain layer is, each non-contract farmer is matched with a contract farmer such that both share the same predicted probability of participating, given their village is selected (*i.e.*, based on predicted $\rho_{c/v}$). The difference in predicted probabilities of village selection and of block selection is computed. In other words, the average difference between predicted $\rho_{v/b}$ is computed for village level exclusion and the average difference between ρ_b^{*} gives the difference in sorting at the block level. For sorting at the farmer level, the matching is made on the basis of predicted probabilities of both estimated predicted $\rho_{v/b}$ and ρ_b. The average difference between predicted probability of the farmer being selected ($\rho_{c/v}$) across contract and non-contract farmers is computed to produce an estimate of farmer level sorting.

Given that the data constitute predictions that are estimated as part of the selection decomposition exercise, there is a prediction error associated with the variables used for matching as well as with those used to compute the differences. The estimation hence allows for biases in matching. In addition, the standard errors correct for heteroscedasticity. Table 1 presents data on the difference in

---

[5] This is implemented using the nnmatch command in Stata (Abadie *et al.*, 2004).

Table 1:   Levels of sorting

Commodity	Difference in Average Predicted Probability at the Region Level Given		Differences in Average Predicted Probability at Farmer Level
(1)	(2)	(3)	(4)
	Village	Block	Farmer
Marigold	0.46***	0.2***	0.30***
Papaya	0.02*	0.02	0.34***
Broiler	0.21***	0.63***	0.47***
Cotton	−0.07***	0.06***	0.16***
Gherkins (Phase 1)	0.01	0.15***	0.15***
Gherkins (Phase 2)	0.28***	0.64***	0.38***

Notes: Significance levels: * = 10%; ** = 5%; *** = 1%.
[a]This is a simple matching estimator, implemented using nnmatch in STATA following Abadie *et al.* (2004).
[b]Matches are based on the predicted probabilities computed as part of the selection decomposition exercise. For the region level (columns (2) and (3)) matching is on predicted $\rho_{c/v}$ and for the farmer level (column (4)) matching of observations is based on predicted block and village selection, ρ_b and $\rho_{v/b}$ respectively.
[c]Since the matching is based on predicted values, the matching is corrected for possibly biased matching.
[d]The standard errors to compute statistical significance are corrected for heteroscedasticity.
Source: Author's calculations, Narayanan (2012b).

probabilities that is associated with the sample farmers for the five commodities. Whenever the difference in estimated predicted probability of the block or village being selected is statistically significant, given matched predicted probabilities that a farmer is selected, one can infer that there is significant domain level or spatial level sorting. So too, if the difference in estimated predicted probability of a farmer being selected is statistically significant given matching propensities for block and village selection, it implies that farmer level sorting is relevant in the process of selection.

The table suggests that contracting status relates significantly to both region level sorting and farmer level sorting. This is true for most cases. In the gherkins sample from phase 2, however, sorting at the region (block level) appears to be significant, while for papaya, farmer level sorting appears to be significant. This implies that for gherkins exclusion of geographies might be relevant and, given a shared propensity for a block to be selected, the farmer level exclusion is less of an issue. In the case of papaya, it appears that farmer level selection is a key driver.

These findings are consistent with evidence from interviews on the contracting firms' approaches to selection. Gherkins firms tend to follow a cluster approach, choosing villages. In papaya, in contrast, social contract drives most initiation of contractual relationships and farmers are scattered fairly widely. Also, because papaya needs significant upfront investments and enterprise, the firm is perhaps discerning in its choice of contract farmers.

Tables 2 and 3, for example, provide data on the proportion of villages and blocks in the study area where the firm contracts and the proportion of farmers within the sample village where the firm contracts. It is evident that firms do not operate uniformly across regions.

Table 2:   Spatial aspects of procurement in the study area

Commodity	Number of Contract Villages (CV)	Average Number of Farmers per CV	Number of Contract Blocks (CB)	Average Number of Farmers per CB	Total Number of Contract Farmers in the Area
Cotton	20	9	6	28	170
Broiler	54	2	11	8	93
Papaya	16	5	11	8	85
Marigold	8	10	2	41	82
Gherkins (Phase 2)	22	20	6	75	449
Gherkins (Phase 1)	21	27	8	72	573
Total	**2,500**		**97**		

Note: Total refers to the total in the study area. Figures have been rounded off to whole numbers.
Source: Author's calculations.

Table 3:   Famer participation pattern in the sample contract villages

| Commodity | Number of Sample Contract Villages | Percentage of Farmers Chosen for Contract Relative to Cultivators in Sample Villages | | | |
		Average	Standard Deviation	Minimum	Maximum
Cotton	7	46.3	6.7	33.3	52.63
Broiler	35	4.9	5.7	1	32
Papaya	10	4.7	4.8	0.3	14.6
Marigold	15	20.6	9.3	6.7	35.7
Gherkins (Phase 1)	6	35	30	6	91
Gherkins (Phase 2)	5	24.0	22.1	6.3	58.8

Note: Figures have been rounded off to whole numbers.
Source: Author's calculations.

Further, the intensity of their presence in terms of the proportion of farmers who contract within a village also varies, both within a particular scheme as well as across schemes. For broiler and papaya, the firms spread out to many villages and blocks relative to the number of farmers they need, so that they account for only a few farmers in each block or village they contract in. For gherkins, cotton and marigold, on the other hand, the firms contract intensively in fewer villages relative to the number of farmers they contract with.[6]

Implications for Public Policy in India

What does the collective evidence on spatial and farmer selection suggest for government policy in the realm of contract farming, or more broadly agro-food supply chains? In India, since 1991, when

[6] These are not adjusted for scale of operation so that cross-commodity comparisons need to be made with caution.

economy-wide reforms began, three broad trends began to put severe pressure on the severely regulated and state-biased agricultural market policies that were perceived to be anachronistic, inefficient, and iniquitous (Narayanan, 2011). First, with the growth of private sector participation and export-orientation in processing industries following industrial delicensing, control over the source of feedstock to ensure quality and traceability became desirable. Second, the emergence of supermarkets and modern retail chains necessitated a steady supply of fresh produce of consistently good quality. Third, against a background of a silent collapse of state extension systems and rising input subsidies to agriculture the state began to disengage from traditional forms of policy intervention in the agricultural sector and sought to create spaces for the private sector. Contract farming began to feature prominently in this effort.

As part of what was termed the "Rainbow Revolution," the National Agricultural Policy (2000) promised that "private sector participation will be promoted through contract farming and land leasing arrangements to allow accelerated technology transfer, capital inflow, and assured market for crop production ...." In 2003, a Model Act (The State Agricultural Produce Marketing Development & Regulation Act) outlined a framework for contract farming operations that would safeguard the interests of both firms and farmers equitably. This act was later complemented by the creation of Agri-Export Zones (AEZ) as part of the EXIM Policy, 2001–2002,[7] across the country, where firms involved in agro-processing for exports would benefit from tax breaks and specific infrastructure facilities. Ever since, the policy thrust has been to increase efficiency in these agricultural supply chains by focusing on an end-to-end approach from farm to market.

The policies listed above are illustrative of different kinds of interventions that reflect assumptions about the transformative power of modern agricultural supply chains. Implicit in the articulation of the

---

[7] EXIM Policy refers to the export import policy announced by the Government of India.

vision for a Rainbow Revolution is an assumption, for instance, that the spread of private sector participation would be a matter of course. Among policies seeking to provide an enabling legislative framework for agribusiness practice, there is no explicit recognition that this might occur only in select geographies. The AEZ provisions, in contrast, explicitly recognize the presence of geographic comparative advantage of clustering, albeit in the restrictive context of export oriented agriculture. Underpinning these latter interventions is the idea that clustering would reinforce geographic comparative advantage and would enhance export competitiveness.

Missing from the current menu of policies are two elements. First, the diverse approaches used by firms dealing with different commodities in the selection of the procurement shed imply that while sorting over geographies is nearly universal, the patterns of spatial selection may vary across commodities and firms. For instance, the example of broiler or papaya suggests that despite being selective in the choice of geographies, there is no evidence of clustering. These distinctions would matter a great deal in the success of policies that presume that clustering entails economies. Second is the prominent absence of any discussion of policy in excluded zones. If modern agricultural supply chains do systematically bypass certain agro-climatic tracts, there needs to be a set of complementary policies that redefine their role in the context of the changes in more favored areas. This is an area that calls for strengthening.

Acknowledgments

This study was supported financially by the American Institute of Indian Studies' Junior Research Fellowship (2006), IFPRI-New Delhi Office, the Borlaug-Leadership Enhancement in Agriculture Program (LEAP) Fellowship (2008), AAEA Foundation's Chester McCorkle Scholarship (2008) and the Ithaca First Presbyterian International Student Fellowship (2007). Thanks are due to Chris Barrett, M. Chandrasekaran, William Lesser, Stefan Klonner, seminar participants at Cornell University and the FAO-Cornell pre-conference symposium at Foz do Iguaçu for valuable comments and insights. The usual disclaimer applies.

References

Abadie A, Drukker D, Herr J and Imbens G (2004) Implementing matching estimators for average treatment effects in Stata. *Stata Journal* 4: 290–311.

Barrett CB, Bachke ME, Bellemare MF, Michelson HC, Narayanan S and Walker TF (2012) Smallholder participation in contract farming: comparative evidence from five countries. *World Development* 40: 715–730.

Barrett CB and Swallow BM (2006) Fractal poverty traps. *World Development* 34: 1–15.

Boselie D, Henson S and Weatherspoon D (2003) Supermarket procurement practices in developing countries: redefining the roles of the public and private sectors. *American Journal of Agricultural Economics* 85(5): 1155–1161.

Carter MR and Mesbah D (1993) Can land market reform mitigate the exclusionary aspects of rapid agro-export growth? *World Development* 21: 1085–1100.

Dev SM and Rao C (2005) Food processing and contract farming in Andhra Pradesh: a small farmer perspective. *Economic and Political Weekly* 40(26): 2705–2713.

Dileep BK, Grover RK and Rai KN (2002) Contract farming in tomato: an economic analysis. *Indian Journal of Agricultural Economics* 57: 197–210.

Glover D and Ghee Lim T (eds.) (1992) *Contract Farming in Southeast Asia: Three Country Studies*. Kuala Lumpur: Institut Pengajian Tinggi/ Institute for Advanced Studies, Universiti Malaya/University of Malaya.

Glover D and Kusterer K (1990) *Small Farmers, Big Business: Contract Farming and Rural Development*. New York: St. Martin's.

Heckman JJ and Smith JA (2003) The determinants of participation in a social program: Evidence from a prototypical job training program. National Bureau of Economic Research Working Paper No. 9818, Cambridge, MA.

Kumar P (2007) Contract farming through agribusiness firms and state corporation: a case study in Punjab. *Economic and Political Weekly* 41: 5367–5375.

Minot N (2008) Contract farming in developing countries: patterns, impact, and policy implications. In Pinstrup-Andersen P and Cheng F (eds.), *Case Studies in Food Policy for Developing Countries*, Vol. 6-3, Ithaca, NY: Cornell University.

Miyata S, Minot N and Hu D (2009) Impact of contract farming on income: linking small farmers, packers, and supermarkets in China. *World Development* 37: 1781–1790.

Narayanan S (2011) Contract farming. In Basu K and Maertens A (eds.), *The Oxford Companion to Economics in India*, 2nd edn. New Delhi: Oxford University.

Narayanan S (2012a) Two kinds of sorting: how agribusinesses choose farmers. Mimeo. Mumbai: Indira Gandhi Institute of Development Research.

Narayanan S (2012b) Safe gambles? Farmer perceptions of transactional certainty and risk return tradeoffs in contracting arrangements in southern India. Working Paper WP 2012-21. Mumbai: Indira Gandhi Institute of Development Research.

Reardon T and Gulati A (2008) *The Supermarket Revolution in Developing Countries: Policies for Competitiveness with Inclusiveness*. IFPRI Policy Brief 2. Washington, DC: International Food Policy Research Institute.

Runsten D and Key N (1996a) Contract farming in developing countries: theoretical aspects and analysis of some Mexican cases. Report prepared for the United Nations Economic Commission for Latin America and the Caribbean, Santiago, Chile.

Runsten D and Key N (1996b) Contract farming in developing countries. *Rural Development* 2: 22–34.

Swinnen JFM (2007) Global supply chains, standards and the poor: How the globalization of food systems and standards affects rural development and poverty. CABI, Wallingford, UK and Cambridge, MA.

Von Braun J, Hotchkiss D and Immink M (1989) *Nontraditional Export Crops in Guatemala: Effects on Production, Income, and Nutrition*. Washington, DC: International Food Policy Research Institute.

Wang H, Dong X, Rozelle S, Huang J and Reardon T (2009) Producing and procuring horticultural crops with Chinese characteristics: the case of northern China. *World Development* 37: 1791–1801.

Warning M and Key N (2002) The social performance and distributional consequences of contract farming: an equilibrium analysis of the Arachide de Bouche program in Senegal. *World Development* 30: 255–263.

Zamora M (2004) The rapid expansion of supermarkets in Ecuador and its effects on dairy and potato production chains. Mimeo.

Chapter 5

CAPABILITIES AND PERFORMANCE IN COLLECTIVE MARKETING: THE IMPORTANCE OF LEARNING TO COPE WITH AGENCY DILEMMAS

Giel Ton,[*,‡] Lithzy Flores,[†] Rubén Monasterios[†] and Evaristo Yana[†]

*LEI – Agricultural Economics Research Centre, Wageningen University and Research Centre, Hollandseweg 1, 6706 KN Wageningen, the Netherlands

†Independent consultants

‡giel.ton@wur.nl

This chapter focuses on the inherent challenges in collective action and the institutional arrangements or regulations that hold market-oriented farmer groups together. It operationalizes the measurement of the capacity to contain these inherent challenges by mapping the presence and effectiveness of internal rules and regulations, related to mechanisms of price-determination, payment systems, quality controls, task delegation, *etc.* Using data from 38 farmer organizations in Bolivia, we show that this capability is strongly correlated with the performance of the group. We illustrate the relevance of learning and experimentation to develop these capacities, and how the policy constrained room for maneuver to do so. We conclude with the importance of policies and legal frameworks that facilitate this search for effective solutions to agency dilemmas in collective marketing, and stress the importance of differentiating between market-oriented and community-oriented farmer organizations.

Introduction

Smallholder farmers need institutional arrangements that facilitate their access to markets. Since they are scattered, they need to aggregate their produce in order to transport it cost-efficiently to urban or regional markets or to the processing industry. The form of coordinating supply varies, from contract farming to trader–agent networks and collective marketing by farmer organizations. The essence of all these different forms is their effectiveness in performing key logistic functions with acceptable financial and managerial costs. The basic form of coordination is a group of farmers that aggregate the crop harvested in a certain location to generate the threshold quantity needed by prospective buyers and in accord with the relevant conventions on qualities and grades and packaging material. Typically, within rural societies, this logistic process is coordinated by village-based farmer–traders who tend to work with a specific urban-based merchant or processor (Fafchamps, 2004; Ton *et al.*, 2010), or by a company or estate that performs this role through contract farming (Prowse, 2012; Shepherd, 2007). More elaborate forms combine the bulking of produce with collective price negotiation and processing. Collective marketing is considered a key strategy for farmers to create added value to their produce (Sjauw-Koen-Fa, 2012; World Bank, 2007). The most prominent legal form of such an organization is the cooperative but, particularly in developing countries, a range of other legal formats are commonly used, especially the civil association or limited responsibility company. In spite of the difference in name and applicable legal framework, these farmer groups share common features (Donovan *et al.*, 2008; Penrose-Buckley, 2007; Robbins *et al.*, 2005).

The incentive for farmer organizations to explore strategies of vertical integration is that, by doing so, the members may have lower marketing costs and thus increase the on-farm price. The decision whether to involve in vertical integration is, consequently, an assessment of cost–benefit comparing the different modalities for coordination of this marketing process. The organization costs can be expected to be relatively high in the start-up years, eventually resulting in a negative cashflow until volumes increase and the break-even point is reached. This negative cashflow is often the biggest threshold for starting collective action in markets. Considering this, most farmer organizations decide not to enter the arena of collective marketing and limit their activities to those functions that are complementary to, and not competing with, the trader–agent networks as bulking nodes in rural agricultural trade. As a result, most farmer organizations in developing countries are community-oriented, not market-oriented farmer groups (Bernard *et al.*, 2008). Nevertheless, in spite of this 'price of empowerment' (Ton *et al.*, 2012), some groups decide to start collective marketing and processing activities and strive for vertical integration in the value chain.

Collective marketing is not easy: structures for coordinated action, in whatever form, face inherent tensions due to the threats of opportunistic behavior by individual farmers toward the group and/ or opportunistic behavior by the group toward group members. Each form of collective marketing needs to establish the rules, trust and discipline to contain these tensions. Effective rules and practices evolve in a learning process as 'organizational intelligence,' and internal formal and informal institutional arrangements develop in a process of organizational learning and adaption. Surprisingly, the struggle of farmer organizations to cope with these challenges in collective marketing functions has not been paid much attention in social research. The literature on collective marketing arrangements in the developed countries is particularly concerned with the distinctive features of cooperatives in having members as owners and investors. In developing countries, however, very few organizations have emerged with significant financial member contribution, and, generally, members do not have rights to the patrimony of the organizations when they withdraw.

The chapter develops a conceptual framework to assess the organizational capacities of farmer groups to resolve the challenges of collective marketing in the face of competition. To do so, we first describe the discussion in Bolivia about community-oriented and market-oriented farmer organizations, and the need for more clarity about the forms and functions of economic farmer organizations. Next, we describe the method of data collection and the constructs used in the cross-case analysis of 38 collective marketing groups in Bolivia, including a construct to assess the organizational capacities of the group to contain the inherent tensions in collective marketing. After this, we present the results of an explorative analysis of the sector by a mix of methods: graphical depiction, statistical analysis and qualitative description of typical cases. We refer especially to the learning and experimentation needed to design balanced internal rules and regulations. We show that there is a strong significant correlation between the organizational performance of these organizations and their capacities to handle tensions that are inherent in collective marketing. In the final section, we reflect on these results and discuss the implications for policy and development practice.

Context

In this research, we focus on the sector of farmer organizations in Bolivia that defined their identity precisely around collective marketing and value addition. The farmer organizations have made the decision to engage in collective marketing and have managed to formalize their existence. Donovan *et al.* (2008) call these groups Rural Community Enterprises (RCE). In Bolivia, the sector auto-defines itself as Economic Peasant Organizations, *Organizaciones Económicas Campesinas, Indígena y Originarias* (OECAs) (CIOEC-Bolivia, 2000, 2009). The special characteristics of OECAs in Bolivia were discussed in academic literature by Bebbington *et al.* (1996), Hellin *et al.* (2009), Laguna (2011), Muñoz *et al.* (2005), and Ton and Bijman (2006).

In Bolivia, the discussion about OECAs and their role in economic development became highly relevant when, in June 2011, the Morales government presented a comprehensive package of policies, Law 144 (Government of Bolivia, 2011), focusing on economic communitarian organizations (OECOMs, *Organizaciones Económicas Comunitarias*), and, in November 2012, Parliament approved a legal proposal, focusing on OECAs. The use of similar abbreviations in both laws caused confusion and triggered discussions on the essential features of both forms of organization and their governance systems.

In the final text, proclaimed law by President Evo Morales in January 2013 as Law 338 (Government of Bolivia, 2013), both forms of organization are defined. OECOMs group all households in a community and rely on the pre-existing village governance structure, while OECAs have a defined membership that often stretches beyond villages and around specific commodities or economic activities. For the latter it is crucial that they have a governance structure independent from the traditional village authorities.

The community organizations tend to channel multiple services to their constituents, including education, health services, *etc.*, where it is easy to see the public interest, while the market-oriented organizations tend to focus on more targeted production. The latter are, as a result, accused of striving for private economic interests and not for 'the public good,' and public investment support to their economic and commercial activities may be considered unfair. There is opposition from both community-oriented organizations and competing private companies. The need to legitimize the collective action for 'private good' against collective action for 'public good' manifests itself in the advocacy strategies toward governmental or development donors. For governments, the transfer of resources to the private sector is constrained by regulations that, to prevent overt corruption, define measures of transparency in the disposal of public investments. The debate in Bolivia is therefore a reflection of a political context where support is available from the state but eligibility of organizations for this support is to a large extent conditional on their being backed up by a legal provision that legitimizes this support.

Research Objective

Thus, more clarity about the organizational form and activities of economic peasant organizations is needed to inform decision-making on appropriate policies and instruments to this sector as agents of rural economic development. This research uses several comparative methods to illustrate the diversity that exists within this sector and to show the importance of specific organizational capabilities for their performance.

Methods and Constructs

Data collection

CIOEC-Bolivia (2009) estimated the number of economic farmer organizations in Bolivia at 778, 64% of which are constituted as civil associations and only 9% as cooperatives. A large proportion (22%) of the organizations in the 2008 Census of OECAs have no legal personality and function as informal groups. This census of the total population of organizations can be considered fairly complete because the presence of support facilities for this associated sector by non-governmental organizations (NGOs), international donors, municipal governments and the existence of apex organizations like CIOEC-Bolivia and AOPEB results in few economic farmer organizations being 'off the radar.' The organizations build on distinct trajectories of change (Flores *et al.*, 2007), work in a wide range of economic sectors, and all propose to seize different niche-market business opportunities in highly dynamic and contested markets (Donovan *et al.*, 2008). The research is based on data from a panel of 38 of these organizations. The sample is largely representative of the regional distribution and variety of sectors in which economic farmer organization in most of Bolivia operate (CIOEC-Bolivia, 2009). Some areas are underrepresented, however, as it does not include community forest enterprises, several of which are engaged in collective processing of timber or non-timber species (Benneker, 2008), or the Chapare area, where before 2006, the year when the Morales Government ended the activities of the United States Drug Enforcement Agency in Bolivia, farmer associations were heavily promoted as instruments for 'alternative development' to restrict the production of coca leaves. Thus, although not a perfectly representative sample, it provides a good profile of the sector.

Three local researchers, co-authors of this study, conducted the interviews between August 2011 and January 2012, using a semi-structured questionnaire about the history of the organizations, the rules and regulations related to agency dilemmas in collective marketing, and the moments of significant change in the internal rules and regulations (Ton *et al.*, 2011). In November–December 2012, the lead author coded this qualitative information in the interview reports with the software application *Atlas.ti_7*, and summarized it in a semi-quantitative form in *SPSS_19*. Complementary to these interviews, data was extracted from the membership lists of CIOEC-Bolivia, from the business plan proposals submitted to *Fondo de Fortalecimiento para las Organizaciones Económicas Campesinas* (FONDOECAS) and, when necessary, from earlier studies on these organizations (Camacho *et al.*, 2005).

To crosscheck the construct we use to represent the organizational performance of the organizations, we developed an Excel application for pairwise comparison of organizations in the sample, applied by a knowledgeable person working in the sector in September 2012. The expert, working in a small-grant facility that caters to these types of organizations, intuitively ranked a subsample of organizations according to a pairwise comparison. His ranking was compared with the ranking based on our construct for organizational performance.

Constructs used

Each case description is considered as a configuration where, depending on certain contextual conditions, internal governance mechanisms influence organizational performance. The dataset for the analysis consists of five constructs (Table 1), derived partly from the original qualitative data extracted from the interviews and partly from the CIOEC member registration and FONDOECAS records. In the following sub-sections, we describe the constructs used for the outcome pattern, then we describe the construct for the tension-containment capacity in detail, and conclude with the key variables and constructs used to map differences in context.

Outcome: Organizational performance

Size of membership. In some interviews, a distinction was made among 'active' and 'passive' registered members. Active members are those currently involved in the organizations' activities, while passive members are those who are inactive in the organizations' activities but still appear on the membership lists. Passive members tend to remain in this situation as formal withdrawal is not a common practice.

Table 1:   Variables and constructs used in the case-based comparative analysis

Category	Construct	Variables
Context	Sector	Main crop or activity in collective marketing
	Level of integration	Mentioning of decentralized operation and delegation in collective marketing
	Intensity of interaction	Assessment of collective marketing process described
	Gender composition	Female members as a proportion of total membership
	Influence of community-oriented organizations	Mentioning the role of community-oriented organizations in the history and governance
Mechanism	Tension-containment capacity (10Cs)	Assessment of the institutional arrangements to resolve inherent tensions on 10 issues (see Table 2)
Outcome	Organizational performance	Size of the membership Size of the patrimony Age of the organization

Therefore, whenever this information was provided, we used the number of active members as the indicator of size. In the sample the average size of an organization is 204, but the distribution is skewed, three organizations being considerably larger than the others. The median is 98, with 25% of the cases having fewer than 37 or more than 320 members. We use the natural log of total membership as our scale variable in the explorative cluster analysis. This variable is normally distributed (Shapiro-Wilk = 0.197).

Size of patrimony. Indicators like profitability are not very useful when assessing the economic performance of farmer organizations (Soboh *et al.*, 2009). Since they all have mechanisms to limit the benefits for the group and maximize the price for the products sold from their members, a better indicator of economic power is the amount of accumulated capital, be it in kind or in cash. The value of the patrimony is leverage for bank credit (as a guarantee for loans) and a proxy indicator for the importance of the organizations as a business. The log-linear representation of this variable lowers the skew of the distribution to 0.539 though, according to the Shapiro-Wilk test for normality (Shapiro-Wilk = 0.015), it deviates from a normal distribution.

Age of organization. We used the natural log of the age of the organization as another component of our construct for organizational strength. While the reproduction of the organization in time seems a sensible indicator of success, it is clear that it alone is not enough. The variable is highly skewed and needs a natural log transformation to be useful in our subsequent analysis. The resulting variable is normally distributed (Shapiro-Wilk = 0.859).

Mechanism: Organizational capabilities

Tension-containment capacity. Organizations deal with the members from multiple positions in multiple agency dilemmas (Shapiro, 2005) that often create 'paradoxes' (Cornforth, 2004) to be coped with through the group's governance system. The essence of any principal-agent dilemma in farmer groups is that the members want the organization to do some things for them (*e.g.*, sell their produce for a good price) and need some assurance that the organization does this well. At the same time, the organization wants members to do something (*e.g.*, provide good quality products) and, in these situations, a workable 'middle way' has to be found to make the deal acceptable to both member and organization: the farmer has to trust the organization to do a good job when negotiating prices for him, while the organization has to prevent possible opportunism in their membership (*e.g.*, related with quality). To contain the tensions that might emerge in the course of action of the group, a successful governance structure is needed that gives both member and organization enough confidence to accept the collective marketing 'deal.' We consider the capacity of an organization to find solutions for different agency dilemmas a key asset: the 'groups' 'organizational social capital'

(Leana and Van Buren, 1999; Ostrom and Ahn, 2009), which enables the containment of the multiple agency dilemmas that present themselves in collective action. As a diagnostic instrument to assess the organizational capacities for collective marketing, we have mapped ten areas where disintegrative tendencies are situated (Ton, 2010). Table 2 summarizes these tensions.

These tensions operate in combination with, and in response to, dynamics in the complex social system that each farmer organization is. The organization must cope with these disturbances, and show resilience. In the literature on Complex Adaptive Systems, resilience is defined as the capacity (of a system) to experience shocks while retaining essentially the same function, structure, feedbacks, and therefore identity (Holling, 1973). The capacity to adapt internal regulations is the main manifestation of the organizational social capital, not the level of detail or the multitude of regulations, nor the conservation of some pre-fixed organizational format or plan of action.

The development of effective rules and regulations is a learning process that takes time and resources (Ostrom and Ahn, 2009). Organizational social capital cannot be assessed in one moment of time with a 'snapshot.' A reflection must be made on the process of adaptation of internal regulations to changing dynamics in a time period still relevant to current decision making in the group. Consequently, the researchers asked the stakeholders in the farmer organization about the current status in regulations to resolve each tension and the events that had triggered changes in these regulations in the last three years. For each tension, we summarized the status of the organizations capabilities to resolve it. We used two questions with three ordinal answer-categories each in a summary sheet. The first question asked about the 'relevance' of the tension, and the second about the 'effectiveness of the organizational solution.' Classification was done in two steps: first directly after the interview by each researcher, and second in the session in which the research team reviewed and compared summary sheets. Afterward, the lead researcher adjusted some of the valuations after data extraction, coding and comparing the information in the interview reports.

Table 2: Ten areas where disintegrative tendencies in collective marketing are located

In Short	Description
'Regulating Member Supply'	Tensions can emerge when individual members increase their supply to the marketing organization, and, by doing so, negatively affect the opportunity for other members to supply.
'Quality Assurance Systems'	When a deal is made, the quality that the organization has promised has to be checked: individual members may tend to deposit lower quality and the organization needs a system to maintain minimum quality requirements.
'Coping with Working Capital Constraints'	Many smallholder farmers tend to face cash constraints and want quick payment, while the organization needs time to complete transactions with the ultimate buyer.
'Anticipating Side-Selling'	The organization might provide a credit service or advance payment system to enable production. However, there is a serious risk that farmers "side-sell" their product to competing traders or processors to whom they have no repayment obligation.
'Ways to Dispose of Profits'	When the organization makes profit, the organization prefers to invest or increase capital reserves, while the members prefer more short-term benefits, *e.g.*, better prices.
'Differentiating Services to Members and Non-Members'	Most economic organizations need contributions from members to realize their business opportunities; however, members face a number of disincentives to do so when benefits that flow from investment accrue to investors and non-investors alike.
'Decision Making on Activities that Benefit Only a Sub-group'	When the type of investment is unlikely to benefit all members, investment decisions that seem economically optimal from the perspective of management are not necessarily desirable from the standpoint of (sub-groups of) members.

(*Continued*)

Table 2: (*Continued*)

In Short	Description
'Task Delegation and Supervision of Professional Staff'	Member-based organizations elect persons to supervise and support management; however, the limited technical knowledge of board members and the lack of transparency of information disclosed by management often limit the effectiveness of this governing structure.
'Liability in Contracts and Loans'	There is an inherent tension between members who want to limit their liability for group actions and the need of the group as a whole to generate as much collateral as possible. Organizations specify procedures for decision making when the board contracts on behalf of the group.
'Managing Political Aspirations'	Economic smallholders' organizations tend to take up a broader representative role in addition to their economic service provisioning to members. Members delegate their political voice to the organization while the political representatives of the organization may never fully discuss all political decisions with them.

Source: Based on Ton (2010).

The valuations of each organization's tension containment capacities are, thus, 'grounded' with information from the interviews and considered to be sufficiently comparable among organizations to enable case-based comparative methods (Byrne and Ragin, 2009).

To derive a quantitative measure for the tension-containment capacity, we used the classification in the two questions, as described before. To calculate a quantitative proxy indicator of the capabilities to contain each of the tensions, we multiplied the values of both questions to one discrete variable (T_x). Table 3 gives the weighing factors used for calculating these scores. To get the overall tension-containment capacity (TCC), we summed these 10 scores to get the construct for the overall TCC.

Table 3:   Weighing factors used for calculating each tension-containment variable (Tx)

		$ScoreQ1_x$		
		This tension is present in their activities	Hardly present	Never present
	They have managed to resolve	9	6	3
$ScoreQ2_x$	They are looking for ways to resolve it	6	4	2
	They do not need to resolve it	3	2	0

$$T_x = ScoreQ1_x * ScoreQ2_x$$

$$TCC = \Sigma_{x=1}^{x=10} T_x .$$

Contextual factors

Sector. Smallholder farmers almost always have a diversified agricultural system. Their economic organizations, however, tend to be specialized in the collective marketing of a certain crop or product. The sample reflects the diversity that characterizes the sector, covering production activities in handicrafts, recollection, cattle raising and agriculture. Different logistic activities create partly different organizational challenges. Differentiation by sector increases the relevance of the comparison of organizations in the sample. We analyze quinoa producers as a separate group, due to their location in the Highlands. The other cereal producers are a diversified group, which includes organizations that specialize in beans, maize, wheat, amaranth, *etc.*, located in the Andean Valleys and Lowlands.

Level of integration. We classify organizations based on their characteristic of being grassroots organizations, with individual households or farmers as members, or being an aggregated, federated organization, with grassroots organizations as members. Although the distinction appeared to be quite straightforward, it became fuzzy when actual performance of organizations was analyzed: various organizations with direct membership had, in practice, an internal sub-division with units that managed different economic activities, *e.g.*, based on geographical distribution or commodities that effectively negotiate their different economic interests within the organization. And, especially in coffee and quinoa, some organizations had a formal second-tier structure but, in practice, they realized their economic activities in direct relation to individual farmers and had their member organizations only as information and logistic channel, not as separate economic units. As a consequence, we reclassified organizations accordingly, resulting in a dichotomous variable with 12 organizations classified as being two-tiered federated organizations and 24 organizations as one-tiered grassroots organizations.

Intensity of interaction. We used the interactions with farmer households as a criterion to rank an organization's intensity. We ranked them as low (on average less than one interaction per month), moderate (once per month) and high intensity (more than once per month). This distinction is important for organizations that are marketing or processing handicrafts and diversified agriculture, where some entities are highly active throughout the year and others function only once or twice a year. The result is a non-normal distributed ordinal variable with 15 cases classified as low intensity, 15 cases as moderate intensity and 8 cases as high intensity in their interaction with supplying farmers.

Gender composition. It is reasonable to believe that the gender balance influences the functioning of the organization and how tensions in collective action are resolved. Some organizations have a predominantly male constituency and others are predominantly female. For the parametric analysis we used the proportion of female members as our variable. A minority of 26%, 10 out of 38 organizations, had a predominantly female constituency (>60% of female members), while 61% (23 out of 38) were predominantly male. A minority of four organizations (10%) of the organizations, AMAGA, APME, APROMAJI and APSU, had a balanced constituency with between 40% and 60% female constituency.

Influence of community-oriented organizations. Based on the case study reports, we make a valuation of the influence that village-oriented organizations have had in the startup and governance of the collective marketing groups. For Burkina Faso, Bernard *et al.* (2010) show that the emergence of market-oriented groups in a village is a process in which the first one tends to have more similarity in objectives with the village organizations, while later market-oriented groups have more room to deviate from this pre-existing organizational structure to prioritize their economic and commercial objectives. We create a variable to establish whether it acts as a contextual factor influencing performance or organizational capabilities.

Empirical Results

Differences in size and patrimony

Since we are particularly interested in exploring the diversity and variation in the sample, as a first step, we used a series of scatterplots for visual examination to discover trends, and similar or contrasting cases (Byrne and Ragin, 2009; Lawson, 2009). The graphical depiction of the relations between size of membership and size of patrimony shows that there is a group of organizations in the sample that can be characterized as being relatively old, big and rich (Figure 1). It also is clear that this group consists of all coffee- and most quinoa-processing organizations in the sample. Both quinoa and coffee need to be aggregated in sufficient volumes (containers) according to quality grades, before being shipped to export markets and both products need processing to convert the raw material to a tradable commodity, especially the washing or polishing of the grains. The need for scale, quality and special administrative arrangements for exports facilitates the emergence of these organizations. Fair Trade contributed to the consolidation of these organizations in the periods of low prices during most of the 1990s.

SOPROQUI and CECAOT stand out as large and capitalized quinoa organizations. Quinoa is one of the booming crops for export. Several varieties of quinoa exist, with key differences in size and color. The most expensive ones are cultivated exclusively on the Bolivian highlands around the *Salar de Uyuni*. Both organizations are similar

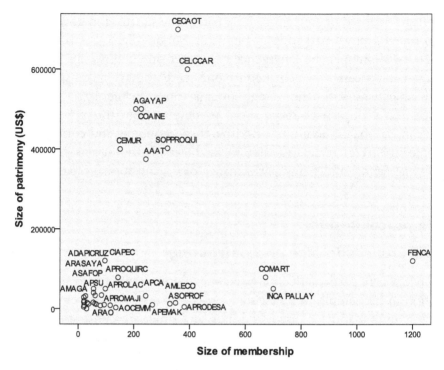

Figure 1. Scatterplot of organizations according to two indicators of economic performance

in size and activities, though CECAOT is a second-tier organization, working through its member cooperatives, and SOPROQUI has primarily individual members. SOPROQUI is one of the nine regional organizations that are members of the national quinoa organization, ANAPQUI. ANAPQUI belongs to the group of oldest and most capitalized farmer organizations. It is much larger than CECAOT, the most capitalized organization in our sample. Until 2000, CECAOT and ANAPQUI dominated the (formal) exports of quinoa, with two-thirds of all exports. Although in the last decade, private trading houses have captured part of the (growing) market, the economic farmer organizations sell at least 30% of production and dominate the market for certified organic production (Laguna *et al.*, 2006; Ton and Bijman, 2006; Verastequi, 2012). For organizations that procure high volumes to back up relations of trust with their members, there is a need for a quality control system. Technology can help make this control more transparent and reduce internal conflicts between group and individual farmer on this issue of quality.

> Quality is a recurrent theme of discussion in our general meetings. We disclose the names of persons that defrauded and, generally, the meeting decides to sanction them, but only when they recidivate. In our last meeting, we decided to start working with a quinoa selection machine. Once the quinoa passes the machine, we pay the product to the farmer. In this way we are assured that we procure a product with the quality that we need to sell it. (CECAOT)

Two other organizations that are highly capitalized are COAINE and CELCCAR. They are second-tier organizations that group local cooperatives and manage the processing and export process for their affiliates. CELCCAR, founded in 1965, and COAINE, founded in 1989, both specialize in organic coffee, generally under the Fair Trade label. CELCCAR, which made its first shipment of organic coffee to the United States in 1981, comprises 11 cooperatives. Cooperatives pay 40% of the price in cash at the moment of delivery, and complete the payment five months later, when the processing and export process has been completed. CELCCAR manages a program to expand production with new coffee bushes, 2 hectares per member. They invest their profits in services, but, due to price competition with a nearby cooperative, they are discussing the possibility to distribute profits in cash, through a price premium.

Farmer organizations often face a challenge of managing ethical business relations with their commercial partners. Sometimes, the management of the organization misuses the organization's market intelligence for personal gain. For instance, in 1999, COAINE suffered an incident that triggered organizational reform. During the period 1995 to 1999, the farmer organization was successfully exporting its produce through contacts of the then-president and administrator. The producers were being paid a fixed price and in a reasonable time interval. In 1999, however, the members discovered that the price was calculated incorrectly and the difference was used for personal enrichment. The two individuals were expelled, but took all information on commercial contacts with them. This left the organization with fiscal liabilities, court cases with providers, liabilities to the banks and it even resulted in the embargo of the processing plant. Logically, this resulted in a severe internal crisis. In response, COAINE created internal structures that guarantee more effective social control. All members have become conscious about the destination of the coffee and its international price.

Another group that stands out in Figure 1 consists of the larger handicraft organizations, COMART and INCA PALLAY, which have a large, extensive membership. COMART is a second-tier organization that manages four shops to market the handicraft products from member organizations. Neither COMART nor INCA PALLAY own their well-located urban shops but rent them. There is a difference between them in their commercial relation with the artisans. INCA PALLAY is a direct-membership organization that manages different production units within two geographically separated cultural regions. INCA PALLAY coordinates the production plans with the representatives of the units of production but buys directly from the individual artisans, paying in cash at the moment of purchase. COMART, on the other hand, deals only with its member organizations, not with the individual artisans, and works with a system of consignation, where no payments are made until the products are sold. Another organization that appears as a special case in Figure 1 is AAAT, a handicraft organization which owns its shop in the city center of Tarija and, therefore, appears as a relatively capitalized artisanal organization. AAAT manages 11 units of production with a two-tiered governance system. Each unit of production does the quality control and decides whether the product is accepted for sale in the shop.

FENCA, the organization with the largest membership, is a federation of 60 rice cooperatives in the lowland area of Santa Cruz, half of them considered to be active members. FENCA's members are producers considered to be small or medium producers in their area, but who have landholdings and household economies much larger than the smallholder farmers in the Andean Valleys and Highlands, who are the overwhelming majority in the other organizations. FENCA manages a rice mill and sells white rice in the national and international market. FENCA realizes its logistic activities directly with the individual producer, as their member organizations do not count on working capital and facilities for processing. In practice, thus, they work as a first-tier organization with direct transaction between FENCA and the individual farmer.

CEMUR and AGAYAP are also located in Santa Cruz, and are both specialized in meat products, CEMUR in chicken and pig husbandry and AGAYAP as a slaughterhouse for cows. CEMUR is an agglomerate of women groups (*Clubes de Madres*), with a strong focus on capacity building and developing income-generating activities. In practice, it worked for many years more as an NGO than as a farmer-led organization, with a central role played by its director. In recent years, the organization has been converting its internal governance system to make it more member-driven, with only the women's groups engaged in economic activities.

AGAYAP is an interesting anomaly. It manages a slaughterhouse, but this had been shut down temporarily, as members took their cattle to cities where the meat price was higher. The site represents a huge patrimony. The property rights of this location were, however, disputed, a legal dispute that resulted partly from the alleged participation of the former president in party politics opposed to the current government. Due to this crisis, the economic activities of AGAYAP are paralyzed. The infrastructure is temporarily used by non-member caretakers, while the group tries to resolve its internal problems.

Difference in organizational performance and tension-containment capacities

As a second step to explore diversity, we generated scatterplots with the organizational capacities of organizations as X-axis. To do so in two-dimensional space, we compiled a construct with three variables: size of membership, size of patrimony and organizational age.

Table 4:   Correlation matrix of performance variables

		Membership (Ln)	Organizational Age (Ln)	Patrimony (Ln)
Correlation	Membership (Ln)	1.000	0.394***	0.433***
	Organizational Age (Ln)	0.394***	1.000	0.502***
	Patrimony (Ln)	0.433***	0.502***	1.000

***Correlations significant at the 0.01 level (1-tailed).

Table 5:   Factor component score for organizational performance

	Initial Eigenvalues			Extraction Sums of Squared Loadings		
Component	Total	Percentage of Variance	Cumulative (%)	Total	Percentage of Variance	Cumulative (%)
1	1.888	62.924	62.924	1.888	62.924	62.924
2	0.619	20.640	83.564			
3	0.493	16.436	100.000			

Note: Extraction method: Principal component analysis.

These are strongly correlated. Some correlations are obvious, such as the correlation between organizational age and size of patrimony: it is highly likely that older organizations have had more time to capitalize themselves, e.g., through donor support and (co)investments. We calculated the construct for organizational strength through Principal-Component Analysis on the three outcome variables: size of membership, size of patrimony and organizational age. These variables are highly correlated (Table 4). The resulting factor explains 63% of the variance (Table 5).

To crosscheck the usefulness of this factor component score as a construct to assess organizational performance, we compared the scores with the valuation of an expert. We used the non-parametric test of the Kendall rank correlation coefficient to compare this intuitive ranking with the ranking according to factor scores. This test compares the number of matching ranks with non-matching ranks.

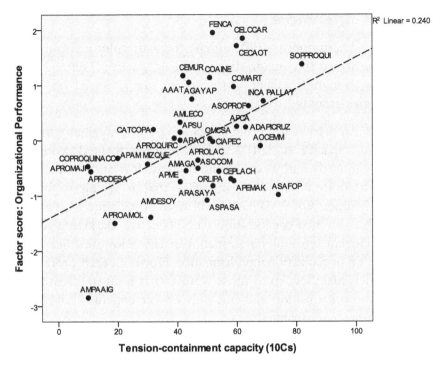

Figure 2. Scatterplot of organizations according to capabilities and organizational performance

The correlation between the ranking by the FONDOECAS expert proved fairly correlated with the outcome factor score on organizational performance ($N = 8$; Kendall $\tau = 0.546$; $p = 0.061$). Considering the small N, a 90% confidence interval ($p < 0.10$) to conclude on significance is considered appropriate.

We used the factor scores as the Y-axis in the visualization of cases in the scatterplot, Figure 2. This scatterplot shows the organizations according to their scores and provides a new perspective with which to select contrasting cases. There is a linear relation between the tension-containment capacity score, measured on all 10 aspects described in Table 2, and the factor score for organizational performance. The correlation is moderately positive and highly significant ($r^2 = 0.240$; $p = 0.002$).

Sectorial differences

To facilitate description, we differentiate the scatterplot according to the sector in which the organizations are mainly active (Figure 3). In each sector, the most salient organizations are reviewed on their organizational learning.

Handicraft. An organization that appears extremely weak in tension-containment capacity is AMPAAIG, a recently formed women's group struggling to find its economic strategy. It is an example of a former community-oriented organization that is trying to better define its membership. AMPAAIG will need some time to develop into a market-oriented organization with collective marketing activities. Their current tension-containment capacity is low, just like their factor score on organizational performance. However, their process of reducing their membership to those women that want to invest their efforts in the organization and not only expect benefits could be a first step to become stronger.

> We are now just 25 members. At the start, we were 60. What happened was that some people thought that the organization would benefit in the short run, and that it would get a lot of support. That's not how it is. As a result, many women have left. Now we are consolidating the group and keeping the door open to anyone who wants to re-affiliate. (AMPAAIG)

We already described the larger handicraft organizations COMART, INCA PALLAY and AAAT. When we analyze the smaller, less capitalized handicraft organizations, we see APSU and ARAO, both artisan groups from various communities. APSU sells most of its products through its own shop in La Paz. ARAO has a similar profile, producing carpets, sweaters, shawls and ponchos, and its own shop in Oruro for distribution. APSU delivers part of its products to COMART (in 2010: 17%), while ARAO uses the two shops of INCA PALLAY to sell part of its handicraft in Sucre and La Paz.

Honey. Outstanding cases in the honey sector are ADAPICRUZ and AOCEMM. Both have a modest patrimony but a sizeable membership

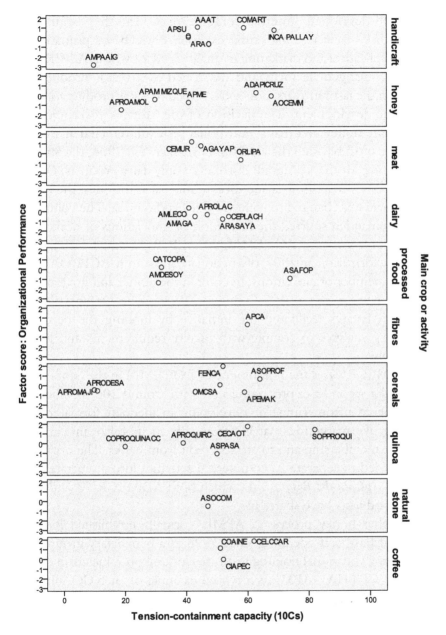

Figure 3.   Scatterplot of organizations differentiated per sector

and well-developed internal organization. In the beginning, AOCEMM's collective marketing experience was based primarily on the multiplication and marketing of quality seed for wheat. AOCEMM, however, changed its focus and developed as a major producer of honey. In the last ten years, honey developed to a star product for local economic development. The decision of the Morales government to incorporate honey in a major nutritional program directed at women who gave birth boosted the local honey market. Till 2004, the Subsidy to Lactating Mothers program distributed only dairy products. Due to pressure of CIOEC-Bolivia and local municipal authorities, the basket of products was changed to include honey and quinoa. The volume of honey demanded spurred the formation of associations of beekeepers in the whole country. AOCEMM, ADAPICRUZ and CIOEC were key in the formation, in 2007, of a national consortium, ACPROABOL, with 17 member organizations, to enter in the tender and government procurement process (CIOEC-Bolivia, 2010). The Organization of American Estates facilitated the initiative by funding the necessary laboratory analyses to comply with quality requirements and health regulations.

ADAPICRUZ is the homologue of AOCEMM in the Santa Cruz area, and a second-tier processing unit with around 200 members. It is considered a front-runner in developing an adequate formal format for collective marketing that is better able to mobilize investments from the membership and to attract credit from banks. The organization decided to separate its commercial activities into a separate legal identity, *Apícola del Bosque S.A.*, which both ADAPICRUZ and individual producers have shares in.

Another honey processor, APME, formally established itself in 2006 but has been operating since 1998 as a beneficiary group supported by a vocational training institute working on value chain development (CETHA). APME is a typical example of an NGO-initiated group, gaining autonomy and learning and experimenting with internal rules for its business, for instance, on the side-selling problem:

> It requires quite a lot of effort to keep members loyal to the organization. First, we decided that the villages should regulate this issue,

but that did not work out well. [Then] we decided that whenever we managed to get support or a grant, we would use the opportunity to say to those that did not supply that they would not benefit from this support. But this did not work either and, till now, we have not found an effective mechanism, though we need to find one to prevent the members leaving the organization. Nevertheless, we have currently only 10% of our members involved in disloyal practices. (APME)

Dairy. The dairy organizations, AMAGA, AMLECO, CEPLACH, APROLAC and ARASAYA, are all of a similar size and type of patrimony. In the 1990s, the dairy farmers associated in these organizations delivered their milk to the dairy company PIL ANDINO, which started as a state company in the 1970 but, since 1988, has been owned by the Peru-based multinational GLORIA. Initially organized around the cooling tank used in the procurement of raw milk, farmers have started to process part of the milk as a group, especially into yoghurt supplied to nutrition programs, specifically the School Breakfast program implemented by municipal governments. Their patrimony is typically a result of donor funding, intended to stimulate local economic development, helping these groups with threshold investments in the processing equipment needed to comply with the quality requirements in these local government procurement processes. As a result of their participation in high-demanding markets and the resulting daily need to deliver quality and quantity, their scores on the tension-containment capacity are also in the same range.

Processed food. ASAFOP, a small organization with predominantly female members active in food processing, stands out. Its high capabilities are due to the fact that it works in a highly demanding market, where quality matters, logistic efficiency is key and the buyer (government) is a notoriously slow payer, resulting in the need for members to pre-finance the groups' activities. Rules and regulations developed in response to these demands. The group started as an informal women group supported by charity NGOs with a diversity of training for 'women as mothers,' and functional in distributing part of the food aid, especially from the US program PL-480. When the latter function disappeared in the 1990s, the group took part in a reforestation project. Based on these experiences, it started to look for other ways of generating income. In 2004, as one of the first organizations in the country, it managed to get a contract with the municipal government to provision part of the school meals (Ton and Mendoza, 2007). Once contracted, the quality that the organizations had promised had to be controlled for. Quality control systems are always a source of tensions: individual members may tend to deposit lower quality and the organization needs a system to maintain minimum quality requirements. ASAFOP developed an effective, though labor intensive, quality control system. An appointed board member, initially assisted by a supporting technician, does the quality control by probing (tasting) the *tarwi* to detect bitterness and deciding to accept or reject the product. To prevent the influence of family ties on this person, the entire group observes and checks that no bad product is allowed. This solution works in a small organization like ASAFOP, but it is obviously inappropriate in larger organizations such as the coffee and quinoa organizations discussed before.

Cereals. OMCSA together with AOCEMM in Tarija, and with APT in Chuquisaca and Cochabamba, started as wheat seed multipliers. Wheat seed was a high-value niche product that received significant governmental support during the 1980s and 1990s. The high altitudes in the Andean Valleys were conducive to the multiplication of virus-free seeds to be used in the extensive agriculture in the Lowlands of Santa Cruz. Technical possibilities for multiplication changed, however, and the market collapsed around the year 2000. Several of the Andean organizations took up other activities, like the production of amaranth, dried beans, *etc.* OMCSA diversified its activities, producing other quality seeds.

An organization with a low score on its capabilities to manage collective marketing activities is APRODESA, a federation of 14 small local associations (with around five members). APRODESA functions more as broker for development support and takes only a limited role in marketing the production of its member organizations. Some of its municipal associations are starting up collective activities like cheese making.

APROMAJI is another illustrative case. It benefited from development investments, because it is situated in an area with high potential for special crops (sweet peppers, peanuts, herbs). It is an example of an association set up from scratch by a value chain development support intervention. In this case, APROMAJI has been supported by FDTA-Valles, an innovation grant facility, part of the national agricultural innovation system, SIBTA (Hartwich *et al.*, 2007; Ton, 2007). APROMAJI started to improve pepper production and develop its own brand. After a kick-start, the group suffered a commercial downturn after the failed intent to export peppers to Argentina through a private company that, in the end, did not pay them. This negative experience resulted in organizational instability. The group is currently reconsidering its business plan.

Quinoa. Besides CECAOT, all other organizations in the sample, SOPROQUI, ASPASA, COPROQUINACC and APROQUIRC, are affiliated with ANAPQUI. Federated organizations are generally among the better performing, larger, more capitalized and older organizations. They provide services and create added value to the products supplied through their membership organizations. In quinoa specifically, they have to face disintegrative tendencies as grassroots organizations are tempted to side-sell to better-paying traders (Laguna, 2011). The legal framework and fiscal policies in which they operate affect the strategies for ANAPQUI to do so. ANAPQUI is a non-profit association, and the tax authorities no longer accept the distribution of profits in this way. In the future, the 'profits' will be used in service provisioning by both national and regional organizations. It is to be seen how members will react to this mandatory change in the main instrument to resolve tension around price determination between group and individual farmer. Service provisioning is an investment that needs to be recovered. Side-selling can become a big issue as a result of this 'disenabling' tax policy.

Coffee. COAINE and CELCCAR, described above, are strong performing organizations with relatively high tension-containment capacities. They are older, and have learned from years of experiences. CIAPEC, the third coffee organization in the sample, is a relatively new organization (2003) and has a direct membership of persons who formerly belonged to other cooperatives and left as a result of disagreement about the price determination system. CIAPEC started with significant member contribution and took several decisions to organize itself differently from other cooperatives, *e.g.*, those related to profit distribution and capitalization.

Other contextual differences

To explore the incidence of contextual factors on organizational capacities and organization performance, we generated graphs, using alternate variables related to the context and functions of the organizations. Additionally, we tested the significance of the visually deducted correlation.

In Figure 4, organizations that had indirect transactions with farmers, the federated organizations, are indicated by black dots. The positive relation between the characteristic of being a second-tier organizations and the factor score for performance is clear (pb = 0.002). More interesting is the absence of any correlation with the indicator that reflects their tension-containment capacities. This shows that the diversity in tension-containment capacity is similar in grassroots and in federated organizations.

Figure 5 shows whether the organizations have a predominantly female (black dots), male (white dots) or mixed constituency (cross). The figure shows the linear correlation between tension-containment capacity and organizational performance seems to hold for women's organizations but is not statistically significant (see Table 6) due to the low sample of organizations with a mixed or large female constituency ($N = 15$; $p = 0.114$). More interesting, however, is the relationship between the percentage of female members and the level of their organizational capacities. Organizations with a high proportion of female members prove to have significant lower scores on their tension-containment capacities ($p = 0.070$).

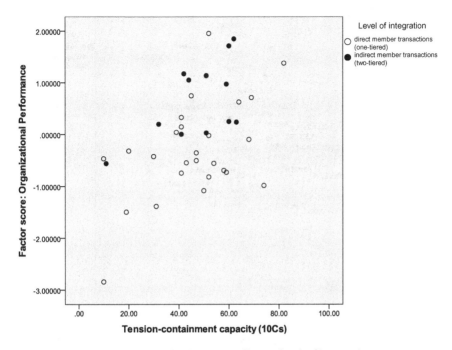

Figure 4.   Organizations according to level of integration

Discussion

Visual inspection of the scatterplots helped to detect and describe the diversity in the sector of economic farmer organizations. To further deepen the analysis, other case-based comparative techniques might be needed to find groupings of organizations with distinct scores on each of the tensions that compose our construct, like Qualitative Comparative Analysis (Rihoux and Ragin, 2008; Schneider and Wagemann, 2012), as certain organizations may perform functions where not all tensions are relevant and for which the absence is not indicative of weaker capabilities. This said, we show convincingly that, on average, there is a causal relation between the capabilities to contain agency dilemmas in collective marketing and their performance.

The major validity threats in the research relate to the constructs used and how the information was collected and converted to

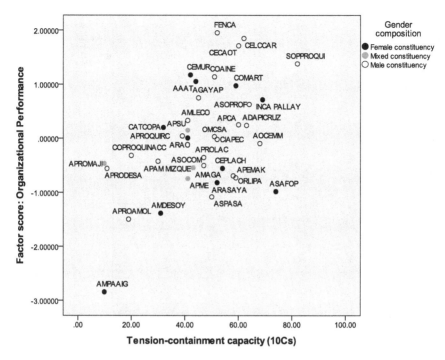

Figure 5. Organizations according to gender composition

quantitative measures. In a previous article (Ton, 2012), we proposed repeating the organizational radiography, the interviews on changes in internal regulations and the valuation of the importance of each tension for their practice, with different compositions of the board to crosscheck if the answers were consistent. We could not implement this, as it already proved difficult to bring together several board members for one interview. This validity threat is especially relevant when, as proposed in that article for an impact evaluation, we compare the changes in this tension-containment capacity for individual organizations, not between them.

The correlation between the tension-containment capacity and the construct used for organizational performance is fairly strong, and the causal effect of the capacities is made plausible in the interview excerpts. This causal inference is important for development agencies that work

Table 6:   Correlation between capabilities and performance

	Statistical Test	Factor Score: Organizational Performance	Tension-containment Capacity (10 Cs)
Influence community-oriented organizations	Spearman	−0.049	0.235
Level of integration	Spearman	0.490**	0.083
Intensity of interactions	Spearman	−0.051	0.212
Gender composition	Pearson	−0.265	−0.315*

*Correlations significant at the 0.10 level (2-tailed).
**Correlations significant at the 0.01 level (2-tailed).

with local economic development and that implement interventions to strengthen these capacities in farmer organizations (Ton *et al.*, 2011). The illustrative events presented help them to better acknowledge the organizational challenges that economic farmer organizations in developing countries face, and the value of experiential learning from friction and success. We show that organizational learning and experimentation is needed to find effective rules and regulations. This provides the rationale for increased support for organizational development, next to investment grants and facilitating market access.

The results are also important for policymakers, who, through the legislation and allocation of investments, define the room for maneuver for farmer organizations to adapt themselves to changing internal and external dynamics and to perform as economic actors in the market. Most organizations in this research have benefited from grants to start up or to develop key competencies and economic services. Often, as in quinoa and coffee, these activities of farmer organizations created the space and initial social infrastructure for private companies to start sourcing products from smallholders, often using the grassroots structures of (formerly) federated organizations. The legal framework for farmer organizations must facilitate learning and adaptation and not impose governance arrangements that may well have been best practices in the past but do not correspond to current conditions. In several countries, governmental and financial institutions still maintain that not-for-profit civil associations are not allowed to distribute profits through final payments in cash, which fails to make the distinction between the profit for the providers of capital and the profit to smallholder farmers who live in poverty-stricken areas and supply their products to the market without power in price determination. The differentiation in legislation in Bolivia between communitarian organizations, which invest in services to all families in a geographical area, and economic farmer organizations, which focus on a restricted membership to take up collective marketing to urban and international markets, seems reasonable. Both village-oriented organization and market-oriented organizations are needed for inclusive rural socioeconomic development. Both types of farmer organization need to be supported, according to their specific objectives and organizational challenges. The results also confirm earlier findings in the literature (Bebbington, 1996; Bosc *et al.*, 2001; Donovan *et al.*, 2008) that federated farmer organizations are a treasure trove of social capital. Their challenges to organize themselves in a way that combines transparency and efficiency are rather different from those of grassroots organizations, as their member organizations have better opportunities than individual smallholders to sell to intermediaries that pay higher prices. These higher-level farmer federations are, however, essential in the provision of services to their member organizations. As a result, these grassroots groups, alone or in alliance with other village-oriented organizations in their area, can develop activities and services to serve rural households and reach poverty reduction and social development outcomes.

Conclusion

We described a method for the comparative analysis of organizational social capital in economic farmer organizations. The collective actions that characterize this sector generate a range of agency dilemmas related to the performance of logistic, social and economic functions. The social organizational capital of the organizations lies precisely in the capacity to contain these tensions. We demonstrate empirically that this tension-containment capacity is highly correlated to their organizational performance: size of membership, longevity and level of patrimony. We found a positive causal relationship, with higher capabilities needed to perform in the market. The various examples of learning processes on internal organization support this causal inference. We show that farmer organizations are creative in developing effective procedures and regulations. They use and develop their 'organizational intelligence' in a continuous struggle to adapt their internal regulations to the changes in their institutional environment and their competitive position in the market. The research in this chapter points to the need to develop effective support and policy instruments that create room to do so, while considering the distinctive characteristics of market-oriented and community-oriented farmer organizations and their respective challenges in organizational governance.

Acknowledgments

The Netherlands' Ministry of Economic Affairs (KB-11-004 and BO-0-010-129) supported this work as part of ESFIM Comparative Research (www.esfim.org). The fieldwork was co-funded by the Dutch Interchurch Development Organizations, ICCO, as part of a baseline for an impact evaluation of the innovation grant fund FONDOECAS. We would like to thank the staff of CIOEC-Bolivia and its regional branches, who facilitated the contacts for the interviews, and, especially, Oscar Chambi and Richard Arguedas in FONDOECAS, who provided data and background information on most of the organizations in the sample.

References

Bebbington A (1996) Organizations and intensifications: campesino federations, rural livelihoods and agricultural technology in the Andes and Amazonia. *World Development* 24(7): 1161–1177.

Bebbington A, Quisbert J and Trujillo G (1996) Technology and rural development strategies in a small farmer organization: lessons from Bolivia for rural policy and practice. *Public Administration and Development* 16(3): 195–213.

Benneker C (2008) *Dealing with the State, the Market and NGOs: The Impact of Institutions on the Constitution and Performance of Community Forest Enterprises (CFE) in the Lowlands of Bolivia.* Wageningen: Wageningen University.

Bernard T *et al.* (2008) Do village organizations make a difference in African rural development? A study for Senegal and Burkina Faso. *World Development* 36(11): 2188–2204.

Bernard T, De Janvry A and Sadoulet E (2010) When does community conservatism constrain village organizations? *Economic Development and Cultural Change* 58(4): 609–641.

Bosc P-M *et al.* (2001) *Reaching the Rural Poor: The Role of Rural Producers Organisations (RPOs) in the World Bank Rural Development Strategy — Background Study.* Washington: World Bank.

Byrne D and Ragin C (2009) *The SAGE Handbook of Case-Based Methods.* London: Sage Publications Ltd.

Camacho P, Marlin C and Zambrano C (2005) *Estudio Regional sobre Factores de Éxito de Empresas Asociativas Rurales.* Mesa Económica: Ruralter-Intercooperación-SNV.

CIOEC-Bolivia (2000) *Agenda para el Desarrollo Estratégico de las Organizaciones Económicas Campesinas.* La Paz: CIOEC-Bolivia.

CIOEC-Bolivia (2009) *1er Censo Nacional de Organizaciones Económicas Campesinas, Indígenas y Originarias.* La Paz: CIOEC-Bolivia.

CIOEC-Bolivia (2010) *Las Organizaciones Económicas Campesinas, Indígenas y Originarias en el Desarrollo del País.* La Paz: CIOEC-Bolivia.

Cornforth C (2004) The governance of cooperatives and mutual associations: a paradox perspective. *Annals of Public & Cooperative Economics* 75(1): 11–32.

Donovan J, Stoian D and Poole N (2008) A global review of rural community enterprises: the long and winding road for creating viable businesses. Technical Bulletin No. 29. Turrialba: CATIE.

Fafchamps M (2004) *Market Institutions in Sub-Saharan Africa: Theory and Evidence.* Cambridge Massachusetts: MIT Press.

Flores L *et al.* (2007) Coaching organisational transitions towards increased market orientation: SNV's experience with producer organisation support in the Bolivian valleys. In Ton G, Bijman J and Oorthuizen J (eds.), *Producer Organisations and Market Chains: Facilitating Trajectories of*

Change in Developing Countries. Wageningen: Wageningen Academic Publishers.

Government of Bolivia (2011) *Ley 144 — Ley de la Revolución Productiva Comunitaria Agropecuaria*. La Paz: Government of Bolivia.

Government of Bolivia (2013) *Ley 338 — Ley de Organizaciones Económicas Campesinas, Indígena Originarias y de Organizaciones Económicas Comunitarias para la Integración de la Agricultura Familiar Sustentable y la Soberanía Alimentaria*. La Paz: Government of Bolivia.

Hartwich F, Alexaki A and Baptista R (2007) *Innovation Systems Governance in Bolivia: Lessons for Agricultural Innovation Policies*. Washington: IFPRI.

Hellin J, Lundy M and Meijer M (2009) Farmer organization, collective action and market access in Meso-America. *Food Policy* 34(1): 16–22.

Holling CS (1973) Resilience and stability of ecological systems. *Annual Review of Ecology and Systematics* 4: 1–23.

Laguna P (2011) *Mallas y Flujos: Acción Colectiva, Cambio Social, Quinua y Desarrollo Regional Indígena en los Andes Bolivianos*. Wageningen: Wageningen University.

Laguna P, Cáceres Z and Carimentrand A (2006) Del Altiplano Sur Boliviano hasta el mercado global: coordinación y estructuras de gobernancia de la cadena de valor de la quinua orgánica y del comercio justo. *Agroalimentaria* 12(22): 65–76.

Lawson T (2009) Applied economics, contrast explanation and asymmetric information. *Cambridge Journal of Economics* 33(3): 405–419.

Leana CR and Van Buren HJ (1999) Organizational social capital and employment practices. *The Academy of Management Review* 24(3): 538–555.

Muñoz D *et al.* (2005) *Small Farmers' Economic Organisations and Public Policies: A Comparative Study*. La Paz: PLURAL-IIED.

Ostrom E and Ahn T (2009) The meaning of social capital and its link to collective action. In Svendsen and Svendsen (eds.), *Handbook of Research on Social Capital: The Troika of Sociology, Political Science and Economics*. Cheltenham: Edward Elgar Publishing.

Penrose-Buckley C (2007) *Producer Organisations: A Guide to Developing Collective Rural Enterprises*. Oxfam Skills and Practice. London: Oxfam.

Prowse M (2012) *Contract Farming in Developing Countries: A Review*. Paris: Agence Française de Développement.

Rihoux B and Ragin C (2008) *Configurational Comparative Methods. Qualitative Comparative Analysis (QCA) and Related Techniques (Applied Social Research Methods)*. Thousand Oaks and London: Sage.

Robbins P *et al.* (2005) *Collective Marketing for Smallholder Farmers: The Territorial Approach to Rural Agro-Enterprise Development*. Bogota: CIAT.

Schneider CQ and Wagemann C (2012) *Set-Theoretic Methods for the Social Sciences: A Guide to Qualitative Comparative Analysis*. Cambridge: Cambridge University Press.

Shapiro S (2005) Agency theory. *Annual Review of Sociology* 31: 263–284.

Shepherd AW (2007) Approaches to linking producers to markets. A review of experiences to date. Agricultural Management, Marketing and Finance Occasional Paper (FAO).

Sjauw-Koen-Fa AR (2012) *Framework for an Inclusive Food Strategy: Co-Operatives — A Key for Smallholder Inclusion into Value Chains*. Utrecht: Rabobank.

Soboh R *et al.* (2009) Performance measurement of the agricultural marketing cooperatives: the gap between theory and practice. *Review of Agricultural Economics* 31(3): 446–469.

Ton G (2007) Farmers' organisations in agricultural research and development: governance issues in two competitive funding programs in Bolivia. In Ton, Bijman and Oorthuizen (eds.), *Producer Organisations and Market Chains: Facilitating Trajectories of Change in Developing Countries*. Wageningen: Wageningen Academic, pp. 271–283.

Ton G (2010) Resolving the challenges of collective marketing: incentive structures that reduce the tensions between members and their group. ESFIM Policy Brief #4. Wageningen: ESFIM.

Ton G (2012) The mixing of methods: a three-step process for improving rigour in impact evaluations. *Evaluation* 18(1): 5–25.

Ton G and Bijman J (2006) The role of producer organizations in the process of developing an integrated supply chain: experiences from quinoa chain development in Bolivia. In Bijman J *et al.* (eds.), *International Agri-Food Chains and Networks: Management and Organization*. Wageningen: Wageningen Academic, pp. 97–111.

Ton G and Mendoza M (2007) *Government Procurement Policies in Bolivia: Creating a Learning Environment for Smallholder Value Chains in*

Serving More Demanding Markets. Regoverning Markets Innovative Policy Series. London: IIED.

Ton G, Opeero DM and Vellema S (2010) How do we get it to the mill? A study on bulking arrangements that enable sourcing from smallholders in the Ugandan vegetable oil chain. VC4PD Research Paper #7. The Hague: LEI Wageningen.

Ton G, van der Mheen-Sluijer J and Castillo L (2012) The price of empowerment. *Capacity.org: A Gateway for Capacity Development* 44: 20–21.

Ton G, Vellema S and de Ruyter de Wildt M (2011) Development impacts of value chain interventions: how to collect credible evidence and draw valid conclusions in impact evaluations? *Journal on Chain and Network Studies* 11(1): 69–84.

Verastequi C (2012) Implications of the quinoa boom on the farmers' income: how do changes in the quinoa market structure mediate quinoa farmers' income. Master's thesis. The Hague: Institute of Social Studies.

World Bank (2007) *World Development Report 2008: Agriculture for Development.* Washington: World Bank.

Chapter 6

SOCIAL INNOVATION, ENTREPRENEURSHIP AND NEW GREEN JOBS: SUCCESSFUL EXPERIENCES IN MEXICO

Artemisa Montes Sylvan

Observatorio Mexicano de la Crisis (OMEC)

Even before the crisis outbreak in 2008, there was a pressing problem affecting both advanced and emerging economies: unemployment. The financial crisis first and the fiscal crisis later have put even more pressure on this issue, leading on many cases to social discontent.

Opportunities in green economy development exist that can offer ways of addressing this problem and provide new solutions. This chapter focuses on identifying successful experiences in Mexico in which social innovation becomes a key element in developing new skills and highly productive alternatives, mainly, in the green sector.

By studying social processes of innovation, this research can help understand the ways in which cooperative social innovation among different economic sectors and social groups can be enabled. Following the literature and as a result of case analyses of successful community development experiences, it is possible to identify five key elements that successful practices have in common: First, creativity, as the starting point to generate a new or novel output; second, value, created when an innovation comes as a solution to a problem; third, a collaborative atmosphere, which fosters individual initiative and cross-pollination; the fourth element is individual expectations, including individual initiative and tolerance for mistakes, which encourages individual effort. Finally, networking based on self-organized special interest groups with informal, horizontal structures, objectives and tasks — these groups tend to have formal leadership and small budgets and are driven from the "grassroots" and/or previous community projects.

In most cases, there are few financial incentives to endorse social innovation, so individuals and organizations have also developed quite interesting recognition instruments to engage new participants and to guarantee their sustainability.

In sum, this work adds to the literature that links social innovation and entrepreneurship, and aims to help build a blueprint towards designing successful development strategies based on this particular type of innovation, by carrying out a systematic compilation and codification of particular cases, in which it has been identified, in Mexico.

Introduction

Even before the crisis outbreak in 2008, there was a pressing problem affecting both advanced and emerging economies: unemployment (OECD, 2009). The financial crisis first and the fiscal crisis later have put even more pressure on this issue, leading to social discontent. As a result, the need to rethink development has become increasingly important because imbalances created in economic, environmental, social and governance sectors pose systemic risks. These imbalances also manifest themselves as rising tensions between local and global environmental and economic priorities, and we cannot know how these imbalances will evolve and how costly they could be.

Recent financial, economic and environmental crises have shown the increasing costs of ignoring or neglecting risks. This is especially so because specific configurations of growth and technological transformations tend to build on one another and therefore economic and policy decisions can have long-lived consequences. This kind of path dependency can set in motion patterns, which can be very costly to reverse (OECD Observer, 2009). Given the interdependency of all sectors and actors, there are risks of a systemic collapse in development, both at a local and global level.

In order to prevent these imbalances, innovative responses have become even more important. When talking about social innovation the main question is how to enhance already existing innovation on the micro level and turn them into competitive advantages for national economies. In this context, micro innovation refers to innovative thinking, information flow to innovative persons, and the flow of critical information to critical actors (Saariluoma *et al.*, 2009, p. 19).

The best thing about innovation is that it is a positive-sum game, where the benefits obtained by a country, region or community do not come as a loss of another. This makes the spreading of new ideas or ways of doing things as significant as the innovations behind them (OECD, 2010). For us to gain the most from innovations, they need to be widely adopted. While extensive data are usually available on technological innovations, much less information is available on non-technological micro innovations, which will also be involved in shifting to a green economy, as defined by the United Nations Environment Programme "a low carbon, resource efficient and socially inclusive economy" (UNEP, 2011). However, there is some evidence that the scope of green innovation is broadening. Due to an increasing scarcity of financial resources and the economic crisis, micro innovations can be introduced in emerging and less developed economies through better practices and integrated strategies that can lead to a range of new business and production models (OECD, 2010).

This chapter focuses on the particular national experience of Mexico to illustrate the case of micro innovations. Mexico, along with the rest of Latin America, is relevant because economic growth in the past two decades has been higher than in the "lost decade" of the 1980s, but still quite irregular, globally insufficient and well below the average of the period 1950–1980. As a result, there are now more poor people than ever on the continent, and the percentage of the population below the poverty line has not changed significantly since the lost decade and, leaving social and environmental sustainability severely challenged (CEPAL, 2010). All this together provides an important reason to look for new solutions to persistent problems and analyze successful experiences based on social innovation, entrepreneurship and green jobs.

By targeting social innovation this work aims to: (i) establish the relevance of social actors, thus going beyond the schematic opposition between state and market; (ii) focus not only on economic matters, but also on political, institutional and cultural issues; (iii) identify processes and interactions between actors, organizations and communities; and (iv) provide a tool for studying the concrete aspects of innovation activities in countries like Mexico. In order to address these issues, this work concentrates on identifying successful experiences in Mexico in which social innovation has become a key element in developing new skills and highly productive alternatives in the green sector (Hamalainen and Heiskala, 2007).

Social Innovation in the Context of Green Economy and Development

This work aims to elaborate the way in which social innovation towards a green economy can offer a useful approach for reconsidering persistent development challenges, representing new solutions. Because at the core of transforming an economy is innovation, it is a key ingredient of any effort to improve people's quality of life. Innovation and creative destruction mean new ideas, new entrepreneurs and new business models. Innovation can contribute positively to the establishment of new markets and leads to the creation of new jobs. From this point of view, innovation means more than invention and more than technology. Technological breakthroughs and their dissemination in the market are obviously very important, but also are the organizational and systemic changes that need to accompany them. Innovation today is as much about people and organizations finding new ways of doing things or using novel technologies as about breakthroughs that take place in formal research environments.

Understanding that a transition can represent a significant expansion of employment in a number of green economic activities, from organic agriculture to clean energy, which will either replace polluting activities with cleaner alternatives or provide environmental services, there are some elements of green jobs and social innovation worth considering. First most green jobs resemble familiar occupations that require a mix of generic skills, which are in wide demand throughout the economy, and specific occupational skills, most of which are familiar but some of which are novel and directly related to the greening of the production activity (CEDEFOP and ILO, 2010). In any case they can both be acquired through social innovation.

Building Richer Communities with Social Innovation

By presenting successful experiences of social innovation, this work can contribute to the understanding of the types of platforms needed to facilitate collaborative social innovation among different stakeholders (Martens and Keul, 2005).

Another important finding introduced is the role that social innovation can play as a tool for development, in the sense expressed by Sen (2000), transforming individuals as activists inside their communities to promote an independent value creation process, that will translate into a "new acquired form of freedom" (Sen, 2000). The research examines this activist role in practice in different community experiences. Considering this, the chapter argues that communities' potential for innovation is fostered by those resources that can be developed and that can shape environmental factors, in particular, social capital, which is understood as set of social relations that have productive benefits. Social capital has been studied at multiple levels, including the individual (Burt, 1995), the organization (Nahapiet and Ghoshal, 1998), and society (Putnam, 1993; Dasgupta and Serageldin, 2001). All these analyses seem to agree on a core proposition, which is also shared by this author: networks of relationships constitute, or lead to, resources that can be used for the good of the individual or the collective.

In this sense, the notion of social capital can be helpful because it makes explicit the interrelation among the four different types of capital production, natural, intellectual and social, plays in the formation of collaborative networks, highlighting the role played by knowledge, development and environmental sustainability in different institutional and national contexts (Arocena and Sutz, 2000, p. 4).

Enacting social innovation in Mexican communities: Monarch Butterfly Sanctuary (Michoacan and State of Mexico, Mexico)

Experiences presented in this section will focus on the value-generating potential of social innovation in community development. Analyses of this case will illustrate the role of collaborative networks have on innovation.

This experience will also help demonstrate that, in countries like Mexico, the notion of endogenous generation of knowledge can be quite helpful providing relevant guides to face present-day-problems. Even more, this initiative have also proven to be very effective as means of creating green jobs, and fighting poverty and its consequences. This is useful because, in many cases, emerging economies, due to particularities of the different kind of problems they face, can find solutions to such problems by developing their own innovation capabilities.

The complete study from which this work draws includes 12 different projects. The most representative is included here as an example, but conclusions presented at the final section are drawn taking into account all cases. It is important to mention, that this research, as a contribution to the literature, that examines the correlation between social innovation and development, has drawn its conclusions from local experiences.

In order to select these 12 projects a series of requirements were established.

(i) Projects with results that could be validated by concrete improvements in people and communities' living conditions;

(ii) Sustainable interventions which results have lasted for a significant period of time, in social policies and sectorial strategies and that could be extrapolated. Experiences that have incorporated during their execution effective, transparent and accountable management systems;

(iii) Contributed to build local leaderships and strengthen community self-sufficiency, including initiatives that inspire innovative

activities and further changes, empower individuals, neighbor-
hoods and communities, and considered social and cultural
diversity;
(iv) Introduced innovations that could be exchangeable and
transferable;
(v) Initiatives that promoted the creation of collaborative networks
among, at least two of, the following entities: community members, civil society organizations or collective bodies, government
agencies and academia.

By focusing on projects operating at the local and regional level it
was possible to work on an important number of interventions while
carrying out controlled comparisons. It also reinforced the capacity to
accurately code cases and accordingly make valid causal inferences.
Finally, it helped deal with the uneven nature of micro innovative
transformations.

Monarch Butterfly Sanctuary Project

This project responds to the particular nature of this worldwide
known region in the states of Michoacan and Mexico in which the
monarch butterfly arrives every year.

Monarch Butterflies became famous because of their amazing
2,000 mile journey from North America to a few specific mountain
tops in Central Mexico. The migration, which takes three to four
generations of butterflies to complete, is key to their survival, but a
number of natural and man-made disasters have put it on the endangered list (Care2, 2012). That is why a sanctuary for its protection was
established in 1986. Currently the Sanctuary covers an area of 56,000
has, that at the time had a population of 500,000 people, whose main
activity was corn farming, with a very low productivity about of
250 kg/ha and 500 kg/ha. So the creation of this reserve represented, both, a challenge and an opportunity to restructure their
economic activities around the provision of environmental services —
understood as "the qualitative functions of natural non-produced

assets of land, water and air (including related ecosystem) and their biota" (OECD, 2012). Under this notion it was possible to start building new conditions for the people living there to acquire new skills and find new products in order to reorganize their economic platform, creating new green jobs.

An innovative solution was designed by social organizations and the community in the form of a local development strategy, based on peasant production units to perform the following activities: agro ecological techniques and orchards for the production of food; forestry production in nursery gardens; recovery of traditional building materials and techniques; building of wood saving stoves and rain harvest, among others.

In order to carry out this strategy a training program for indigenous instructors was implemented. The training group is self-managed by the participants who design a work plan with objectives, tasks, products and time table. The objective is to promote organized collective work. Participants also select a committee to represent and motivate them to fulfill their tasks; these committees meet every three months in order to share their experiences, achievements and problems. To support their efforts there is a Training Center in which they can learn and practice different techniques on the sustainable use of resources; they must attend this center three times a week for a year. The project, oriented towards creating green jobs, helped resemble familiar occupations with specific occupational skills, most of which were familiar but some of which were novel and directly related to the greening of the production activities.

So far, 858 training workshops have taken place, and this region is in the path of consolidating a strong sustainable development model grounded on seven generations of peasant instructors who keep replicating the model. They are, also, obtaining recognition inside their communities and have been elected for public office. Over 3,000 people have been trained and 600,000 families received the benefits of new green economy activities, with over 1,000 projects set in place and 18,269 trees planted. These activities have provided an environmentally friendly setting for the monarch butterfly and better living conditions for communities.

Lighting the spark: Six key steps to social innovation

Following the literature (Praszkier and Nowak, 2012) and as a result of these case analyses, we have been able to identify the key elements that these successful practices have in common.

First of all, in most cases the development of skills related to green jobs are built by a formal training process, that involves a large group of community members and organizations which play a double role as triggers and catalyst for change. The process includes practices that promote active participation and integration oriented to problem-solving, team work, trust and fulfilling expectations. This is the role played by training groups in the Monarch Butterfly project.

A second characteristic of successful social innovation is the construction and strengthening of social values and prevailing mores. Common values can have a positive impact on transforming perceptions towards gender, environmental protection, expectations, equality, and relation with public authorities, among others. By introducing new practices in terms of decision making and priority settings based on people's empowerment new values are formed and new behaviors emerge (Portes and Sensenbrenner, 1993).

The role of education, training and social values foster creativity as a starting point to generate a new or novel output, consequently it can be said that the way in which a community functions is the result of a particular form of organizational culture (Hennessey and Amabile, 2009, pp. 64–68). This culture is based on a set of values that can promote or limit creativity and innovation (Martins and Terblanche, 2003). Therefore, a collaborative framework for open and transparent communication, supported on trust is fundamental for this to take place. Thus when innovation comes as a solution to a problem it can easily be converted into value.

The next key element is a collaborative atmosphere that fosters individual initiative and cross-pollination. By this process it is possible to draw links between apparently unconnected ideas or concepts and obtain new results and possibilities. Learning and teaching encourage the search for new experiences, expands interests and the ability to translate acquired knowledge and transferable skills. In the meantime, former students become trainers and are able to generate new knowledge and inspire others inside and outside their communities. People who achieve the transition can be recognized by their open mindedness, diligent note-taking, tendency to think in metaphors, and ability to reap inspiration from constraints, as well as room for individual initiative and tolerance for mistakes (Hennessey and Amabile, 2009).

All projects and initiatives studied had in common, as a fifth element, individual expectations. The introduction of new ways of doing things in a community is usually supplemented by excitement, public attention and high rising expectations about the potential of the innovation. This excitement is usually followed by a considerable decline of attention and adjustment to initial expectations. In the first stage, enthusiasm attracts an increasing number and variety of actors inside and outside the community, as well as, resources. If expectations are widely shared, they can bring together heterogeneous actors. A decrease in attention can have negative effects on the innovation process, reducing participation and resources. That is the reason the promotion of institutional structures inside communities lead to increasing positive expectations, which contribute to stabilizing ongoing innovation activities (Borup *et al.*, 2006).

Lastly, all these elements combined contribute to build networking structures based on self-organized special interest groups with informal, horizontal structures, objectives and tasks. These groups tend to have formal leadership and small budgets and are driven from the "grass roots" and/or previous community projects. In most cases, there are few financial incentives to endorse social innovation, so individuals and organizations have also developed quite interesting recognition instruments to engage new participants; instruments, which, are also presented in this work.

Considering these five elements, social innovation can be perceived as the foundation of actual and potential benefits that communities and individuals can obtain when working together (Nahapiet and Ghoshal, 1998). This type of innovation can also have an impact on productive structures, on local and social development and enlightening how communities can turn into local arrangements that can have a greater impact on social innovation, as they contribute to the building of mutual trust, co-operation, and entrepreneurial spirit, with complementary specialized competencies (Saxanian, 1994). This can translate into spaces shared by small, but, dynamic communities with strong interactions that will favor micro innovations through the direct involvement of local social, economic and political actors. In many cases with better achievements than those obtained by large firms, with relatively low investments (Granovetter, 1973, 1985). This is the case of communities settled in the Monarch Butterfly Sanctuary who have shared for many years, even for centuries, the same 56,000 has of land. This proximity has made it easily to exchange new trained workers after their participation in the workshops and to share the Instruction Center facilities.

Social innovation helps develop a cognitive dimension based in attributes like a common program or shared visions that contributes to build collective goals and working styles (Portes and Sensenbrenner, 1993). This dimension enforces positive communal outcomes produced by individual and group actions, that build upon trusting relationships, establishing "common goals and values have brought and kept them together" (Barber, 1983, p. 21), moving away from opportunistic behavior (Ouchi, 1980). Building trust is so important because one of the main obstacles for team work is the perception that other community member will take advantage of someone's work. Civil society organizations participating in the implementation of projects, as in the case of the Sanctuary contribute to create new expectations and establish communicative vessels among different participants.

In most of the cases studied, we discovered a strong link with this cognitive dimension, in particular in highly innovative projects, and the ability of certain actors to acquire new visions or perspectives according to new established relations and commitments with other individuals or groups inside or outside their community. Individuals inside a community started to move in a similar direction based on setting new goals and plans. In the meantime, this collective orientation became a common vision.

A common vision goes beyond objectives and it turns into a way of relating to one another, communication codes, resource and ideas exchanging mechanisms and rewarding systems. By promoting local leaderships and empowerment of the participants in the Monarch Butterfly Project has helped fortify links inside the community around common goals.

Therefore, as part of further research we expect that a process of social innovation occupying a central location in a network of various interacting communities would be likely to create a common vision and values with similar practices, in a manner that a regional path to a green economy can be developed. If we conceptualize interactions as "channels for information and resource flows, through different interactions" (Salaran, 2010, p. 136), it is possible for individuals to exchange resources through informal processes, fostering innovation (Kanter, 1988). As these interactions can be built inside communities and with external actors it becomes easier to remove traditional obstacles to the creation of common knowledge. Once knowledge becomes a social construction inside a community its creation, updating and dissemination is normalized, and it can be shared to others. As a result of the projection of the Monarch Butterfly communities their experience has been reproduced by others elsewhere in Mexico.

These interactions combined with common goals and visions can help integrate heterogeneous actors around a project, promoting Sen's idea of freedom through development. When we put this in terms of a model shift to a green economy a shared vision as a bonding mechanism can help different communities to participate or to combine resources. The project in Michoacan has now brought together Federal, local, regional government efforts, as well as academic and other key actors.

As many authors, like Kanter (1988) have stated, innovation involves different resource inputs and combinative capacities in order to become a source of value. It is thus necessary to build the necessary mechanisms to guarantee that a new development strategy, such as the promotion of green jobs, will create value.

Lessons to be Learned

Following this, the chapter proposes the creation of integrated social clusters that can help mobilize specialized knowledge and resources resulting on an operative system, successfully merging education and training, environmentally friendly products, technologies and techniques, creating jobs, attracting capitals and integrating enterprises, individuals and communities. As the Monarch Butterfly Sanctuary Project shows, this can also be a long-term solution, so far the project has been functioning for over 10 years and has become sustainable, due to the engagement of different counterparts and is in fact operating as an integrated social cluster. A key element is to set in motion existing activities, knowledge and relations and leaderships. This will contribute to the design of effective policy packages that can replicate *ex-novo* the most effective innovation ecosystems, and promote their development, by supportive R&D, enabling infrastructure, and institutional platforms for collaboration (OECD, 2012).

Finally, experiences in this chapter comprise a series of best practices to be replicated in the process of stimulating development and green jobs through social innovation:

- For community development process to consolidate, it is necessary to design long-term intervention strategies and guarantee support for at least three years;
- A clear identification of existing opportunities is the key to design alternatives to unattended issues;
- Capacity building is easier when there is an immediate application of acquired knowledge;
- Recognizing different forms of knowledge to incorporate them into strategies and projects to sum up people, practices, problem solving experiences and ideas to the innovation process;
- Money should not have a negative or positive influence on the way work is carried out. Fundraising even when it is an important element, should not consume energy and resources that can be used to develop a project. On the contrary, most practices include innovative forms of obtaining and managing resources with transparency and efficiency;

- Recording and organizing experiences, processes contribute to developing of successful and innovative models and programs;
- Integrate a well-trained and committed team in each area is an important feature to move towards specialization and consolidation of innovative structures and job creation processes;
- Identifying useful methodologies that can help organize and categorize organizational, individual and communitarian knowledge and procedures is a useful tool to communicate and replicate successful practices and instruments;
- Hands-on programs are not sufficient for social innovation to take place; it is necessary to carry out complementary research and to be aware of the state of the art in our field.

What Have We Learnt and Where Do We Go from Here?

Several studies (Tidd *et al.*, 2011; OECD, 2010; Von Braun and Pandya-Lorch, 2009) have already found a link between social innovation and entrepreneurship. Findings of this work are consistent with the literature and help build a blueprint towards designing successful development strategies and new public policies to promote green growth, together with job creation, particularly at the local level. The findings are based on the analyses of successful cases in collaborative solutions helped face vast difficulties bringing together non-governmental organizations, community leaders, researches, social workers faculty teams. Social innovation helps create situations and stable networks that favor the emergence of innovative space, their innovative nature contributes to their consolidation and renewal, mainly because they operate in environments and settings that tend to be ignored by traditional institutional designs and programs on innovation.

This research worked on the analysis of social innovation and its potential for development, outside traditional models and standard programs. The case studies have shed a light on the role community organization can play in creating new solutions to old or new challenges. People in Michoacan have learned the strength that can come from working together and protecting their natural heritage. Their experience is now shared by other communities and a successful bottom-up innovation process is in motion. If this process is consolidated it can become an innovative fashion in the usually adverse context of crisis, underdevelopment or poverty. As these examples can be seen as a model for social innovation, their multiplication and interconnection can favor larger innovation process. Therefore, identifying, informing and endorsing such spaces seem to be a win–win situation for actors involved.

Another way to support social innovation is to eliminate financial obstacles for small, social and independent projects, or to create innovative forms of credit and rewards. In particular, access to finance is especially difficult for social entrepreneurs in green sectors, due to the relative immaturity of the market (OECD, 2012). Policies to boost financing of immature green and/or social projects can contribute to the furthering innovation in general.

There is also an important question for governments on how to focus their own national efforts, towards promoting social innovation, creating jobs and social innovation. Not many countries are aware of the benefits that can come from promoting bottom-up solutions and independent community efforts, especially when it comes to unemployment and job creation. This will lead them to ignore effective and cheaper solutions occurring in the social innovation arena and benefit from the experience and knowledge acquired in these sectors and communities.

Conclusively our findings provide strong support for the initial claim about an association between social innovation, job creation and development while also providing inquiries for future research on the areas of social innovation, development and its possibilities in the context of a new green economy.

References

Arocena R and Sutz J (2001) Desigualdad, tecnología e innovación en el desarrollo latinoamericano. Iberoamericana, Madrid, Vol. I.1, 29–49.

Barber B (1983) *The Logic and Limits of Trust*. New Jersey: Rutgers University Press.

Borup M *et al.* (2006) The sociology of expectations in science and technology. *Technology Analysis and Strategic Management* 18(3/4): 285–298.

Burt R (1995) *Structural Holes: The Social Structure of Competition.* Massachusetts: Harvard Unversity Press.

Care2 (2012) Available at http://www.care2.com/ [accessed on 12 December 2012].

CEDEFOP and ILO (2010) *Skills for Green Jobs: European Synthesis Report.* Luxembourg: Publications Office of the European Union.

CEPAL (2010) Equidad, desarrollo y ciudadanía. Santiago de Chile, CEPAL.

Dasgupta P and Serageldin I (2001) *Social Capital: A Multifaceted Perspective.* Washington: World Bank Publications.

Granovetter MS (1973) The strength of weak ties. *American Journal of Sociology* 78(May): 1360–1380.

Granovetter MS (1985) Economic action and social structure: the problem of embeddedness. *American Journal of Sociology* 91: 481–510.

Hamalainen J and Heiskala R (2007) *Social Innovations, Institutional Change and Economic Performance: Making Sense of Structural Adjustment Processes.* London: Edward Elgar Publishing.

Hennessey BA and Amabile TM (2009) Creativity. *Annual Review of Psychology* 61: 569–598.

Kanter M (1988) When a thousand flowers bloom: Structural, collective, and social conditions for innovation in organizations. In Staw BM and Cummings LL (eds.), *Research in Organizational Behavior*, Vol. 10. Greenwich, CT: JAI Press, pp. 169–211.

Martens B and Keul A (2005) *Designing Social Innovation: Planning, Building, Evaluating.* Boston: Hogrefe & Huber Pub.

Martins EC and Terblanche F (2003) Building organisational culture that stimulates creativity and innovation. *European Journal of Innovation Management* 6(1): 64–74.

Nahapiet J and Ghoshal S (1998) Social capital, intellectual capital, and the organizational advantage. *Academy of Management Review* 23: 242–266.

OECD (2009) Economic outlook interim report, March. Available at www.oecd.org/oecdeconomicoutlook [accessed on 18 December 2012].

OECD (2010) Green growth strategy interim report: Implementing our commitment for a sustainable future, Paris, May.

OECD (2012) Green growth and developing countries: A summary for policy makers, Paris, June.

Ouchi WG (1980) Markets, bureaucracies, and clans. *Administrative Science Quarterly* 25(1): 129.

Portes A and Sensenbrenner J (1993) Embeddedness and immigration: notes on the social determinants of economic action. *The American Journal of Sociology* 98(6): 1320–1350.

Putnam RD (1993) *Making Democracy Work. Civic Traditions in Modern Italy.* Princeton, New Jersey: Princeton University Press.

Saariluoma P, Kannisto E and Kujala T (2009) Analysing micro-innovation processes: universities and enterprises collaboration. *Communications of the IBIMA* 9: 19–23.

Salaran M (2010) Research productivity and social capital. *Australian Higher Education: Higher Education Quarterly* 64(2): 133–148.

Saxanian A (1994) *Regional Advantage: Culture and Competition in Silicon Valley and Route 128.* Cambridge: Harvard University Press.

Sen A (2000) *Development as Freedom.* New York: Anchor Books.

Tidd J, Bessant J and Pavitt K (2001) *Managing Innovation: Integrating Technological Market and Organizational Change*, 2nd edn. Chichester: John Wiley & Sons.

UNEP (2011) Towards a green economy: Pathways to sustainable development and poverty eradication. www.unep.org/greeneconomy.

Von Braun J and Pandya-Lorch R (2009) *The Poorest and Hungry: Assessment, Analyses, and Actions.* Washington: International Food Policy Research Institute.

Chapter 7

SWEET SORGHUM: A SMART CROP TO MEET THE DEMANDS FOR FOOD, FODDER, FUEL AND FEED

G. Basavaraj,* P. Parthasarathy Rao,* C. Ravinder Reddy,*
A. Ashok Kumar,* S. Datta Mazumdar,* Y. Ramana Reddy,[†]
P. Srinivasa Rao,* S.M. Karuppan Chetty*
and Belum V.S. Reddy*

*International Crops Research Institute for the Semi-Arid Tropics
[†]International Livestock Research Institute, Patancheru 502 324,
Andhra Pradesh, India

Sweet sorghum is a C4 plant with high photosynthetic efficiency producing high biomass with sugary stalks in a short time (4 months) under rain-fed conditions. The stalks can be crushed to make juice, which can be fermented to produce ethanol or boiled to produce syrup. The syrup can be converted to ethanol or to food grade quality syrup to be used as sweetener by the food industry. This chapter highlights income generating opportunities for smallholder farmers from sweet sorghum cultivation and processing through small scale agro-enterprise. This pilot project was conducted by ICRISAT by establishing a Decentralized Crushing Unit (DCU) at the village level to crush sweet sorghum stalks, extract juice and boil it to produce syrup to be used for various industrial uses (ethanol and food). The bagasse (fiber left over after crushing) was used as livestock feed or as fuel. The benefit–cost ratios (BCR) for the options explored indicate that a simple value addition in the form of chopping sweet sorghum stover provides the highest BCR of 2.56, though the sustenance of the agro-enterprise depends on the availability of multiple feedstocks like maize and sorghum stover for optimum capacity utilization and profitability. This is followed by syrup production for the food industry. The establishment of small scale enterprises will pave the way for micro-entrepreneurship at village level and enhance income and employment opportunities, in the process reducing rural poverty.

Background

At present, energy demand for transport in India is primarily met through non-renewable energy sources like fossil fuels. Being short in domestic production, India depends mainly on crude oil imports for its energy needs. In the near future, oil imports are slated to rise further with no major breakthrough in domestic oil production. A compounding factor is the rise in the number of vehicles on the road, which has grown by 10% each year between 2001 and 2006,[1] and is expected to rise further. Against this backdrop, there is a renewed interest in energy augmentation through biofuel crops. One such promising biofuel crop is sweet sorghum, whose sugar-rich stocks can be crushed to produce juice, then fermented into bioethanol, and used to make a blended fuel replacing conventional gasoline (Reddy *et al.*, 2005).

Sweet sorghum is a C4 plant with high photosynthetic efficiency. It produces a high biomass (upto 40–50 tha^{-1}) in a short time (4 months) under rain-fed conditions (Reddy *et al.*, 2005). One advantage of sweet sorghum compared with other crops is that using sweet sorghum for fuel does not reduce its contribution as a food source because the grain can be harvested for food, and the bagasse — the fiber that remains after the juice used for biofuel has been extracted — may be used for fodder (Nalini Kumari *et al.*, 2011). Hence, sweet sorghum is a "smart" crop, which meets the triple requirements of food, fuel and fodder.

To assess the potential benefits of sweet sorghum as feedstock for bioethanol production, a new pilot program is being tested in the state of Andhra Pradesh, under the partnership of International Crops

---

[1] Authors' estimate based on MoRTH (2006).

Research Institute for the Semi-Arid Tropics (ICRISAT), Indian Council of Agricultural Research (ICAR), and National Agricultural Innovation Project (NAIP). The project promotes a value-chain approach to augment farmer incomes, while promoting a sustainable sweet sorghum–ethanol value chain. The overall objective of the project is to provide greater employment and income-generating opportunities for farmers and other stakeholders in the value chain, while supplying an environmentally friendly energy source. Through the example of a successful sweet sorghum value chain for ethanol production, this paper explores the opportunities for agro-enterprise development from sweet sorghum.

Sweet Sorghum Syrup for Bioethanol

Working with a centralized distillery

The project adopted the value chain model called "Seed to Tank" (ICRISAT, 2008), which encompasses sweet sorghum production, processing, value addition and marketing.

After harvesting, sweet sorghum stalks have to be crushed within a short time to avoid loss of juice due to drying. Hence, the harvesting and crushing of stalk to process into ethanol have to go hand-in-hand and the cultivation area of the crop ideally should be no more than 50 km from the distillery. In the case of this project, sweet sorghum was initially processed into ethanol in a distillery established by a private sector partner M/s Rusni Distilleries Pvt. Ltd., located in Medak district of Andhra Pradesh. The distiller had the capacity to produce 40 kiloliters of ethanol per day, and it was incubated in ICRISAT's Agri-business and Innovation Platform.

The M/s distillery was a 'centralized unit,' meaning that farmers were linked to the distillery through a partnership with a local nongovernmental organization (NGO), whose role was to deliver the stalks to the distillery and to process payments to farmers. The NGO also liaised with research organizations to promote the program in general and to provide technological assistance. A schematic presentation of the value chain under a centralized unit is presented in Figure 1.

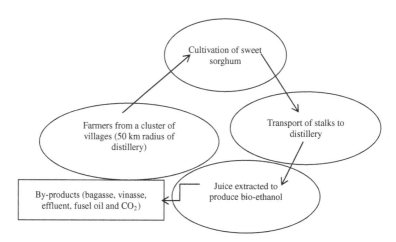

Figure 1. Schematic sweet sorghum value chain for ethanol production — centralized unit

Using the centralized distillery presented several challenges, namely:

- Using a centralized distillery, a typical ethanol yield of 40 kiloliters per day requires raw material from 8,000 ha of crop area per year spread over two seasons — 3,500 ha in the rainy season (rain-fed) and 4,500 ha in the post-rainy season (irrigated), which requires the mobilization of a large number of farmers (on average 1 farmer would cultivate 1 ha under sweet sorghum) preferably within a 50 km radius of the distillery. This presented significant limitations, namely: Finding 4,500 ha with irrigation facilities during the post-rainy season was a daunting task in the semi-arid tropics with limited access to irrigation.
- Organizing such a large number of farmers (3,000) to undertake sweet sorghum cultivation within the specified area (<50 km) also proved difficult.
- Farmers located more than 50 km from the distillery were burdened by high transportation costs owing to the bulkiness of stalks.
- A 24-hour delay in transportation of stalks to distilleries after harvest led to a reduction in stalk weight by up to 20%, depending on climatic conditions, causing economic loss to grower and processor.

Given these limitations, project coordinators decided to establish decentralized crushing units (DCU) at the village level, which had the added benefit of being a small-scale agro-enterprise.

DCU: An innovative approach to making sweet sorghum syrup

A crushing unit at the village level was established (Ravinder Reddy *et al.*, 2009) in the close vicinity of farmers' fields at Ibrahimbad village, Medak district of Andhra Pradesh. The site of the unit was established in consultation with the local NGO, village leaders, and farmers and was based on several socio-economic criteria, namely, the existing natural resource base, social harmony, agro-ecology and the feasibility of cultivating sweet sorghum. A total of 514 households spread across seven villages of Ibrahimbad cluster were selected to cultivate sweet sorghum. Having a DCU means that the harvested sweet sorghum stalks can be crushed and juiced on the same day, after which the juice is boiled into syrup (Figure 2). The brix content of syrup (between 70% and 80%) allows syrup to be stored longer than juice — over 24 months — without loss of fermentable sugars, and

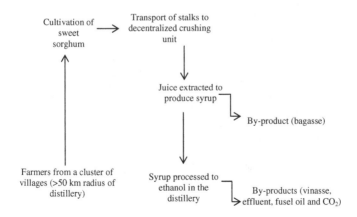

Figure 2. Schematic sweet sorghum value chain for syrup production to ethanol — DCU

can be processed to produce ethanol at the distillery. The decentralized approach makes the supply chain more efficient by reducing the volume of feedstock to be supplied to the centralized crushing units and by increasing the period of feedstock availability (supply of syrup) to industry (Figure 3). Further, the establishment of DCUs benefits the farmers farther away from the distillery as long as they have a crushing unit relatively close to them.

The crushing of sweet sorghum into syrup continued for 4 years under this project, and was carried out using a modified sugarcane crusher. (A crusher customized for sweet sorghum had not been designed.) The crushing capacity was 2 tons per hour and

(A)   (B)

(C)

Figure 3.   Decentralized sweet sorghum crushing unit: (A) crushing; (B) bagasse; (C) boiling the juice to produce syrup

the crushing efficiency depended on the sweet sorghum genotype, crushing season, time lapse between harvesting and crushing, and temperature. During the rainy season (sweet sorghum is presently grown only in rainy season), in 30 days, working 8 hours a day, the crushing unit could crush sweet sorghum cultivated on 25–30 ha. The initial cost of the unit for the pilot phase was jointly financed by ICAR and NAIP (Ravinder Reddy *et al.*, 2009).

To meet the raw material requirements of the DCU, forward and backward linkages had to be established (Figure 4). The linkage established between Farmers' Association, local NGO, and crushing unit facilitated the mobilization of farmers, the distribution of seed, and the dispensation of technical advice related to production and harvesting schedules to supply sweet sorghum stalks to the unit. Inputs such as fertilizer and herbicides were supplied on credit to farmers, payment for which was later deducted from the payment made to farmers. Other forward linkages included the technical advice on crushing the stalk to produce juice and syrup, assistance with contract agreements between farmers and distillery, and

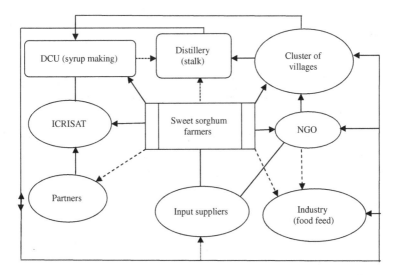

Figure 4. Flow chart of linkages in sweet sorghum value chain[2]

---

[2] Solid lines in the figure represent strong linkages, dotted lines weak linkages.

information on value addition of the bagasse being provided by consortium partners.

Economics of syrup production

Under the pilot project, the crushing unit produced sweet sorghum syrup between 2008 and 2012. Below, we provide an overview of the economics of syrup production for the years 2008–2010. Our discussion is in two parts: the cost of sweet sorghum cultivation and the cost of processing sweet sorghum to syrup.

Economics of sweet sorghum cultivation

Data on the cost of cultivation was collected from farmers who were part of the project and analyzed for various costs, gross and net returns, and input–output ratios of the crop. The cost of cultivation included both paid out costs and imputed costs. In 2008, total cost of cultivating sweet sorghum was Rs 15,804 (US$316)/ha with an average stalk yield of 15 t/ha during 2008.[3]

Economics of cost of processing sweet sorghum to syrup

Data for syrup production was analyzed for the stalks supplied to the crushing unit by 102 households in 2008–2009 and 94 households during 2009–2010. A total of 600 tons of sweet sorghum was crushed in 2009 with an average crushing capacity of 22 tons per day (Table 1). The average labor requirement was 54 person days, with an average production of 5,897 liters of juice per day. The total quantity of juice extracted from crushing 600 tons of sweet sorghum was 161,565 liters with a total quantity of 28.8 tons of syrup.

The total cost of production of 28.8 tons of sweet sorghum syrup was Rs 739,528 (US$14,790) and on average, the cost incurred in processing 1 kg of syrup was Rs 25.65 (US$0.50) during 2009.

---

[3] Rs is the abbreviation for India currency rupees. At 2012 exchange rate, US$1 = Rs 50.

Table 1:   Sweet sorghum crushing indicators under
DCU, Ibrahimbad, Andhra Pradesh

Indicator	2008	2009
Number of farmers	102	94
Stalks crushed (tons)	557	600
Stalk yield (t/ha)	15	20
Average stalk crushed (t/day)	13	22
Crushing days	43	27
Juice extracted/t of stalk	261	269
Syrup/t of stalk	40	48

Table 2:   Cost of syrup production under DCU (2009), Ibrahimbad,
Andhra Pradesh

Cost Item	Total Costs (Rs)	Percent of Total Costs
Cost of raw material		
Stalk yield (tons)	600	
Cost of stalk (Rs)	419,930	57
Processing costs		
Labor costs	210,830	29
Chemical costs	20,850	3
Firewood	10,825	1
Operating expenses		
Fuel costs	47,359	6
Repair and maintenance	15,869	2
Miscellaneous	13,265	2
Total costs	**739,528**	**100**

The cost of syrup progressively decreased to Rs 22 (US$0.44) per
kilogram during 2011. Table 2 shows that raw material (sorghum
stalks) accounted for 57% of the total costs of production, followed
by labor costs (29%) and fuel (6%) (Figure 5). Currently farmers manage the crushing unit; there is still significant scope for reducing the
cost of syrup production with the proper protocols in place.

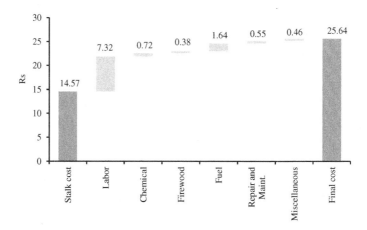

Figure 5. Item-wise break-up of costs of processing sweet sorghum to syrup production

Table 3:   Costs and returns to syrup production for ethanol

Indicator	Per Ton of Stalk (Rs)	Per Hectare (Rs)
Cost of syrup production	1,232	24,783
Gross returns (@ Rs 10/kg)	480	9,670
Net returns	(752)	(15,113)
Benefit cost ratio	0.38	

Note: Syrup was sold to the distillery at Rs 10/kg.

The gross returns realized per hectare and per ton of sweet sorghum stalk produced for syrup were Rs 9,670 (US$193) and Rs 480 (US$10), respectively (Table 3). Currently, the purchase price of syrup by the distillery for ethanol conversion is Rs 10 (US$0.02)/kg. The pricing is based on ethanol recovery from syrup, processing costs of syrup to ethanol, and the selling price of ethanol (based on discussions held with the distillery). The distillery requires about 3 kg of syrup to convert to 1 liter of ethanol. The government of India regulates prices for ethanol to be blended with gasoline and the 2012 administered price of ethanol was Rs 27 (US$0.5)/l. It is not feasible for the distillery to pay more for the syrup unless and until the government revises the ethanol price.

Several other alternatives were also explored to reduce the operating cost of syrup production, namely:

- Reducing labor costs (labor efficiency);
- Further mechanization of production (improving crushing efficiency and extraction efficiency);
- Increasing the brix (sugar content) of stalks through improved genotypes.

The above-mentioned efforts resulted in increasing the amount of syrup extracted by 50% and reducing labor costs by 28%.

Benefits of the DCU as an agro-enterprise

The long-range goal of establishing a village-level small-scale agro-enterprise is to reduce poverty and unemployment. Achieving this was envisioned through producing value-added agricultural produce and creating new employment opportunities in the villages to enhance the livelihoods of the rural population. Establishment of a DCU in Ibrahimbad village had both tangible and intangible benefits. The tangible benefits included increased employment opportunities, especially during the post-rainy season, which tends to be a lean period for agricultural activities in the drylands. On average, the project generated about 40 additional person days of employment per household. The monetary value of the additional employment generated was about Rs 6,400 (US$128) per household annually (the wage rate prevailing during 2012 was Rs 160 (US$3) per day). Some of the intangible benefits were an improvement in farmers' ability to manage a small-scale village-level agro-enterprise and enhanced food security due to increased incomes.

Besides developing sweet sorghum syrup as a fuel source, two more alternatives for agro-enterprise development have been explored to make the DCU viable and provide alternative opportunities to smallholders from sweet sorghum:

- Sweet sorghum syrup for use in food industry and,
- Value addition for bagasse.

Alternative Options for Agro-Enterprise Development from Sweet Sorghum

Syrup for use in the food industry

An alternative use for sweet sorghum syrup is in the food industry, provided the product is food grade. Food grade syrup can be used as a sugar replacement in certain value-added food products. In addition, the syrup, which is rich in iron, calcium and potassium, also has potential pharmaceutical applications.

If sweet sorghum syrup were tó compete with sugar cane, it could claim a share of the country's sugar industry, which in 2011 produced 24 million ton of sugar (Indian Sugar Mills Association, 2012) valued at US$144 million (at current prices of Rs 27 (US$0.5) per kilogram of sugar). If just 1% of sugar market value were tapped, the market potential for sweet sorghum would be US$1.44 million.

The processing of sweet sorghum juice for food grade syrup involves the removal of leaves and leaf sheath from the stalks before crushing. The juice is then pre-heated and clarified. The clarified juice is then further concentrated to syrup by heating and slow evaporation ensuring the taste profile is not compromised. Some of the products developed by the NutriPlus Knowledge Program of the Agri-business and Innovation Platform, ICRISAT, using food grade sweet sorghum syrup include ready-to-serve beverage, tamarind–sweet sorghum sauce, sweetened tomato sauce, and energy bars (Figure 6).

When it comes to making value-added food products from sweet sorghum, opportunities exist for the entrepreneur to establish an agro-enterprise that integrates production and processing at the village level. Strict regulations and stringent quality requirements of the food industry need to be observed, however, which is likely to increase the costs of production.

The economics of syrup for food industry

The entrepreneur has the option to either cultivate sweet sorghum and produce syrup or purchase stalks from the farmer and convert it to syrup. The economics of syrup production presented below in

Figure 6. (A) Ready-to-serve sweet sorghum-based beverage; (B) Tamarind–sweet sorghum sauce; (C) Sweet sorghum-based tomato sauce; (D) Sweet sorghum crispies

Table 4 is for a stand-alone agro-enterprise producing only syrup and only the returns realized from by-product (bagasse) value addition are included in the economic analysis.

Value addition to bagasse

The by-product of bagasse is obtained regardless of whether the syrup is produced for ethanol or for the food industry. Bagasse is a good livestock feed and value addition to bagasse in the form of chopping or producing feed blocks or pellets provides additional income opportunities for farmers. The processing of bagasse can also be integrated into facilities that produce syrup for ethanol or for the food industry. The additional returns generated from the value addition of this by-product can enhance the attractiveness of the business proposition for entrepreneurs.

Table 4:   Economics of syrup production for food industry

Indicator	Value (Rs)
Cost of sweet sorghum per ton of stalk	800
Processing cost of sweet sorghum to syrup per ton of stalk[a]	531
Total cost of syrup per ton of stalk	1,331
Returns from syrup per ton of stalk[b]	1,755
Returns from bagasse per ton of stalk[c]	115
Gross returns per ton of stalk	1870
Net returns per ton of stalk	539
Benefit cost ratio	1.40

[a] The cost escalation in producing food grade syrup is not accounted for in the analysis.
[b] The sale price of syrup is assumed to be Rs 27/kg which is equivalent to price of sugar at 2012 prices.
[c] Returns from sale of bagasse is at the rate of Rs 1.2/kg (the value realized may go upto Rs 4/kg in distant locations) for surplus bagasse of 115 kg/t of sweet sorghum crushed.
Source: Authors' estimates.

The economics of bagasse processing

The current rate of conversion of a ton of stalk to juice is 27% to 30% (269–350l), leaving 650–700 kg of wet bagasse. The wet bagasse is dried and used as a source of fuel during the process of syrup production. Even after using the bagasse for fuel, about 55% of it remains as surplus, however, which can serve as a good livestock feed. Consortium partner International Livestock Research Institute (ILRI) conducted research on the quality and composition of bagasse fodder, as described in Blümmel et al. (2009).

During 2009, the surplus bagasse was sold directly to fodder traders by an arrangement facilitated by ILRI and partners in the project. During 2010, the fodder traders chopped the bagasse and transported it by truck to their customers in Hyderabad, 70 km away. This type of value addition resulted in selling the bagasse at higher prices of Rs 0.70 (US$0.014) per kilogram during the start

Table 5: Economics of bagasse value addition to different end products

Cost or Returns Parameters	Bagasse Based Value Added Products	
	Feedblock	Chopped Bagasse
Feedstock cost (Rs/t)	800	800
Cost of other raw material[a] (Rs/t)	8,840	—
Processing cost (Rs/t)	260	85
Transport cost (Rs/t/100 km)	260	675
Total cost	10,160	1,560
Gross returns[b]/t	20,000	4,000
Net returns/t	9,840	2,440

[a] Cost of other raw material includes molasses, bran, husk and cotton seed cake for preparation of feedblock.
[b] The selling price of a feedblock is Rs 150 and chopped bagasse is Rs 4/kg.
Source: Rows 3 and 4 are from Anandan *et al.* (2010) and the rest are authors' estimates.

of season and a higher Rs 1.2 (US$0.24) per kilogram at the end of season, which was remarkable given that the whole (*i.e.*, unextracted) sweet sorghum stalks were valued only slightly higher at Rs 0.80 per kilogram. The scope for further value addition to different end products (feedblock, pellets, mashed and chopped) was demonstrated by ILRI under the project. The economics of value addition is presented only for two end products: feedblocks and chopped fodder (Table 5).

The small-scale entrepreneur may set up a stand-alone small-scale stover and bagasse processing agro-enterprise, which will suit prevailing labor and infrastructural conditions or integrate with the syrup-based DCU. In case of a stand-alone stover and bagasse based agro-enterprise the returns realized per ton of stalk will be in the range of Rs 2,440–9,840 (US$49–197) depending on the end-products. The bagasse based agro-enterprise has to be integrated with either syrup production for ethanol or through production of food grade syrup.

Conclusions: Viable Sweet Sorghum Agro-Enterprise Options

This chapter has discussed three different options for agro-enterprises from sweet sorghum. The benefit–cost ratios (BCR) for each of the options are presented in Table 6. Through simple value addition in the form of chopping, the sweet sorghum stover provides the highest BCR of 2.56, though the sustenance of the agro-enterprise depends on the availability of multiple feedstocks like maize and sorghum stover for optimum capacity utilization and profitability. Syrup production from sweet sorghum for the food industry as an agro-enterprise integrated with chopping of surplus bagasse with a small-scale processing unit provides a BCR of 1.40. The bagasse can be stored and processed to chopped form after the syrup has been produced. This practice aids in increasing the operating window and optimum capacity utilization of the agro-enterprise. However, since setting up of an agro-enterprise for processing sweet sorghum to food grade syrup would require strict regulations, the cost of syrup would increase to meet the quality standards and cost of establishment. The benefit cost ratio of producing and processing syrup for ethanol was the least at 0.38 relative to other options explored.

The DCU was established to overcome some of the shortfalls of the centralized unit. The establishment of the crushing unit on a pilot

Table 6:   BCR of different agro-enterprises from sweet sorghum

Sweet Sorghum Agro-Enterprise[a]	BCR of Agro-Enterprise	Ranking Based on BCR
Syrup for ethanol only	0.38	5
Syrup for ethanol with by-product bagasse valuation	0.98	4
Syrup for food industry only	1.31	3
Syrup for food industry with by-product bagasse valuation	1.40	2
Stover/bagasse value addition only	2.56	1

Source: Authors' estimate.

[a] Investment cost of establishing the agro-enterprise is not considered in the calculations.

basis to aid in supply chain management for the centralized unit led to alternative options for syrup utilization and establishment of alternate agro-enterprises. The direct benefits of DCU establishment as an agro-enterprise for supply of syrup to the ethanol industry provided 40 person days of employment with monetary benefits of Rs 6,400 during the lean season of agriculture.

The results of crushing sweet sorghum over a four-year period show a gradual decline in costs of syrup production by 31%. The existing costs of syrup production still are on the higher side for converting it to ethanol and there is significant scope for reducing the cost through mechanization of the DCU. Policy options and enabling environment also play a significant role in promoting the DCU as a village level agro-enterprise complementing ethanol production from the centralized unit. Capital assistance for establishment of the DCU and increase in procurement price of ethanol will help in sustainability and economic viability of the DCU.

Alternative options explored for establishing an agro-enterprise producing food grade syrup integrated with bagasse value addition has also shown to be a promising avenue. Setting up an agro-enterprise producing food grade syrup requires strict regulations to meet the quality requirements of the industry, however. Hence, these parameters and their cost implications need to be taken into consideration before establishment of the unit.

Given the scarcity of fodder and the growth of the livestock economy at the rate of 4% *per annum* in India, alternate options of sweet sorghum stover-based and bagasse-based agro-enterprise are promising. Hence, establishing a small-scale agro-enterprise for sweet sorghum stover value addition might be an economically viable proposition taking into consideration the availability of multiple feedstocks for processing (enabling utilization of capacity for more than 6 months in a year), prevailing labor supply and infrastructural conditions.

The DCUs will pave the way for micro-entrepreneurship development at village level and bring income and employment opportunities, in the process reducing rural poverty. At the same time, they may prevent (or at least slow down) rural-to-urban migration, thereby mitigating the growth of urban slums.

Acknowledgments

This research work was carried out the under National Agricultural Innovation Project (NAIP) — Indian Council of Agricultural Project, Government of India project and Common Fund for Commodities (CFC). The funding support from both NAIP and CFC is greatly acknowledged.

References

Anandan S, Khan AA, Ravi D and Blümmel M (2010) A comparison of two complete feed blocks based on sorghum stover of two different cultivars on weight gain in sheep and economy of feeding. *Animal Nutrition and Feed Technology* 10S: 101–104.

Blümmel M, Rao SS, Palaniswami S, Shah L and Reddy BVS (2009) Evaluation of sweet sorghum [*Sorghum bicolor* (L.) Moench] used for bio-ethanol production in the context of optimizing whole plant utilization. *Animal Nutrition and Feed Technology* 9: 1–10.

Indian Sugar Mills Association (2012) *Statistics.* Available at www.indiansugar. com/Statics.aspx [accessed on 24 April 2012].

ICRISAT (2008) *ICRISAT-NAIP Sub-Project on Value Chain Model for Bioethanol Production from Sweet Sorghum.* Patancheru, Andhra Pradesh, India: International Crops Research Institute for Semi-Arid Tropics.

Ministry of Road Transport and Highways (MoRTH) (2006) *Road Transport Year Book 2006–07.* Available at http://indiagovernance.gov. in/files/road-transprt-annual-report.pdf [accessed on 20 March 2012].

Nalini Kumari R, Reddy Y, Blümmel M, Nagalaxmi M, Pavani, Sudhakar Reddy, Ravinder Reddy C and Reddy BVS (2011) Effect of feeding different processed sweet sorghum bagasse based complete diet on growth and carcass traits in growing ram lambs. Paper presented at the 8th international symposium on nutrition of herbivores at Wales, UK, 6–9, September 2011.

Ravinder Reddy C, Ashok Kumar A, Reddy BVS, Karuppan Chetty SM, Sharma KK, Gowda CLL, Parthasarthy Rao P, Wani SP, Rao SS, Umakanth AV, Srinivas I, Kamal Ahmed, Blummel M, Ramana, Reddy Y and Palaniswami AR (2009) Establishment and maintenance of decentralized sweet sorghum crushing-cum syrup making unit. Information bulletin No. 79, Patancheru, Andhra Pradesh, India: International Crops Research Institute for Semi-Arid Tropics.

Reddy BVS, Ramesh S, Sanjana Reddy P, Ramaiah B, Salimath PM and Rajashekar Kachapur (2005) Sweet sorghum — A potential alternative raw material for bioethanol and bio-energy. *International Sorghum and Millets Newsletter* 46: 79–86.

Chapter 8

PROMOTING FOOD PROCESSING THROUGH FOOD PARKS AND FOOD PROCESSING SPECIAL ECONOMIC ZONES: THE INDIAN EXPERIENCE

Aradhna Aggarwal

National Council of Applied Economic Research, Parisila Bhawan,
11 Indraprastha Estate, New Delhi 110002

This study evaluates the performance of food processing clusters and their role in the development strategy of the food processing industry in India. We focus on two major cluster development initiatives of the Government of India: one, a food park scheme of the Ministry of Food Processing, and two, a special economic zone (SEZ) policy of the Ministry of Commerce. While analyzing the performance of these initiatives, the study adopts a comprehensive framework which covers not only the quantitative measures of investment, employment, and production but also qualitative indicators such as dynamism of the parks and backward and forward linkages with the rest of the economy, regional economy and cluster-induced benefits. The analysis is based on interviews with chief executive officers of the selected parks, officials of the Ministry of Food Processing and developers of selected parks and SEZs. It is complemented by secondary data based analysis. The study shows that overall the schemes have failed to generate critical mass of economic activity and their achievements have been unimpressive, apart from a few exceptions. It concludes that implementing successful, large-scale industrialization programs involving private participation requires of policymakers a long-term vision, strong commitment, a pragmatic and flexible approach, and dynamic learning and institution building.

Introduction

There is a growing realization that in order to meet the twin national objectives of "inclusive growth" and "food security," it will not be enough only to increase agricultural production; it is equally important to reduce wastages through food processing. In addition to reducing wastages, food processing also ensures value addition, generates additional employment opportunities, improves farmers' income and economic viability of agricultural operations as well as export earnings and thus leads to improvement in socio-economic condition of millions of families in both urban and rural communities (Henson and Cranfield, 2009; Wilkinson and Rocha, 2009). There are clear indications that agro-industries have a significant global impact on economic development and poverty reduction (Da Silva *et al.*, 2009).

In India, the recent realization by policymakers that growth of the food processing sector would be key to "growth with food security and inclusion" in the country has prompted the government to recast its efforts of promoting the industry on a much wider scale and in an integrated manner. In this context, cluster initiatives are an important new direction in economic policy. Two major cluster initiatives of the Government of India are: one, food parks of the Ministry of Food Processing, and two, dedicated special economic zones (SEZs) for food processing under the SEZ policy of the Ministry of Commerce. The development of these agro-industrial clusters involves large investments. There has been no comprehensive evaluation of their performance to date from an economic perspective, however. This study aims to fill this gap by evaluating the performance of these programs. The objectives of this study are three-fold:

- To provide an overview of the evolution of the food park and SEZ policies.
- To analyze their progress to date.
- To evaluate the performance of the selected operational food parks in terms of selected parameters; while doing so, the study investigates experiences of food park developers/units in cluster development and cluster building (success stories, bottlenecks, and success factors).

The analysis is based on the primary survey of selected parks and SEZs and is complemented by secondary data based analysis. The study has important policy implications for policymakers to refine and adjust strategy in (future) cluster building and improve cluster induced benefits.

We begin by providing a brief overview of the global and Indian food processing industry in the next section. The section that follows will focus on the evolution of government policy. We then address the question whether clustering is the way forward in promoting food processing, followed by an evaluation of the performance of food parks and SEZs and a section discussing case studies. Finally, conclusions complete the analysis.

Food Processing Industry: A Brief Overview

Global food and beverage (F&B) sector

Globally, the F&B sector, which comprises farming, food production, distribution, retail and catering, was valued at US$5.7 trillion in 2008 (IMAP, 2010). It is expected to continue to grow at a compound annual growth rate of 3.5% to US$7 trillion by 2014. Both developed and developing countries contribute to the growth of this industry. Historically, the global industry of food processing has been dominated by the developed countries with Europe still accounting for the largest share in the global F&B industry, generating revenues of US$1.4 trillion in 2007 and employing 4 million workers and the United States following closely with US$1 trillion of this market in the same year (IMAP, 2010).[1] In recent years, however, the contribution of the developing countries has been rising faster. According to FAO (2007), the percentages of global manufacturing value addition for the main agro-industry manufacturing product categories generated by developing countries have nearly doubled in the last 25 years. Growing population, favorable demographics, rising income levels, increasing urbanization and growing numbers of women in the

---

[1] These countries will continue to contribute to the growth of the industry due to rising health consciousness and increasing demand for high quality, nutritional products and pre-packed and home-cooked food.

workforce are contributing to this shift with Russia, China and India increasing their production capacities in this sector. The prospects for continued growth in demand for value-added food and agricultural products constitute an incentive for increased attention to agro-industries development within the context of economic growth, food security and poverty-fighting strategies in developing countries.

Food processing in India

Contribution to the economy

The food processing industry in India is witnessing quick growth in terms of consumption, production and growth. The total food market in 2009–2010 was approximately US$274 billion (at 2004–2005 prices), which was more than 36% of total private consumption. The overall size of the food processing sector has been estimated at US$132 billion in 2009–2010 (at constant price), which accounts for more than 50% of the domestic food market. It stood at US$69.4 billion in 2004–2005. This means the sector has grown at an average annual rate of above 13% since 2004–2005 (in constant prices). Over the same period, the registered industry grew faster at an average annual rate of over 17% from US$43 billion in 2004–2005 to US$96 billion (CSO data, online). Over one-fifth of the factories and over 18% of the total workforce in the organized manufacturing sector have been accounted for by this sector.

Between 2004–2005 and 2009–2010, the contribution of the sector remained almost at 1.7% of total GDP. The National Sample Survey on Employment and Unemployment shows that 25.6 million people were employed in agri-processing industry in 2009–2010. In addition to direct contribution, the industry also has the potential to generate significant indirect employment and income effects. Table 1 reveals that the investment in the sector has multiplier effects that are larger than in any other industrial sector.

Structural transformation of the industry

Induced by the opening of the economy, changing food habits, entry of multinationals, low cost technology and rise in commodity

Table 1: Income and employment multipliers in India

	Output	Income	Employment	Tax
Agriculture	1.652	1.059	4.645	–0.059
Mining	1.514	0.962	0.632	0.038
Food processing	2.541	0.978	2.778	0.022
Industry	2.471	0.883	1.059	0.117
Services	1.745	0.958	0.943	0.042

Source: Based on CSO.

branding, the industry has been undergoing structural transformation. These factors have fundamentally changed the way agricultural products are produced, processed, packaged, distributed and sold. In what follows, I briefly summarize the changes taking place in this industry.

- The industry has grown more than tenfold between 1950–1951 and 2006–2007. Most growth has come from the formal sector, which has grown 25-fold over the same period (Figure 1). In 1950–1951, informal players contributed more than 73% of value added in the industry. By 2009–2010, their share had declined to less than 35%. There has been a sharp decline in the ratio of informal to formal sector.
- Over the years large players have emerged in the organized segment of the industry. The level of concentration has been increasing with large domestic and foreign players entering the market as shown by both concentration ratios and Hirschman–Herfindahl Index (Table 2). Five companies that have remained at the top over the past five years are: ITC, Ruchi Soya, United Spirits, Adani Food and Nestle. Their share has grown rapidly over time from 21% in 2005 to 34% by 2011.
- There has been a steady increase in the use of capital per unit of labor in the industry (Figure 2). The capital used per unit of labor increased continuously from close to 0 in 1980–1981 to over US$9,000 in 2007–2008. Evidently, food processing is becoming increasingly automated with increasing sophistication in processing, preservation and packaging processes.

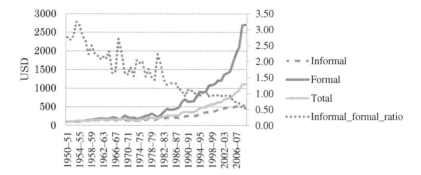

Figure 1. Size of the informal and formal food processing industry in India: 1950–1951 to 2009–2010 (base year 1950–1951 = 100)

Source: Central Statistical Organisation.

Table 2: Market concentration in the food processing industry

	Concentration Ratio			
	4 Firms	5 Firms	8 Firms	H-index
2005	19.4	21.0	25.2	2.02
2006	22.5	24.5	28.6	2.09
2007	22.8	24.5	29.1	2.13
2008	21.9	23.7	28.1	2.29
2009	22.4	24.5	29.3	2.33
2010	23.5	25.9	31.4	2.36
2011	31.0	33.8	41.2	3.66

Source: CMIE, PROWESS (2012).

- The industry is becoming technologically more sophisticated because of increasing desires by customers for products with high nutritional value, palatability, safety and convenience; the emergence of new technologies, in particular, in the biotech sector; expansion of the organized segment; and growth of large brands. Increasing growth of the packaged food industry[2] appears to have

---

[2] According to an ASSOCHAM study the Indian packaged food industry alone has been growing at a compound annual growth rate of about 15% to 20% annually.

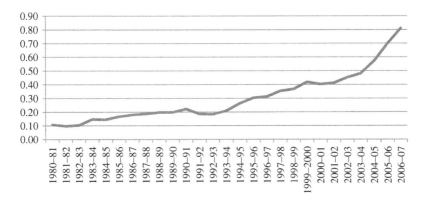

Figure 2. Capital used per unit of labor (in US$1,000)

Source: ASI (various years).

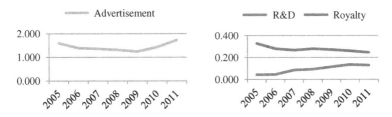

Figure 3. Technology and marketing intensity of the industry (%)

Source: CMIE, PROWESS (2012).

fueled the demand for advancement and development of a variety of packaging that can lead to increase in shelf life and also satisfy needs of a variety of customers. As shown in Figure 3, domestic R&D expenditures have risen faster than not only technology imports but also sales. Expenditures on marketing and brand building have also grown faster than the sales in recent years.

• Despite the increased concentration at the top, industry profit margins have declined reflecting increasing dynamism in the industry (Figure 4).

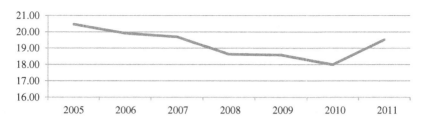

Figure 4.   Trends in profit–sales ratio in food processing
Source: CMIE, PROWESS (2012).

The fast growing industry notwithstanding food processing still remains rather small in India when compared with the potential (Table 3). It is 2.2% in case of fruits & vegetables, 35% in milk, 21% in meat, 6% in poultry produce and 26% in marine products.

There is thus a need for a major push to the industry. Vision 2015 of Ministry of Food Processing Industries aims to raise the processing of perishables in the country from existing 6% to 20%, value addition from 26% to 35% and the share in global food trade from 1.5% to 3% by 2015. To realize Vision 2015, the government of India has initiated concerted efforts. Promoting food parks is a critical component of these initiatives.

Evolution of the Food Park and SEZ Schemes

Food parks

The food park scheme has evolved through four phases over the past 20 years. The scheme was introduced in 1992–1993 with the objective of making available common infrastructure facilities for the food processing industry, especially small and medium entrepreneurs. Under the scheme, state governments were entrusted with the responsibility of promoting food processing industrial estates or parks. Food park is a business park for agricultural and food companies providing common facilities such as analytical and quality control laboratories, cold storages or modified atmosphere cold storages, warehousing facilities, supplementary pollution control facilities, *etc.* Under the scheme, these common facilities were to be funded by the central government, subject to a maximum of US$1.38 million. In

Table 3:   Current processing by item

Item	Production	Level of Processing
Food grains (million tons)	230	n.a.
Vegetables (million tons)	125	2.2
Fruits (million tons)	63	2.2
Spices (million tons)	4	n.a.
Milk (million tons)	105	35
Fish (million tons)	7	26
Livestock (million)	485	21
Poultry population (million)	489	6
Egg (million)	45	n.a.
Total value addition		26%

Source: 12th Plan Working Group Report.

2002–2003, the quantum of grant was enhanced to 25% of the project cost in General Areas and 33.33% in Difficult Areas.[3] Other facilities and concession were also enhanced to make it more attractive. Under the scheme, 56 food parks were sanctioned up to March 2007. These food parks were conceptualized in a traditional industrial estate mode with no forward and backward linkages.

In order to provide a major thrust to food processing, therefore, a paradigm shift was introduced in the Scheme in 2007–2008 when a Mega Food Parks Scheme (MFPS) replaced the food park scheme. In contrast to the earlier scheme, the new scheme lays thrust on attracting private investment in creating state of the art infrastructure for food processing in the country. It is essentially based on the public–private partnership mode with government stake in ownership restricted to less than 26% to maintain the private character of these parks. The scheme operates in "hub and spoke model," comprising Collection Centers (CCs), Primary Processing Centers (PPCs) and a Central Processing Center (CPC). The CPC is promoted as a hub. It has food processing units with need based common infrastructure

---

[3] Difficult Areas comprise North Eastern Region including Sikkim, Jammu & Kashmir, Himachal Pradesh, Uttarakhand, Andaman & Nicobar Islands, Lakshadweep & Integrated Tribal Development Project areas.

required for processing, packaging, environmental protection systems, quality control labs, trade facilitation centers, *etc.* This facility is connected with PPCs, which offer cleaning, grading, sorting and packing facilities; dry warehouses; and specialized cold stores including pre-cooling chambers, ripening chambers, mobile pre-coolers and mobile collection vans. The PPCs in turn are connected with farm proximate CCs. The CPC spreads over 50–100 acres of land for central processing. In addition, 2–5 acres of land is required in surrounding region for setting up PPCs. The CCs are considered optional. This infrastructure, *i.e.*, the PPCs and CCs may be located in a radius of 100–120 km from the CPC, though this distance would depend upon the business plan of the project. The objective is to promote efficient supply chain management from farm gate to retail outlets.

Government offers financial assistance (grant-in-aid) up to 50% of the project cost in general areas and 75% for NE Region and Difficult Areas subject to a maximum of US$10.38 million for creation of common Infrastructure facilities and facilities for backward and forward linkages.

Under the guidelines, each mega food park must benefit at least 6,000 farmers or producers directly and 25,000–30,000 farmers indirectly and generate about 40,000 direct and indirect jobs. The actual configuration of the project may vary depending upon the business plan for each mega food park. In all, approval has already been given to 30 mega food parks during 2007–2012.

Since 2012, the MFPS has entered the next phase when, in view of the experience gained in implementation of the scheme, it has been suitably revised. In the earlier version, each project required at least three independent entrepreneurs or business units to get together to develop the project. This restriction discouraged large food processors to invest in these projects. In the revised version, any one business entity may be eligible to promote a mega food park project. Further, it being a central government scheme, its implementation in the erstwhile version was carried out by the executing agencies of the center. This led to a problem of "lack of ownership" from the state governments. The revised scheme provides for a greater role of state governments in both selection and implementation of the mega food park projects.

Finally, in this phase, a scheme for "Mini Food Parks" has also been proposed to cater to the need for smaller states, especially in the northeastern region, as well as in disadvantaged regions of other states. Mini food parks will be spread over a minimum area of 30 acres. The private developers will be entitled to a maximum grant of US$4.17 million from the central government. Initially, the target was to set up 30 additional mega and 15 mini food parks during 2012–2016. Recently, however, the ceiling on the number of mega food parks that can come up in this period has been done away with and this is an open-ended scheme now.

SEZs

In 2005, Parliament passed the SEZs Act, 2005. The act became operative in February 2006 when the SEZ rules were also finalized. Like food parks, SEZs also aim at promoting cluster-based industrialization. SEZs are industrial parks that, unlike the food parks of the Ministry of Food Processing, cater primarily to the export markets. Further, unlike food parks, SEZs cover a wide range of economic activity. They may be sector specific or multiproduct. Sector specific SEZs in turn cover several sectors, food processing being one of them. As of March 2011, seven food-processing SEZs were operational.

Can Clustering Yield Benefits to the Industry?

There is a global trend towards the adoption of industry clustering as a key component in economic development policy. There appears to be a growing consensus that if done right, this model can provide a foundation for sustainable economic growth (Delgado *et al.*, 2011; Dobkins, 1996; Porter, 1998, 2000; Saxenian, 2006 among several others). A pertinent question is: can clustering benefit the food industry? This requires investigation into the spillover effects associated with the demand-driven and supply-side externalities in the location of food manufacturing industry. Agglomeration effects on the firms' location decision in the food processing industry are of interest because this sector is fundamentally connected both with agricultural production in rural areas, and consumption demand usually concentrated in urban areas (Cohen and Paul, 2001). Accordingly, Connor and Schiek (1997) classify three types of food processing units: demand oriented, supply oriented and footloose, which require different types of infrastructure and support services.

- First, demand oriented firms producing bakeries, breweries, milk processing facilities, and pasta makers. These firms tend to produce fragile, perishable, or bulky food items. Their cost structure is dominated by distribution costs — costs associated with getting their product to market. They tend to locate near urban centers well connected by physical infrastructure and logistic services and are benefited by the agglomeration effects generated on the demand side including transport, and marketing and distribution infrastructure.
- Second, supply oriented firms that have cost structures dominated by what they use to make their products. Examples include flour milling, fruit and vegetable canning, animal slaughtering, and cheese manufacturing businesses. They choose to locate in locations that offer ready access to the raw material that dominates their cost structure to reduce their procurement costs.
- Third, footloose firms, which do not have cost structures dominated by either input or distribution costs. These firms include breakfast cereal, chocolate, cracker, and spice manufacturers. They prefer to locate in areas where business schools and junior colleges provide a pool of trained and productive potential employees, and transportation and business services are available. These cost savings occur because inputs and service providers are nearby.

Apparently, all three food manufacturing types share some common location needs. Considering that the location characteristics are important for food manufacturing firms, spatial agglomerations should emerge. There are several measurers in the literature to assess them. I use the following index to gauge spatial agglomeration of food processing sector by state:

$$AG = \frac{\text{The food industry's } i \text{ in the state industrial sector}}{\text{The industry's } i \text{ share in country's industry}}$$

where i: output, value addition, employment.

Agglomeration effect is "revealed" if AG > 1. If AG is less than unity, the state is said to have a comparative disadvantage in the industry.

Of the 28 states, only 10 offer a clear advantage in the industry. These are Andhra Pradesh, Assam, Bihar, Kerala, Madhya Pradesh, Manipur, Nagaland, Punjab, Uttar Pradesh and Tripura. Interestingly, all these states except Kerala have the agrarian structure of their economy. This means that food processing establishments have been clustered into main agricultural production regions. In other words, significant economies seem to be associated with locating directly in a state with a high agricultural output level, possibly resulting from poor connecting infrastructure for transporting materials in rural areas, labor market effects and supply orientated character of the industry.

Further, when a group of similar manufacturers locates in the same geographic area, considerable "agglomeration (or localization) economies" arise from labor market pooling, knowledge interactions, specialization, and the sharing of inputs and outputs. The agglomeration economies are associated with economic benefits for member firms in the form of access to specialized human resources and skills, lower input and service costs, knowledge spillovers, and pressure for higher performance. There may also be opportunities for recycling wastes and/or using rejected products from the one processing stream as the raw material for the next. A well-designed agro-industrial park located near rural areas with all the requisite facilities thus has considerable potential for commercial success in India. Figure 5 presents the food park eco system.

In this eco-system, food parks are integrated backward with the producer and forward with the consumer markets. In the intermediate stages they are linked with the labor and capital markets on the one hand and knowledge generation institutions on the other. They enhance the competitiveness of members through

- linkages between parks and the domestic economy;
- different competencies within the cluster, and interrelations with related clusters (other sectors), and
- sharing competencies and joining forces with similar clusters in international networks.

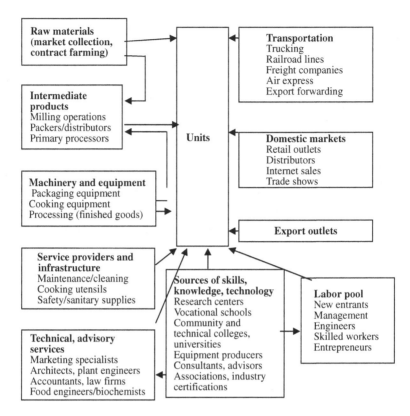

Figure 5.   The food park ecosystem

Performance of the Food Parks and SEZs: An Evaluation

Much has been written on clusters in the past two decades. Nonetheless, knowledge on their performance indicators remains highly fragmented. In a recent study National Research Council, which supports cluster development in Canada, has developed a framework for evaluating the performance of clusters (Davis *et al.*, 2006). The framework as depicted in Figure 6 has two sets of components:

- current conditions and
- current performance.

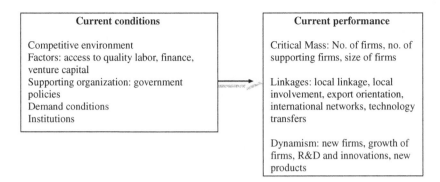

Figure 6.   Cluster evaluation framework

Source: Adapted from National Research Council (2006), Canada.

While these indicators do not capture several aspects of clusters such as tacit knowledge creation, social capital and collective leanings, they indeed are useful for evaluating the cluster performance from a broad perspective. I follow the above framework for evaluating the performance of India's food parks.

Current performance

Critical mass

A prerequisite for the success of food parks is that they are able to generate sufficient amounts of activity. Our analysis indicates that none of the food processing clusters in India has succeeded in generating a critical mass of activities.

Food parks

In the first two phases of the scheme (1992–2002), about 56 parks were approved. Of them none could be fully operational. Further, none of the functioning parks was able to attract large investment and units.

In 2004, the Ministry contracted the Entrepreneurship Development Institute of India, Ahmedabad to review the progress of 45 parks approved until then. The review found that the objective of setting up of food parks for providing common infrastructure facilities for food processing units was far from being achieved. Over all, US$74.38 million were invested in these parks. Of this, US$24.07 million (almost one-third) was government investment. None of the parks became fully operational as of March 2007, however, as detailed in Table 4.

A detailed audit scrutiny of the Ministry's records relating to 20 food parks, disclosed the following:

- In none of these 20 parks, the implementing agencies (IAs) could adhere to the stipulated time schedule for completion. There was no provision for recovery of unutilized grants from the defaulting IAs, nor any penalty for non-adherence to the stipulated time schedules.
- In nine parks, the state governments, nodal agencies or promoters had not contributed their share of funding. These projects were affected by resources constraints and other problems, thus resulting in delays.
- In five parks, despite release of funds four to six years ago, the projects were still in progress.

Table 4:   Operational status of food parks

Operational Status	Number of Food Parks
No physical or financial progress; entire funds lying unutilized with the IAs	5
Not operational and did not attract any entrepreneur for setting up units	13
Operational but only 109 units out of a total availability of 3,154 units/plots (3.46%) commissioned as of March 2007	22
Operational with 50% of the units being commissioned	2
Operational with more than 50% of the units commissioned	1
No grant released	2

Source: Ministry of Food Processing.

- In four parks, the promoters had changed the site location and/or substantially modified the project.
- In one park, the Ministry had not released funds, due to non-fulfillment of the prescribed conditions.

The poor record of performance notwithstanding, the government continued to sanction additional parks in the pipeline, taking the tally of food parks from 45 to 56. In a performance evaluation, the Committee on Agriculture instituted by the Ministry of Food Processing in 2010–2011 reveals that hardly 18 out of 56 food parks were able to claim the entire amount of financial assistance. An internal study conducted by the parent Ministry[4] reveals that even the sanctioned grant could not be fully utilized (Table 5). Of the total 4,150 plots approved only 475 were commissioned. Of them, 140 units were in Rai (Haryana) Food Park only.

Clearly, the parks failed to generate critical mass of activity. The dynamism of firm growth and expansion was also missing.

Table 5: Performance of food parks

Performance Indicators	Statistics
Number of parks	56
Grant involved (US$ million)	45.82
Grant released by government (US$ million)	35.08
Number of parks fully funded	29
Number of parks partly funded	24
Number of parks for which no grant could be released	3
Number of plots approved	4,150
Number of plots allotted	2,345
Units commissioned	475

Source: Based on an internal study conducted by the Ministry of Food Processing.

---

[4] I would like to thank the Ministry of Food Processing for letting me have partial access to this study.

Mega food parks

The MFPS also failed to take off, like its precursor in the previous years. Initially, the Cabinet Committee that had approved the scheme envisaged setting up 30 mega food parks but the Finance Ministry reduced the count to 10 keeping in view the below-expectation performance of the earlier scheme. Subsequently, the proposal for upscaling of the scheme had been considered by the Expenditure Finance Committee, which recommended taking up five more such projects during the remaining period of the 11th Plan. Eventually, the government approved all 30 mega parks. Of them, 15 ongoing projects involve a government grant of US$173.04 million.

In an evaluation of mega parks, the Committee on Agriculture observes that of the 10 mega parks approved in the first phase only 6 have made some progress (Table 6). Combined project cost of these six parks is about US$138.43 million. This includes government assistance of US$65.92 million. Of these six projects, four have started construction work, while two others have completed other formalities to initiate the process for construction. Only two mega parks — the Patanjali Food & Herbal Park in Uttarakhand and Srini Food Park — are partially operational. But, the units commissioned by the developers themselves have inhabited both these parks. They have had little success in attracting other units.

SEZ

As of March 2011, six SEZs reported investment across five states: Andhra Pradesh, Haryana, Karnataka, Kerala and Maharashtra. Of them, state governments have developed four while three involve private participation. Only two have become operational in terms of exporting activity. These SEZs reported employment of only 213 persons as of 31 March 2011. The export volume amounted to a mere US$45.48 million.

Dynamism

Food parks. It was expected that (mega) food parks would attract large players as anchor investors for triggering dynamism in these parks.

Table 6: Performance of mega food parks (operational and in pipeline)

State	District	Park	Comments
Andhra Pradesh	Chittor	Srini Food Park Pvt. Ltd. (Ravindra Nalluri)	Construction of various components of basic enabling infrastructure as well as core processing facilities has already commenced and is under various stages of development. Integrated aseptic pulping line in park has commenced operation.
Jharkhand	Ranchi	Jharkhand Mega Food Park Pvt. Ltd. (Nitin Shenoy)	Land development at the site of CPC is completed and construction of boundary wall is progressing.
Assam	Nalbari	North East Mega Food Park Ltd. (HK Sharma)	Construction work has started.
Uttarakhand	Hardwar	Patanjali Food & Herbal Park Ltd.	Work toward land development, road, water, power, ETP, *etc.* has been completed. The construction of certain other components of basic enabling and core processing facilities are nearing completion. Plots are allotted to processing and packaging units. The processing unit of Patanjali Ayurved Ltd. has already commenced operations.

Source: The Committee on Agriculture (2011).

But big multinationals such as Britannia, Coca-Cola, ITC, Nestle and PepsiCo have shown little interest in them. Among the big players only the Futures Group, a large domestic retail group, appears to have shown some interest. The group's mega food park is taking shape at a 110-acre site in Karnataka and is planned to be complete by 2014. Another park is proposed to be set up in Maharashtra. The progress has, however, been rather slow.

SEZ. Of the six SEZs that have reported investment, three have been set up by state governments and are developed as any other industrial estate, while private developers have developed the other three.

Of the three private developers two are real estate developers; only one is being promoted by a food processing company (Parry Foods). Parry Food SEZ is the only successful zone that has attracted investment of over US$87.89 million and direct employment of 100 persons. Other SEZs are of marginal significance.

Linkages. One of the reasons for discontinuation of the food park scheme was that these parks could not forge forward and backward linkages. The state government developed them as any other industrial estate without acknowledging the specific characteristics of the industry. The MFPS is a paradigm shift in the sense that it emphasizes on the backward and forward linkages through primary processing and CCs. Until now, however, these spokes have not been developed; the focus has essentially been on the development of the hub (central processing unit) itself.

Conditions

Infrastructure

Food parks have been operating as any other industrial estate. Most companies have to develop their own infrastructure including the cold storage facilities. While the focus has been on enabling infrastructure (such as roads, plots, water, electricity, *etc.*), common infrastructure facilities have yet to develop. Even if these facilities are developed, they are rather inadequate. In Rai Food Park, for instance, it was observed that the building created for the purpose of providing common testing and R&D facilities was being used for office purposes. The cold storage facility indeed existed but it was inadequate for the companies. Most companies have their own cold storage.

Supporting institutions

Approval process. The process of approval for these projects has often become long and even progress of the projects under implementation has been found to face some serious challenges. At present, MFPS provides for a two-stage approval process comprising in-principle approval and final approval. The approval process, as per existing guidelines, may take up to around 10 months to accord final approval to a project. In the event of a project failing to meet conditions for final approval, this process gets further stretched. It has been found that such delays have been caused primarily due to inability of applicants in meeting condition of possession of land and structuring of project ownership. It has also been found that the initial policy of allocating one project to each state has led to some very good proposals not being selected in larger states.

Incentives. There is no incentive system in place for processing companies to move into food parks. These parks have been created away from the cities and suffer from poor connectivity due to infrastructure constraints. There is no incentive offered to offset these handicaps. SEZs enjoy certain special tax benefits stipulated under the SEZ policy. But these incentives will also be withdrawn after 2014.

Ownership patterns. The weak response to the scheme from large corporates of the sector has been discussed extensively during recent months and it has been found that the requirement of the scheme, in terms of at least three independent entities (initially it was five entities), discouraged large food processors. It has been suggested that any business entity, proposing to invest around US$10.99 million (through equity or debt) in such projects, would not like to be constrained by conditions such as inclusion of at least two more equity partners in project.

It has also been seen that many projects under implementation have suffered due to lack of trust and coordination among various equity holders. In some cases, such conflicts have even endangered the projects, as various entities seek to have control over the ownership. In other cases, it has been found that this mandatory requirement has encouraged related entities, though with no direct evidence of such relationships, to pose as independent entities to be eligible under the scheme, thus nullifying the proposed advantages of a collective structure.

Bureaucratic delays. The Committee on Agriculture (2010–2011) finds that the Ministry has displayed a total lack of commitment and professionalism in implementing this scheme. There are tenuous delays in bureaucratic decisions. In the case of 10 food parks, state governments, state nodal agencies or promoters had not contributed their requisite share. For two parks, the Ministry had late released or not released the funds, due to non-fulfillment of prescribed conditions. The private promoters of at least five mega food parks have returned the money received as government subsidy for the capital cost and backed out from the project. The chairman of Western Agri-Food Park, which was to be set up at Shirval near Pune reportedly said, "There was huge bureaucratic delay in setting up of the Mega Food Park. Hence, we submitted a letter to the government stating that we are not interested in the Mega Food Park." He added, "We are still interested to set up the Mega Food Park if the government changes its procedures" (*Economic Times*, 2011).

Factor conditions

Supply of material. The CCs are subject to Mandi tax under the State Agricultural Produce Marketing Act. This discourages farmers to sell the products to CCs.

Possession of requisite land for project. These projects have been beset with problems like non-clearance of project site, improper selection process of consultants or contractors, opposition from or agitation by locals, to name a few. Acquisition of suitable land for the project along with change in land use has been found as a major reason for delay in according final approval to a project. As per existing guidelines, a project may need to acquire requisite land within six months of in-principle approval of the project. Many projects in the first phase have been delayed due to inability of the selected bidder to procure land. In fact, in some cases like Uttar Pradesh and Punjab, the projects had to be canceled and proposals had to be invited again due to this reason. At the same time, it would be difficult to find promoters who would have with them readily available land of the requisite area.

Capital availability. On average, a project costs US$52.19 million to US$62.62 million. The government grant has the ceiling of

US$10.99 million. The rest of the money has to be raised in the market. High cost of capital and delays in the sanctioning of loans can also delay and even lead to cancelation of the approved projects.

Case Studies

Rai food park (Haryana): A successful food park

Rai industrial estate is about 7 km from the Delhi border. Haryana State Industrial and Infrastructure Development Corporation (HSIIDC) is developing nearly 568 acres of land into a modern industrial park here. HSIIDC has been promoting two parks here, the IT and food parks. The food park is spread over 118 acres.

Performance

Scale of activity. This is one of the best operational food parks in India in terms of occupancy. There are 223 plots in the park (as of 31 May 2012). Of them, 217 have been allotted. Production has started on 144 plots; others are under construction. Only a few plots are vacant. Some of the prestigious companies that have started operating in the park are, for instance, Danone (France), Sky Lark and Yakult (Japan). In 2011–2012, the total turnover of the park was approximately US$417.5 million and the park had generated direct employment for 2,500 persons.

Dynamism. Encouraged by the success, HSIIDC has also acquired 595 acres of land to create a mega food park. The project will not seek the central government grant and will be fully developed by the state government. It has already attracted some large companies: Bikanerwala (large domestic company), Rajdhani Flour Mill (large domestic company), Shakti Bhog (large domestic company) and Surya Agro (NRI).

Spillovers. The success of the park has attracted other companies in the proximity, for instance, Glaxo Smith Kline on land measuring 150 acres just 9 km away from the park. Other companies are: M/s Satnam Overseas, M/s L.T. Overseas, M/s Sunstars, and M/s Nova Ghee.

Training. While the park has access to qualified labor, a food processing training institute is being developed at Rai. It has been conceived
as an international center of excellence with state-of-the-art infrastructure, and research and training facilities in the field of food technology and management.

Conditions

Location. Haryana has an impressive agricultural base. Almost 88% of
its geographical area ($44,212$ km^2) is arable and 98% of this is under
cultivation. It is the second largest contributor of wheat and the largest contributor of rice to the national pool. It is also the largest
exporter of basmati rice and contributes significantly to the production of mustard and cotton. Over time, however, its industrial base
has also been expanding. It has 25 well-developed urban centers with
well-developed industrial infrastructure. The state government has
adopted a pro-active approach to reap the benefits of its connectivity
and proximity to Delhi. HSIIDC is also creating residential infrastructure around the park.

Infrastructure. It has a basic infrastructure in place both within the
park and outside it. It has regular infrastructure of 132 KVA power
station, water effluent treatment plant, cold storages, road, water and
sewage plant. It also has a shopping complex with food courts. Finally
and most importantly, it is located at a national highway and is well
connected with Delhi.

Factor conditions. Due to its proximity to and easy connectivity with
Delhi, the capital city, it has abundant supply of qualified labor force,
largest consumer market, and entrepreneurial capital. The state's large
agricultural base ensures supply of materials to park inmates. The sale
of agricultural products is not subject to Mandi tax within the state.
Agricultural products from outside the state are subject to entry tax
into the state, however, which is a disincentive for producers.

Incentives. Low land price is an important incentive. The immediate
trigger for its success, however, was the government order to shift

factories out of Delhi. This led to massive outflow of industrial under-takings to outside Delhi. Since the conditions were ripe in this park, which is only 7 km from the Delhi border, companies started shifting to this park. While the trigger for the success of this park was acciden-tal, it is clear that good industrial and connecting infrastructure is critical for success.

Patanjali food park: A successful mega park

This mega food park is coming up at Haridwar. Backed by yoga guru Baba Ramdev, it aims to eliminate middlemen in the farm-to-retail chain for a host of products ranging from branded basmati rice to herbal creams and fruit juices. Patanjali Ayurved Ltd. has a 49% stake in Haridwar Park. With the project cost of US$20.87 million, the central processing facility is being developed on 85 acres of land. In addition, five PPCs and several CCs are also planned. This is not a greenfield mega food park. Processing was already being done in this area even before the announcement of the MFPS. It was brought within the fold of the scheme later. Thus, the development of this area into a mega food park was quite natural.

Performance

The park has the capacity of developing 30 to 40 units. Developers project this number to go up to 65. These units process juices from gooseberry, apple and aloe vera, corn, soybean, barley, oats, pearl mil-lets and produced packaged spices and soaps. Currently seven units are operating and processing fruits, herbs and vegetables. According to the chief executive officer of the park, they require 20 tons of gooseberries per hour for processing for more than a month. This means 200 tons of the fruit every day, which is transported by 20 trucks every day. In addition they require several tons of other fruits, grains and vegetables. They have engaged contractors who in turn engage farmers for procurement. Currently 2500 persons are employed in the CPC in addition to persons employed in the PPCs in construction and processing works. The park expects a turnover of

US$988.79 million and direct employment of 20,000 persons once full capacity production is achieved.

Forward linkages

The developer is manufacturing several herbal products, which are sold through direct outlets developed by the developer. The retail channels are being expanded and strengthened. Further, both Future Group and Patanjali Ayurved are firming up deals with modern retail and cash-and-carry chains. The products of the food parks are available in defense and police canteens and wellness stores also.

Backward linkages

The launch of the mega food park at Haridwar has significantly benefited the farmers in the state. The park houses factories for processing juices of vegetables, wheat grass, and herbs. There have been training programs for the cultivation of exotic fruits, vegetables and herbs. In addition to CPC, one PPC is also operational and houses units of multigrain milling and ripening chambers. Other PPCs are also in various stages of construction. Finally, there are a number of CCs, which have been procuring fruits and vegetables. The project has already begun to have socioeconomic impact on the farmers of the region. The park is expected to generate as many as 20,000 jobs in the initial phase. According to park authorities, plans are to promote cooperative farming in collaboration with local farmers to transfer technology to them.

Location

The park is located in Haridwar district, which also has the world's largest center for Ayurveda and Yoga and includes facilities for treatment, research and a teaching university. Patanjali Ayurved college, medical facility, village, herbal botanical garden, and organic agricultural farm are some of the institutions successfully run by the developer in the same area. The park is one of the most successful parks and is expected to generate significant socioeconomic impact on the regional economy.

Srini mega food park: A not-so-successful park

Srini Food Park sanctioned by the Union Ministry of Food Processing Industries for development as a public–private partnership venture at an outlay of US$23.9 million is coming up near Mogili village, Chittoor district, Andhra Pradesh. Promoted by professionals, the park is also supported by the Andhra Pradesh Infrastructure Investment Corporation. It was approved in March 2009. The central processing unit is spread over 140 acres with a total installed capacity to process 100,000 tons of agricultural produce. The park can accommodate more than 100 units. There is a provision for 30 to 40 small-scale units also.

The food park has proposed to have four attached PPCs at Anantapur, Gudur, Kodur and Madanapalle to take care of crops in their early hours of harvest to ensure an enhanced shelf life. However, there is little progress in that direction yet.

Performance

Units. The park is still waiting for the units to set up their business here. The promoters themselves have put up three units for mango pulping and tetra packs.

Dynamism. Since the park could not attract units, it has little dynamism. The units put up by the developer have, however, introduced the latest technology for fruit pulping. The United Kingdom-based equipment manufacturer Starfrost is supplying an innovative quick freezing system for mango to Srini Food Park. Starfrost has also been contracted to supply a special dual action vibratory conveyor to ensure continuous product separation at the in-feed to aid faster freezing.

Backward linkage

A CC has been set up but with little success. Meetings are being held with farmers at the central processing unit and outside to educate farmers about the initiative. The units are facing constraints, however, in the supply of raw materials. Developers' units have entered into contract farming with growers of tomato, but they are facing problems in the implementation of the contract.

Forward linkage

Developers have been participating in trade fairs nationally and internationally. They have tied up with big retailers including Bharti-Walmart, More, and Spencers for fresh fruits and vegetables from the PPC. Tie-ups have emerged with export houses such as Keventer, Mysore foods, Safa Agros and Shimla Hills.

Conditions

Location. Chittor has a long tradition of mango cultivation. It has more than 50 canning units. It has thus natural advantage in mango pulping and the park enjoys locational advantages to that extent.

Enabling infrastructure. The park has extensive enabling infrastructure. The outside infrastructure, however, is rather inadequate. The park is situated 30 km away from the city, but there is no connecting infrastructure. There is a small dormitory in the park but it is not meant for the regular stay of labor. It is being used as a guesthouse for the stay of officials.

Factor conditions. The availability of labor is inadequate to meet both quantitative and qualitative needs of the park due to poor connectivity of the park with the city. There is little social infrastructure in the surrounding areas. Further, even while the area is known for mango, supply of raw material poses severe constraints. Farmers are unwilling to sell raw material to the units in the park due to overpayments by (outside) competitors and procedural delays in payments by the park units.

Conclusion

Though food parks have attracted huge public and private investments there has been little analysis of their performance. Even as there is no comprehensive assessment of the existing scheme, the government is extending the program during the next Five Year Plan.

In addition to 56 food parks, 30 mega food parks, and 6 operational SEZs, the government is planning to set up 30 mega parks and 15 mini parks. This raises serious concerns over the seriousness of the policymakers in promoting these parks.

There have been delays in approval and implementation. Most projects are languishing in the absence of facilitating institutions for land acquisition, labor recruitment and availability of capital. These are large projects that require constant government support and incentives throughout their implementation, but there is no such institutional support mechanism. Further, this has been a central government scheme which is being implemented by state governments. It has been experienced that many projects under implementation have faced delays in getting requisite approvals from state agencies (approval for sub-lease of land, land use changes, *etc.*) due to "lack of ownership" from state governments. Most of these projects are implemented outside the city, in rural areas in particular. In the absence of connecting infrastructure, they face severe constraints in the availability of labor and materials. The cost of production goes up further making the projects unviable. Thus most cluster based industrialization programs have been languishing. Finally, the challenge is how to integrate the informal agricultural economy with the formal industrial sector. There is no clear road map for that. The upshot is that it requires long-run vision, strong commitment, patience, an imaginative incentive structure, and institution building to implement government-induced cluster initiatives successfully.

References

ASI (various years) Annual Survey of Industries, Central Statistical Organisation, Government of India.

CMIE, PROWESS (2012) Centre for Monitoring Indian Economy, PROWESS Database.

Cohen JP and Paul CJM (2001) Agglomeration economies and industry location decisions: the impacts of vertical and horizontal spillovers. Working paper 01-010. Department of Agricultural and Resource Economics, University of California Davis: California Agricultural Experiment Station.

Committee on Agriculture (2011) Demand for Grants (2010–2011). Twenty Fifth Report.

Committee on Agriculture (2010–2011) Fifteenth Lok Sabha, Ministry of Food Processing Industries, Government of India, presented to Lok Sabha on 29th August 2011.

Connor JM and Schiek W (1997) *Food Processing: An Industrial Powerhouse in Transition,* 2nd edn. New York: John Wiley and Sons.

Da Silva *et al.* (2009) *Agro-Industries for Development.* Wallingford: The Food and Agriculture Organization of the United Nations and The United Nations Industrial Development Organization by arrangement with CAB International.

Davis CH, Arthurs D, Cassidy E and Wolfe D (2006) *What Indicators for Cluster Policies in the 21st Century?* Available at http://www.oecd.org/sti/inno/37443546.pdf [accessed on 6 April 2014].

Delgado ME, Porter M and Stern S (2011) Clusters, convergence, and economic performance. Mimeo, Harvard University.

Dobkins LH (1996) Location, innovation and trade: the role of localisation and nation-based externalities. *Regional Science and Urban Economics* 26(6): 591–612.

FAO (2007) *Challenges of Agribusiness and Agro-industries Development.* Committee of Agriculture, Twentieth Session, COAG/2007/5. Rome, Italy: FAO.

Henson and Cranfield (2009) Building the political case for agro-industries and agri-business in developing countries. In Silva CA, Baker D, Shepherd AW, Jenane C and Cruz SM (eds.), *Agri-Industries for Development.* Wallingford: Food and Agriculture Organisation.

IMAP (2010) *Food and Beverage Industry Global Report — 2010.* Available at http://www.imap.com/imap/media/resources/IMAP_Food__Beverage_Report_WEB_AD6498A02CAF4.pdf [accessed on 7 April 2014].

Porter ME (1998) Clusters and competition: new agendas for companies, governments, and institutions. In Porter ME (ed.), *On Competition.* Boston: Harvard Business School Press, pp. 197–299.

Porter ME (2000) Location, competition and economic development: local clusters in a global economy. *Economic Development Quarterly* 14(1): 15–34.

Saxenian AL (2006) *The New Argonauts: Regional Advantage in the Global Economy.* Cambridge, MA: Harvard University Press.

The Economic Times (2011) *Union Budget 2011: Promoters Return Subsidy Received for Mega Food Parks.* Available at http://articles.economictimes. indiatimes.com/2011-02-28/news/28641928_1_mega-food-park-subsidy-promoters [accessed on 6 April 2014].

Wilkinson J and Rocha R (2009) Agro-industry trends, patterns and development. In Silva CA, Baker D, Shepherd AW, Jenane C and Cruz SM (eds.), *Agri-Industries for Development.* Wallingford: Food and Agriculture Organisation.

Chapter 9

AUTONOMY, COMPETENCE AND MARKET STRUCTURE: SELF-DETERMINATION THEORY APPLIED TO SMALL AGRICULTURAL EXPORTERS FROM LATIN AMERICA

Linda M. Young*,‡ and Theresa C. Bushman†

*Department of Political Science, Montana State University P.O. Box 172240, Bozeman, Montana, 59717
†Montana Conservation Corps, Bozeman, Montana, USA
‡lmyoung@montana.edu

The success of small agricultural producers in meeting the challenges of exporting high value products may be enhanced if interactions with intermediaries and market institutions support basic human needs. We use self-determination theory from social psychology to identify and examine the factors that support producer autonomy and competence in their relationship with the market, focused on their specific relationship with intermediaries. Focus groups were conducted with producers of trout and quinoa in Peru and rice, broccoli, passion fruit in Ecuador. Questions focused on producer interactions with intermediaries and include questions on dispute resolution, quality standards, price formation, market information, and the terms of their informal or formal agreement with intermediaries. These focus group interviews were translated and transcribed by native Spanish speakers from Ecuador and Peru and coded by the authors using Nvivo 8. The conceptual framework developed for coding facilitates examination of how support for competence, autonomy and relatedness is associated with market structure and the effectiveness of underlying institutions. Producer expressions of competence and autonomy are associated with the realized ability to make choices of intermediaries, clear and observed quality standards, and are further enhanced by higher levels of market knowledge. An NGO played a significant role supporting the competence, autonomy and relatedness of quinoa producers.

Introduction

Many governments, aid agencies and non-governmental organizations (NGOs) are involved in efforts to increase the income of small agricultural producers in Latin America through the production and export of high value agricultural products. One critical aspect of this effort is building supply chains linking these producers with world markets. Currently, these supply chains include diverse types of intermediaries between producers and world market, including commercial actors like traders and processing plants; producer organizations and cooperatives; and social institutions including a diversity of NGOs and fair trade associations. In many cases, governments, aid agencies and NGOs are constructing new supply chains to increase producer success in the export market. This chapter investigates how the structure of the transaction between producer and intermediary impacts producer success.

The transition to exporting to the world market involves many significant challenges for small producers. Many high value products have niche markets and limited information on world prices and export demand, standards for quality and food safety are high and specific, lack of contracts creates uncertainty about the quantity, quality and price that intermediaries will purchase, and intermediaries may have local or regional market power. Producers and their associations, NGOs, and other agencies have grappled with these challenges by attempting to create market institutions to reduce these obstacles. Aid agencies, NGOs and government agencies have funded and implemented these activities with the desire to promote pro-poor growth. Illustrating this trend is the conclusion by Springer-Heinze (2005, p. 1) that "'Pro-poor growth' has become the leitmotif running through much of the recent development debate. In agriculture, pro-poor growth is increasingly associated with the diversification and development of those markets for high-value food and natural products that generate employment and allow a broad-based participation of farmers and small enterprises."

Different measures can be used to assess the success of a supply chain, including its growth and continuation, and profitability for producers and intermediaries. As many programs are constructing supply chains to alleviate poverty, a measure of their success is increased income for producer households. Another measure is the empowerment of the producers, recognized as key in creating change that extends beyond a particular market opportunity (Alsop and Heinsohn, 2005; Samman and Santos, 2009). Research to measure empowerment has used the concept of agency first advanced by Sen (1985, 1999), and, more recently, has incorporated concepts and measures from self-determination theory. Self-determination theory is a theory of psychological needs and motivation, and it is used here as a framework for evaluating the extent to which the structure of the interaction between producers and intermediaries meets the basic psychological needs experienced by all humans of autonomy, competence and relatedness.

Background

The construction of supply chains to meet specific policy goals held by the government is not new. Historically, governments in many developing countries used a package of policies to assist agricultural producers. In many cases, governments empowered state trading enterprises (STEs) to act as intermediaries between producers and the world market (Anderson *et al.*, 2010; Young, 1999). In other cases, large plantation owners exported directly to world markets. Between the 1970s and 2000, governments in many developing countries eliminated or reduced the role of their agricultural STEs, due first to the reforms contained in structural adjustment programs required by the International Monetary Fund and the World Bank, and, more recently, to meet the norms and requirements of the World Trade Organization. New supply chains have developed to connect producers to markets, but in many cases larger producers have benefited disproportionately.

In the 1990s, a nexus of factors contributed to the emergence of new opportunities for agricultural producers in developing countries, leading to a redefinition of their comparative advantage (Reardon and Berdegué, 2002). These factors include growth in global demand for high value agricultural products and the adoption of policies to facilitate trade, supporting the growth of trade in differentiated high value products. Many small producers have been unable to take advantage of the opportunities created by trade reform (Winters *et al.*, 2004). New opportunities created by the growth of retail grocery stores and new export markets have mostly benefited larger farmers with higher levels of technical skills. For example, Escobal *et al.* (2000) examine how the growth of the asparagus industry on the Peruvian coast benefited larger producers who signed contracts with processing firms. Small farmers were largely excluded from these developments and relegated to less profitable cotton production. In addition, Reardon and Berdegué (2002) examine the entry of supermarkets into Latin America, and conclude that the displacement of small producers is a consequence of the development of these new supply chains.

The Governments of Latin America face numerous limitations in attempting to address the poverty of their small producers, including fiscal constraints and policies emphasizing free markets and trade. de Janvry *et al.* (1997) conclude that Latin American governments have been adopting rural policies compatible with an orientation to the market.

One market-oriented policy to address poverty has been to encourage producers, including small producers, to produce high value agricultural products for export to the world market. Governments, multilateral institutions and aid agencies have promoted this concept (McCullough *et al.*, 2008; Swinnen, 2007; The World Bank, 2005). For example, in 2009, the Government of Peru began a program, Sierra Exportadora, to promote the export of agricultural products from small producers in Peru. ProChile, an export promotion agency of the government of Chile sponsored the "Internationalization Program Peasant Agriculture" to promote the exports of peasant agriculture.

Drawing on economic perspectives, many analysts have discussed the challenges of involving producers, particularly small producers, in new global supply chains for high value products (da Silva *et al.*, 2009). We propose a new, interdisciplinary approach. We apply a theory from social psychology to market settings with the goal of evaluating the extent to which characteristics of market environments foster the motivation and success of producers.

Self-Determination Theory

Self-determination theory provides a well-developed and empirically tested framework from social psychology to assess how conditions within different contexts, including the workplace, family, schools or hospitals, meet the individual's basic needs for competency, autonomy, and relatedness. These basic needs are considered "innate psychological nutriments" that are essential for well-being, and when met, spur an individual's motivation (Deci and Ryan, 2000, p. 229). Self-determination theory was first proposed by Deci and Ryan in 1985, and should not be confused with Maslow's hierarchy of needs dating from 1943.

Conditions that provide opportunities for people to satisfy their basic needs enhance intrinsic motivation and spur them to action. Environments, including work, school, hospital, and other environments, that satisfy basic needs encourage self-motivation and foster behaviors that are conducive to success (Ryan and Deci, 2000). For example, Baard *et al.* (2004) evaluate how dimensions of the work environment impact the autonomy of workers, with the goal of delineating the dimensions of the workplace that lead to positive outcomes. They found that when management provides meaningful information to subordinates, understands and acknowledges worker perspectives, removes obstacles created by excessive work rules, and provides elements of creative engagement, an increase in positive work outcomes results. These outcomes include job satisfaction, worker motivation, reduced absenteeism and higher supervisory ratings of work quality.

Deci (1996) summarizes the importance of choice for subordinate agents involved in interactions within institutional environments. Even when an outcome is prescribed to students, patients, workers or other participants in a subordinate situation, clear information on why a particular outcome is important, and choice on how to achieve it, is valued by subordinate agents. Interactions in institutional settings are more likely to spur motivation if desired outcomes, and choices in meeting those outcomes, are clearly articulated in a manner that transforms the interaction into one of an alliance rather than being characterized by power.

Self-determination theory proposes that individuals' basic human needs include competence, autonomy and relatedness. Competence refers to an individual's ability to affect their environment and to attain valued outcomes. Feelings of competence result from success at optimally challenging tasks and attaining desired outcomes (Deci *et al.*, 2001). Autonomy is the experience of choice and volition. It is similar to Amartya Sen's concept of agency, expressed in the desire to self-organize experience and behavior and to have one's activities align with one's sense of "*the good*" (Sen, 1985, p. 206). In self-determination theory, Deci *et al.* (2001) define autonomy as being the initiator of one's own actions. Relatedness is the desire to feel connected to others, requiring a sense of respect, caring, and reliance with others.

We propose that producers' success in exporting high value products is likely to be enhanced if the conditions governing the transaction between the producers and intermediaries support the satisfaction of producers' basic needs, thus promoting the motivation necessary to be entrepreneurial and to compete in the world market.

Following the initial examination of the data, self-determination theory was chosen as a lens for analysis for the focus group interviews, as many elements of the data would not be fully captured by an economic framework. This choice follows a general principle of grounded theory (Glaser and Strauss, 1967), a method of data analysis that encourages iterative interplay between researchers and the data. Researchers begin with examination of the data and then choose an existing theory for interpretation or use the data as the basis for the development of a new theory. Self-determination theory offers several advantages as a framework guiding analysis of the relationship between producers and intermediaries and the fulfillment of basic human needs. It provides a widely accepted theory of motivation. It was developed in the discipline of social psychology, has been empirically tested, and is widely used in diverse applications to understand motivation, basic needs and how to construct domains to maximize individual well-being. The concepts of autonomy and agency are closely related, but self-determination theory provides insight about how autonomy is supported by competence and relatedness.

While supply chain relationships, specifically the interaction of producers and intermediaries, exist in the market, both society and the state play critical roles in structuring and supporting this market relationship. In this research, we identify and examine the structural factors that support producer autonomy, competence and relatedness in their relationship with the market, focused specifically on producer relationships with intermediaries. We use information and perspective from focus group interviews conducted with producers to assess market structures that support producer autonomy and competence, and we provide limited discussion of relatedness as a supporting theme.

Data Analysis Questions and Methods

The following questions guided data analysis:

1. What is the experience of small agricultural producers exporting to world markets? This question encompasses both the structure of the relationship between producers and intermediaries and producer assessments of that relationship.
2. What obstacles exist to producer success and what factors contribute to their success?
3. What is the relationship between market structure and success?

Methods

Focus group interviews were used to obtain information, data, and producer perspectives on their interactions with intermediaries. Focus group interviews were conducted in early 2009 with producers of trout and quinoa in Peru, and rice, broccoli, and passion fruit in

Ecuador. A local facilitator contacted producer groups and interviews were conducted in a variety of informal settings, including offices of producer groups, common outside meeting areas, and producer's homes.

For this preliminary research, products were chosen to provide perspectives from a range of marketing structures, including three commodities with processing plants, the involvement of NGOs in the supply chain as exporters or providing technical and marketing assistance, and a mix of reliance on the domestic and international markets.

High value crops are usually defined as a group of commodities including vegetables, fruits, meat, fish, and milk. Realization of the value of high value crops depends, however, on where it is marketed. Historically, non-organic quinoa marketed domestically is not considered as a high value product, but organic quinoa exported to the world market is. The bifurcation between a domestic market accepting lower standards and remunerating producers with lower prices than world markets has ramifications on the level of choice experienced by producers. Trout produced to high standards for the export market is sold on the domestic market at a lower price, while broccoli produced for export has almost no domestic market due to a lack of domestic demand for broccoli. The experience of rice producers described here provides a contrast to the experience of the producers of other commodities, as in this situation rice is not a high-value crop.

A standard set of questions was posed to each group of producers interviewed. Following Hennick (2007), interviews were conducted to allow participants to suggest and explore new themes. Questions focused on producer interactions with intermediaries and included a description of the supply chain, the terms of their informal or formal agreement with intermediaries, quality standards, price formation, market information, and dispute resolution. (A complete list of interview questions is available upon request.) Interviews were transcribed and translated by native Spanish speakers from Ecuador and Peru.

The unit of analysis is formal or informal producer groups. Interviews were coded using Nvivo 8, a software package used in qualitative analysis. Two researchers independently coded focus group interviews. Following Corbin and Strauss (2007) and Hruschka *et al.* (2004), researchers coded two focus group interviews initially, discussed and reconciled differences, and then refined the codebook. All interviews were then independently coded using the revised coding framework, and coders discussed differences and converged on coding to create a final dataset. Results of the coding process were reconciled between the two researchers to gather data on their initial level of agreement. Table 1 presents the Cohen's kappa and other indicators of agreement for the coding for all focus group interviews.

We conducted several layers of coding including descriptive coding (how the transaction between the producer and intermediary is conducted); topic coding (activities performed by the producer, and within the spheres of the market, state and society); and analytical coding (how the structure of the transactions impacts autonomy, competence and relatedness) to understand relationships and assess their importance. Due to space constraints we report here only the results of the analytical coding.

Coding framework

The goal of the coding is to be able to identify information, key themes and patterns in the interview data to inform the questions listed above. Following self-determination theory, we coded for autonomy, competence and relatedness by assessing statements by producers or actions described by them embodying those needs. Table 2 provides examples of text from the focus group interviews and how they were coded.

Findings

Autonomy

We developed indicators of autonomy, based on characteristics associated with autonomy in the literature, after the initial coding of the interviews. One indicator of autonomy is the existence of choice, in production and marketing, and the ability of the producer to learn about options, evaluate them, and then exercise choice. The existence

Table 1:   Measures of coding agreement

	Cohen's Kappa	Agreement (%)	A and B (%)	Not A and Not B (%)	Disagreement (%)	A and Not B (%)	B and Not A (%)
Broccoli							
Competence	0.29	83	5	78	17	10	7
Autonomy	0.23	80	6	74	20	12	9
Relatedness	0.03	89	0	89	11	1	10
Passion fruit							
Competence	0.55	78	46	32	22	11	11
Autonomy	0.48	74	40	33	26	11	15
Relatedness	0.68	94	8	86	6	2	4
Quinoa							
Competence	0.60	80	41	39	20	14	6
Autonomy	0.53	76	41	35	24	20	4
Relatedness	0.09	81	1	80	19	1	17
Rice							
Competence	0.45	74	26	47	26	9	17
Autonomy	0.46	73	36	37	27	19	8
Relatedness		89	0	89	11	1	11
Trout							
Competence	0.48	80	14	66	20	20	0
Autonomy	0.47	82	12	70	18	18	0
Relatedness	0.71	94	9	85	6	6	0

Notes: Hruschka *et al.* (2004) discuss the divergence of opinion in the literature over acceptable scores for the Kappa coefficient. The Kappa coefficient is a statistical measure that takes into account the amount of agreement that is expected to have occurred by chance. A kappa of 1 indicates perfect agreement, 0 indicates agreement that is no better than chance. The larger number of codes used and greater length of segments that are coded can decrease the kappa. Nvivo (QSR International, 2012) suggests that Kappa < 0.4 is poor; 0.4–0.75 is good and >0.75 is excellent. Percentage agreement is calculated as the sum number of characters coded by both coders and characters not coded by either divided by total characters.

Table 2:   Definitions and examples of coding

Autonomy

Definition: Volition, agency, experiencing choice and initiating action. Also includes opportunities that increase autonomy, such as increasing income and introduction of new market opportunities.

Narrative Examples of High Levels: "Despite all the colors the white ones have less proteins than the colorful ones. Markets do not know that. We have to tell them and put this product in markets. Each variety has its benefits."

Narrative Examples of Barriers: "They are (intermediaries) always right; everyone has to do what they say. There is no other way out. Because if you say I am not going to sell this to you anymore, and I will give you your money back, you will never have money again."

Competence

Definition: Mastery, ability to attain valued outcomes, knowledge of alternative options, expressed largely as an understanding of production practices and marketing.

Narrative Examples of High Levels: "Market asks us for top quality and we are capable of complying with that, we have become specialized.... We had support and assistance from engineers and we prevented diseases from attacking our trout."

Narrative Examples of Barriers: "What we are pretty sure about is the fact that we are in debt. We are always in debt. Nobody has heels on their shoes anymore. Each year you only see more poverty."

Relatedness

Definition: Connectedness, mutual respect, recognition of mutual self-interest.

Narrative Examples of High Levels: "We have to get together and organize ourselves with the help of some advisors."

Narrative Examples of Barriers: "(Government) Ministers come and deceive people, just like a child." "We are forgotten here, forgotten by every government."

---

of choice means that alternatives exist and that producers can and do make choices to fulfill their needs. The existence of choice frequently depends on structural factors, such as the existence of alternative crops for production and competitive markets for their products. Table 3 summarizes structural factors that impact autonomy (as well as competence and relatedness). Another indicator of autonomy is the ability to initiate action. Initiating action differs from choice in that

Table 3:   Structural factors impacting autonomy, competence and relatedness

Crop	Autonomy	Competence	Relatedness
Broccoli	Broccoli sold only to processing plant for export, no domestic market	Receive production assistance from plant, limited market knowledge	Small informal group of large producers
Passion Fruit	Production experience in multiple crops, choice of domestic and international markets	Limited technical and marketing assistance received	New producer organization
Rice	Bound by debt to particular intermediary	No technical assistance in evidence	No producer organization
Trout	Limited domestic market; sole export market processor collapsed	Technical production and marketing assistance provided by NGO	Producers worked together to negotiate with plant or to achieve volume in other transactions
Quinoa	Choice of domestic and international market	Technical production and marketing assistance provided by NGO	Producer organization required to receive technical and financial assistance

the producer, alone or with other agents, is involved in conceptualizing and/or taking actions to create new alternatives. A third indicator is the condition of clarity surrounding transactions, which influences both the autonomy of the producers and their competence, and will be further explained in a subsequent section.

Choice

Rice producers describe having produced rice for 3 to 60 years, but they do not mention having experimented with alternatives to rice production. They state their local rice market has many intermediaries that they could sell to. Several producers, however, describe being bound for multiple years to a particular intermediary, to whom they owe money, effectively limiting their choice of intermediary. Additionally, they explain that their debt to a particular intermediary limits their ability to negotiate prices and quality classifications. One producer said, "They are always right; everyone has to do what they say. There is no other way out, because if you say, 'I am not going to sell this to you anymore and I will give you your money back,' you will never have money again, you do not pay 10% anymore, you will have to pay 15 or 20% of interest" (R-26). Another producer stated, "There is no other way out, right now we are supposed to sell rice at US$28, but we are selling it at US$23" (R-28).

Quinoa producers give evidence that they have experienced choice in their production decisions between non-organic quinoa, organic quinoa and other crops, and indicate that they have increased the amount of acreage devoted to quinoa substantially over the past 5 years due to its profitability. They describe choice in their marketing decisions, between the local market (largely non-organic) and international market (exclusively organic). Higher prices for organic quinoa have induced many producers to invest in the more costly production practices necessary to meet the standards for organic production.

Passion fruit producers describe several types of choice. They recount the history of crop production in their area, which has evolved rapidly through several crops due to changing market conditions, a new buyer for passion fruit due to a new processing plant, and technical assistance and support offered by the government. Their history of adapting to changing market opportunities, and the fact that they produce crops for both the domestic market and the passion fruit processing plant, may explain why lack of choice was not voiced as a concern. Broccoli producers made 17 statements (see Table 4) coded as representing a low degree of choice, largely related to their reliance on a single processor with a regional monopoly and no domestic market, as domestic consumers do not eat broccoli. Trout producers faced a similar situation, relying on one processor for access to the export market. When this processor closed, the regional market could not absorb their production, and of the ten producers interviewed that were producing trout in 2008, only two were still involved in trout production in 2010.

Table 4:   Low and high indicators of autonomy and competence

Indicators	Rice		Quinoa		Trout		Broccoli		Passion Fruit	
	Low	High	Low	High	Low	High	Low	High	Low	High
Choice	3	0	0	14	14	12	17	2	1	22
Initiate Action	11	0	2	28	14	13	9	2	2	23
Act on Values	12	0	0	6	0	1	0	0	0	0
Knowl Prod.	0	2	0	12	0	12	0	7	4	7
Knowl Mkting.	3	2	0	12	4	23	6	10	0	23
Clarity Standards	6	1	0	6	0	0	0	4	0	0

Quinoa producers described having the greatest level of choice due to their ability to shift between other crops and quinoa, and between non-organic and organic quinoa. The flexibility of trout and broccoli producers is limited by their dependence on a processing plant, and trout producers had to find an alternative when their processing plant closed. Both broccoli and passion fruit producers produce crops for local markets in addition to the processing plant. Passion fruit producers made a high number of statements (22) indicating satisfaction with their ability to make choices. This may be in part due to the fact that the processing plant they sell to has not yet reached operating capacity, so producers have choice in how much they sell to the plant. They also described a long history of switching crops due to changing market conditions.

Initiate action

An important indicator of autonomy is the ability to initiate action on behalf of oneself and in accordance with one's beliefs. Rice producers presented themselves as unable to successfully initiate action on their own behalf. Their responses in the interview included the statement with respect to intermediaries "Them, they have gotten us" (R-47) and with respect to government officials "They trick [treat] us as we were child" (R-48). Table 4 summarizes the number of statements made by rice producers under the category of initiating action. Coders assessed 11 statements as indicating an inability to act on their own behalf and that producers felt strongly ill-treated, and no statements were coded as representing a high level of ability to act on their own behalf.

In contrast, quinoa producers provided many examples of initiating action "We need to create strategies..." (Q-39) with respect to discussion about meeting quality standards for quinoa by preventing stains due to rain, and "We have to work harder, because of the price" (Q-37) with respect to the incentive provided by the high price for organic quinoa. Finally, "We have to get together and organize ourselves, with the help of some advisors" (Q-40) in reference to the challenge of meeting quality standards for organic quinoa. There were 28 statements in the quinoa interview that were coded as indicating a high level of ability to initiate action and two statements coded with a low ability to initiate action.

Trout producers made statements indicating that they had initiated action by responding to changing market conditions both as individuals and as a producer group. They explained that they are able to produce trout to the standards required by the export market, but since the collapse of the processing plant they previously relied on they had been unable to export. Trout producers stated they had met with firms interested in being an intermediary to the export market but that they were unable to aggregate enough production to meet the minimum volume required to be viable for these firms (T-29, T-30, T-31).

Lack of access to credit emerged as an important theme in the focus group interviews. The impact of indebtedness on rice producers has already been discussed. Trout producers mentioned lack of access to credit nine times (see Table 4), explaining that they need financing to be able to increase production. "To finance us we were asked too many requirements and we did not comply with many of them, we are farmers, we know nothing about requirements, mortgages and stuff like that, we did not know how to handle that, we work the land

and that is the only thing we have" (T-7). Passion fruit producers described that the Government of Ecuador has a program, Competitividad Agropecuaria, assisting them with the purchase of inputs for passion fruit and pepper production for 2 years, with the government paying for 60% of the inputs. Producers described this program as an important source of financing for their investment in passion fruit, although they expressed difficulty in paying for the 40 percent they are responsible for.

Acting and being treated in accordance with values

In some cases, producers described marketing situations with reference to their values. Rice producers indicated that their indebtedness impacts both their negotiations with intermediaries and also violates their standards of fairness. For example one producer said, "We keep on working knowing that we have to pay this or that person, I owe some money and I have to hide I can pay you. We are called 'monkeys' because of that" (R-57).

Quinoa producers displayed 20 varieties of quinoa during the interview and discussed their long history of quinoa production. They expressed pride in the healthfulness of quinoa. One quinoa producer stated, "We would like to keep our varieties (of quinoa), and we also want to market our quinoa varieties, the ones which are non-commercial. Despite all the colors, the white ones have less proteins than the colorful ones… We have to even try to recover all varieties our ancestors had. We have to re-teach people about the importance of eating the different varieties" (R-60). This quinoa producer is making a proposal for action that would expand their markets and allow them to recover varieties that have been important to them historically.

Clarity

A key finding from analysis of the focus group interviews is the importance of clarity for producers in their interactions with intermediaries. Clarity about both the price of the product and the quality standards required to achieve a particular grade is important for producers to engage in transactions effectively. The authors hypothesize that clarity about the price paid for an associated level of quality affects both producer competence and autonomy. Competence is impacted as producers do not possess relevant information to use in marketing decisions and negotiations, and thus autonomy, or the ability to act on their own behalf, suffers as a result.

Rice producers expressed a lack of clarity about both the price and the quality standards expected by intermediaries. They depicted intermediaries as opportunistically using violations of rice standards to penalize them on the weight of rice sold, and, due to their indebtedness, producers were not free to break ties with these intermediaries. Additionally, they described intermediaries as discussing and agreeing on the price to pay producers and 10 comments were made that intermediaries routinely violate the government set minimum price for rice.[1]

Quinoa producers explained the process of price formation in local markets for non-organic quinoa and several participants confirmed that this market is competitive. They also explained in detail the quality standards required to produce and sell organic quinoa. No complaints were stated about intermediaries exercising market power or manipulating quality assessment to reduce the price paid to producers.

Broccoli producers stated that the quality standards required by the processing plant were well defined. They clearly explained the standards and how the price paid was discounted when standards were not met. The processing plant has technicians who meet with the producers on their farm regularly to consult about production issues and improve the quality of production. Producers communicated, however, that the plant routinely downgraded the quality assessment of the broccoli submitted by producers for processing when periods of favorable weather resulted in larger than expected yields. Producers stated that the plant engaged in this practice in

---

[1] The government of Ecuador has not officially set a minimum price for rice since the 1980s. Government does, however, use variable import tariffs and controls exports to impact domestic rice prices.

order to maintain a constant volume of broccoli processed through the plant.

Passion fruit producers and trout producers both discussed the quality standards expected by the processing plants they sold to, and did not express concern about the clarity of price and quality standards as communicated by the plants.

Rice producers strongly communicated a lack of clarity in their interactions with intermediaries, and broccoli producers voiced some concern over the manipulation of standards during times of larger than expected harvests.

Competence

Indicators of competence include the knowledge and ability to be effective in the production and marketing of the commodity.

Rice producers discussed having difficulties meeting standards including rice that was too green and/or too wet to receive the full price (R-22 and R-26). They did not explicitly discuss their production practices, a need to change them, or a desire for research or technical assistance to help them solve particular challenges. As discussed previously, their comments focused on the lack of clarity of standards and how intermediaries did not honor what producers view as the minimum price for rice set by the government. They did not display knowledge of other marketing channels for their production on their national or the international market for rice.

Quinoa producers demonstrated knowledge of the local market in Peru, the relationship between supply–demand balance and price, the normal price margin relationship between the non-organic and organic prices, and the connection between the Peruvian and Bolivian markets for quinoa. Quinoa producers also discussed quality standards for organic quinoa for the export market, including a uniform size and color, coliform analysis, and stones and contamination from animal feces (Q-33).

The level of competence indicated by quinoa producers in the focus group has been influenced by the work of a local NGO, Centro de Investigación de Recursos Naturales y Medio Ambiente (CIRNMA), that has been active in providing technical assistance in production and marketing. Additionally, CIRNMA developed a marketing arm that buys organic quinoa from producers for the export market. CIRNMA has given quinoa producers technical assistance about the production practices required to qualify for organic certification and pays for the certification process conducted by an international firm.

Relatedness

Relatedness did not emerge as a strong theme from focus group interviews. And when it did emerge it was usually in reference to the role of producer associations. The rice producers interviewed did not have a producer association. Their expressions of relatedness focused on their pride at their history of being "the best rice producers" and their association through time with rice production, due to long personal histories of rice production. Broccoli producers also did not have a formal producer group and explained that the nine producers assembled for the focus group interview accounted for 80 to 90% of production for their plant, so that a formal organization was not required.

CIRNMA requires that quinoa and trout producers organize into producer groups before it works with them, and consequently trout and organic quinoa producers had producer groups, including one solely for organic production. Quinoa producers explained the cooperation required to receive organic certification and described the certification process: "There is an external supervision but we have to organize the internal supervision, 100 percent of producers have to participate" (Q-4). Their expressions of relatedness focused on understanding the individual interests of producers and also in getting group agreement. They spoke about the value of producer groups: "I think we are trying to organize ourselves and show our capabilities" (Q-8). Passion fruit producers explained that they had recently formed a producer group and so had not started to work together. One producer, however, stated, "Looking for development is our goal," and another producer added "It is our vision" (P-5).

Conclusions

Of the five groups interviewed, rice producers demonstrated the lowest level of autonomy, competence, and relatedness, and quinoa producers the highest. Lack of clear quality standards, combined with debt, misunderstanding about government set prices for rice and/or lack of enforcement, lack of trust in the government, and little support from producer or other groups combine to create an environment unsupportive of rice producer's competence and autonomy. In contrast, quinoa producers illustrate a high level of autonomy and competence, which can be at least partially credited to the support and opportunities created by CIRNMA. This result is instructive as both rice and quinoa produce a grain that has not historically been a high value crop. CIRNMA was key in creating the opportunity for producers to export a high value crop by providing technical and marketing assistance. Requiring the formation of producer groups to receive assistance spurred relatedness between producers. CIRNMA also developed a marketing arm for the exportation of organic quinoa. Both their role as an NGO working to assist producers and the clarity of the standards required for the sale of organic quinoa appear instrumental in creating an environment supportive of producer autonomy and competence.

All producer groups mentioned lack of access to credit in varying degrees. The lack of adequate institutions for credit or the inability of producers to use existing possibilities for credit has significant ramifications for their autonomy. Additionally, their competence is limited by lack of information about local and world prices and price formation.

Producers face a difficult transition between producing and selling for the local markets to reliance on the sale of high value products to world markets through intermediaries. Self-determination theory provides a lens to evaluate if a supply chain and the institutions that support it meet the basic human needs of producers. Extensive empirical research in a wide range of social domains indicates that meeting basic human needs for autonomy, competence and relatedness has a positive impact on the level of intrinsic motivation and the success experienced by agents. For this reason, self-determination theory is particularly relevant to analysis of markets used by the government to promote social and economic goals for designated groups.

Acknowledgments

The authors would like to acknowledge Edward Deci, University of Rochester, and Jessi Smith and Elizabeth Shanahan of Montana State University for generously sharing their insights.

References

Alsop R and Heinsohn N (2005) Measuring empowerment in practice: structuring analysis and framing indicators. World Bank Policy Research Working Paper 3510. Washington DC: World Bank.

Anderson K, Cockburn J and Martin M (eds.) (2010) *Agricultural Price Distortions, Inequity and Poverty*. Washington, DC: World Bank Publications.

Baard PP, Deci EL and Ryan RM (2004) Intrinsic need satisfaction: a motivation basis of performance and well-being in two work settings. *Journal of Applied Social Psychology* 34(10): 2045–2068.

Corbin J and Strauss A (2007) *Basics of Qualitative Research: Techniques and Procedures for Developing Grounded Theory*. Los Angeles: Sage Publications.

da Silva CA, Baker D and Shepherd AW (eds.) (2009) *Agro-Industries for Development*. Oxford: CABI Press.

de Janvry A, Key N and Sadoulet E (1997) *Agricultural and Rural Development Policy in Latin America: New Directions and New Challenges*. FAO Agricultural Policy and Economic Development Series. Rome: Food and Agriculture Organization of the United Nations. Available at http://www.fao.org/docrep/W7441E/W7441E00.htm [accessed on 20 October 2009].

Deci EL (1996) *Why We Do What We Do: Understanding Self-Motivation*. New York: Penguin Books.

Deci EL and Ryan RM (1985) *Intrinsic Motivation and Self-Determination in Human Behavior.* New York: Plenum.

Deci EL and Ryan RM (2000) The "what" and "why" of goal pursuits: human needs and the self-determination of behavior. *Psychological Inquiry* 11(4): 227–268.

Deci EL, Ryan RM, Gagne M, Leone DR, Usunov J and Boyanka PK (2001). Needs satisfaction, motivation, and well being in the work organizations of a former eastern bloc country: a cross-cultural study of self-determination. *Personality and Social Psychology Bulletin* 27(8): 930–942.

Escobal J, Agreda V and Reardon T (2000). Institutional change and agro industrialization on the Peruvian coast: innovations, impacts and implications. *Agricultural Economics* 23(3): 267–278.

Glaser BG and Strauss AL (1967) *The Discovery of Grounded Theory: Strategies for Qualitative Research*. New Brunswick and London: Transaction Publishers.

Hennick MM (2007) *International Focus Group Research: A Handbook for the Health and Social Sciences*. New York: Cambridge University Press.

Hruschka D, Schwartz DJ, Cobb St. John D, Picone-Decaro E, Jenkins RA and Carey JA (2004) Reliability in coding open-ended data: lessons learned from HIV behavioral research. *Field Methods* 16(3): 307–331.

McCullough EB, Pingali PL and Stamoulis KG (eds.) (2008) *The Transformation of Agri-Food Systems: Globalization, Supply Chains and Smallholder Farmers*. London: Earthscan.

QSR International (2012) *Run a Coding Comparison Query*. Available at http://help-nv10.qsrinternational.com/desktop/welcome/welcome.htm [accessed on 1 March 2012].

Reardon T and Berdegué J (2002) The rapid rise of supermarkets in Latin America: challenges and opportunities for development. *Development Policy Review* 20(4): 317–334.

Ryan RM and Deci EL (2000) Self-determination theory and the facilitation of intrinsic motivation, social development, and well-being. *American Psychologist* 55(1): 68–78.

Samman E and Santos ME (2009). *Agency and Empowerment. A Review of Concepts, Indicator's and Empirical Evidence*. University of Oxford: Oxford Poverty and Human Development Initiative, Department of International Development. Available at http://ophi.org.uk [accessed on 15 January 2012].

Sen A (1985) Well-being, agency, and freedom: the Dewey lectures 1984. *The Journal of Philosophy* 82(4): 169–221.

Sen A (1999) *Development as Freedom*. New York: Alfred A. Knopf.

Springer-Heinze A (2005) *Shaping Value Chains for Development — Experience in Development Assistance.* Stuttgart–Hohenheim: Conference on International Agricultural Research for Development. Available at www.tropentag.de/2005/abstracts/full/611.pdf [accessed on 10 october 2011].

Swinnen JFM (ed.) (2007) *Global Supply Chains and the Poor.* Cambridge: CABI.

Winters A, McCulloch N and McKay A (2004) Trade liberalization and poverty: the evidence so far. *Journal of Economic Literature* 42(1): 72–115.

The World Bank (2005) Linking small-scale producers to markets: old and new challenges. A Workshop of the ARD Rural Infrastructure, Markets and Finance (RIMFI) Thematic Group, The World Bank, December 15.

Young LM (1999) Prevalence and reform of state trading importers in world grain markets. *Canadian Journal of Agricultural Economics* 47(4): 351–362.

Chapter 10

PROMOTING AGRO-ENTERPRISES IN THE HIGHLANDS OF ETHIOPIA THROUGH IMPROVED INSTITUTIONAL SUPPORT SERVICES: EXPERIENCES OF MARKET-ORIENTED DAIRY AND FATTENING DEVELOPMENT

Berhanu Gebremedhin,* Dirk Hoekstra and Azage Tegegne

International Livestock Research Institute (ILRI)
*b.gebremedhin@cgiar.org

Ethiopia's agriculture-led industrial development strategy (ADLI) stipulates that smallholder-led commercial transformation of agriculture is vital for the social and economic development of the country. The improving productivity and market success (IPMS) of Ethiopian farmers project is intended to demonstrate market-oriented transformation of smallholders in Ethiopia. This five-year project, operating in 10 districts distributed in four Regional States, follows innovation systems perspective and value chains framework, and participatory commodity development approach in identifying and implementing various interventions. Action research is an integral part of the project designed to draw and synthesize lessons for scaling out and up of successful practices. This chapter presents syntheses of the results and lessons of the development of institutional support services in promoting market-oriented dairy and livestock fattening to transform smallholder farms into rural agro-enterprises. Major conclusions and implications include: (1) the traditional production and technology focused extension service approach is inadequate for market-oriented agricultural development; market-oriented extension service is required; (2) provision of market information in various forms, facilitating virtual or physical linkages of producers with buyers, and formal and informal collective action for produce marketing increase bargaining power of farmers; (3) different input supply systems including community-based, farmer-to-farmer, the private sector, cooperatives and the public sector can be appropriate and effective for different value chains; (4) creating linkages between producers, input suppliers and other value chain actors is an important part of value chain development and a task for the extension service; (5) market-oriented agricultural development is a continuous and dynamic process that requires different types of interventions at different stages of development; (6) community-based insurance for small ruminant fattening enterprises can be successfully developed, benefiting especially female-headed households; and (7) credit systems to support small-scale commercial livestock production and agribusinesses can be successfully used to boost production and the supply of inputs and services.

Introduction

Commercial transformation of subsistence agriculture is a key strategy of agricultural development in the agriculture-based economies (Pingali and Rosegrant, 1995; Timmer, 1997; von Braun, 1994; World Bank, 2008). Commercial transformation of subsistence agriculture promotes sustainable household food security and welfare (Pingali, 1997). The benefits of commercial transformation of subsistence agriculture come from the possibility to realize comparative advantages, gains from economies of scale, and the promotion of technological, organizational and institutional[1] changes arising from the flow of ideas due to market-based interactions (Romer, 1993, 1994).

There are a number of success stories where agriculture serves as the basis for economic growth in the development process. Such a role requires a productivity revolution and market orientation in

---

[1] Institutions are defined as 'rules of the game' and comprise formal laws, rules, regulations, *etc.*, and informal norms, traditions, *etc.*

smallholder farming. In the recent past, a number of agriculture-based Asian economies (China, India, Indonesia, Malaysia, South Korea, Taiwan, Thailand and Vietnam) have managed to achieve sustainable growth through consistent long-term investment in market-oriented smallholder agriculture. A study on the Asian Green Revolution by the Swedish International Development Agency (SIDA) concluded that the revolution was a state driven (through direct action as well as creating enabling environment), market mediated, and small farmer-based strategy (SIDA, 2006).

Ethiopia's agriculture-led industrial development strategy (ADLI) stipulates that smallholder-led commercial transformation of agriculture is vital for the social and economic development of the country. Agriculture has risen to the top of the list of the public sector investment agenda. Since the 1990s, the total investment in Ethiopian agricultural research has almost doubled. Ethiopia is one of the few countries in Sub-Saharan Africa (SSA) where the public expenditure on agriculture is above the 10% target set by the Maputo Declaration.

Consistent with the agricultural development strategy of the government of Ethiopia, the improving productivity and market success (IPMS) of Ethiopian farmers project is intended to demonstrate, on a pilot basis, market-oriented transformation of smallholders in Ethiopia. Its purpose is to strengthen the effectiveness of the government's efforts to transform agricultural and rural development through market-oriented agricultural development based on a sustainable natural resource base. This five-year project, operating in 10 districts distributed in four Regional States, follows an innovation systems perspective (ISP) and value chains framework, and participatory commodity value chain development approach in identifying and implementing various interventions. In addition to introducing new production technologies, the project played an active role in promoting innovative institutional arrangements for input supply and marketing, enhanced knowledge sharing mechanisms, credit supply, and building capacity of value chain actors and service providers and creating linkages between them vertically and horizontally.

Action research is an integral part of the project designed to draw and synthesize lessons for scaling out and up of successful practices. This chapter presents syntheses of the results and lessons of the introduction and development of institutional support services of the IPMS project in the development of market-oriented dairy production and livestock fattening. Policy and strategic implications for commercial transformation of smallholders to develop into rural agro-enterprises are drawn.

The chapter is organized in five sections. The next section presents an overview of the strategies for commercial transformation of smallholder agriculture, which serves as a conceptual framework for the IPMS project. Followed by a section that deals with the approaches and methods followed by the project. The fourth section discusses the results and lessons of the project in introducing and promoting agricultural institutional services for the development of market-oriented dairy and livestock fattening. The last section concludes the paper and distills key implications for policy and market-oriented development strategy.

Strategies for Commercial Transformation of Smallholders

Commercial transformation of smallholders entails market orientation and market participation (Gebremedhin and Jaleta, 2012). Market orientation involves producers finding out what consumers want and producing a product that satisfies those needs in the expected quality, time and place (Jaworski and Kohli, 1993, 1996; Selnes *et al.*, 1996). The product choices could be determined more by comparative and competitive advantages than by food needs of the particular household, which eventually leads to product specialization and possibly expanded scale of operation. The key to success is rapid adjustment of the producers to changing national, regional and international market opportunities. Output market participation can be through market orientation or surplus selling. Surplus selling refers to the situation where many small farming families engage in selling almost as an afterthought, a way of handling any production left over after fulfilling own consumption needs and social obligations. Here the production signals are derived from the consumption patterns and needs of producers and the existing agro-ecology.

Commercial transformation of smallholders also requires increasing integration of farmers into input markets, thus enhancing the links between the input and output sides of agricultural markets. Commercial agriculture promotes demand for modern technologies and can enhance the adoption of technological innovations (von Braun, 1994). The use of modern technologies in turn may increase productivity, marketable surplus as well as the use of purchased inputs (Gebremedhin *et al.*, 2009).

The agricultural commercialization process usually takes a long time from subsistence to semi-commercial and then to fully commercialized agriculture (Pingali and Rosegrant, 1995; Timmer, 1997). In the real world, therefore, we do find smallholder producers operating at all three stages, *i.e.*, three distinct groups of smallholder farmers operating in the agricultural sector and at times in the same production system and geographical area. The characteristics, needs and aspirations of these groups may be different. Hence, for any transformation to be effective, we need to develop multi-pronged approach, and all-inclusive, more context-specific, target group(s)-oriented options and programs that are sustainable.

Based on past experience, it has been established that five basic prime movers work in tandem to achieve sustainable market-oriented agricultural development, *viz.*, technology, improved human capital at all levels, sustainable growth in physical capital (markets, roads, dams, irrigation systems, energy *etc.*), effective organizations, and enabling political and institutional environment. It is important to acknowledge two important characteristics of the prime movers. First, no prime mover on its own can get agriculture to grow on a sustainable basis. The second characteristic of all prime movers is that long-term investment is necessary to strengthen them (Tsakok, 2011). This calls for greater commitment by governments for sustainable investment in agriculture. In addition to the prime movers, the transformation process is also influenced by three other factors, namely, macro-economic and political stability, secure property rights and incentives, and real income growth in the non-agricultural economy to induce demand for agricultural products and services. The most recent experiences also emphasize the importance of partnerships and institutional innovations, and the role of the non-government actors in this transformation process.

Hence, what is needed in Ethiopia is a homegrown, integrated strategy to promote smallholder-led market-oriented agricultural development. This integrated strategy should incorporate the following elements: technologies to enhance innovations; human capacity development at all levels (especially the key change agents and farmers); connecting smallholders to markets; increasing access to assets and services; institutional innovations; reducing the risk and vulnerability in smallholder production systems; sustainable management of natural resources; and an environment for enhanced participation of public, private and the third sector (NGOs). There is also a strong need to promote active engagement of the private sector and civil society in this process. The strategy should also call for enhancing the skills of rural people to get them gainfully employed in other sectors. The challenge for policymakers and development practitioners, therefore, is to get the right investment, policy instruments and partnerships needed to design and implement such a strategy.

Project Approaches and Methodologies

The IPMS project is an action research project aimed at demonstrating, on a pilot basis, market-oriented agricultural transformation of subsistence agriculture in Ethiopia. Action research and impact analysis generate knowledge and distill lessons. Ten pilot learning districts were selected for demonstration. Priority market-oriented commodities were selected in a participatory manner based on the development priorities expressed by the farming communities, frontline agricultural extension agents, researchers, experts, the private sector and other relevant stakeholders. All research and development activities in the pilot districts focused on the selected market-oriented commodities and institutional support services to develop them, and were geared toward addressing critical value chain constraints.

The project has five major components: (1) improved knowledge management, (2) capacity building of value chain actors and service providers, (3) participatory commodity development, (4) research, and (5) promotion of lessons and experiences for scaling out and up. The knowledge management component of the project focuses on increasing access for value chain actors and service providers to agricultural knowledge and information. The capacity development component of the project focuses on strengthening capacity of value chain actors and service providers in commodity value chain development. The main beneficiaries of the capacity building component were producers and agricultural staff.

The participatory commodity development component of the project mainly engages in identifying and promoting appropriate technologies, processes and institutional innovations to develop the market-oriented commodities. The research and promotion components focus on activities related to generating, synthesizing, and promoting innovative lessons and recommendations to inform policies and strategies. All project activities give explicit attention to the three cross-cutting issues of gender, HIV/AIDS and the environment. The project has an inbuilt M&E system that monitors and evaluates outputs, outcomes and impact.

Project implementation is guided by four key principles: (1) participatory commodity value chain development, (2) ISP, (3) market-oriented extension, and (4) mainstreaming gender, HIV/AIDS and the environment. Below we give brief descriptions of these key concepts.

Participatory commodity value chain development

The IPMS project makes a distinction between commodity development and technology development, and follows the commodity value chain development approach rather than a production technology transfer approach. Commodity value chain development approach is based on the 'commodity value chain system,' which consists of the value chain actors involved in value addition at different nodes of the value chain, the support services, and the institutions and the institutional environment (laws, regulations, policies and other institutional elements) (da Silva and de Souza Filho, 2007). In other words, the development of a crop or livestock commodity is based on interventions[2] in production, input supply, service provision, output marketing, and the institutional environment. In the commodity development approach, the commodity is the center of focus and priority interventions are identified based on analysis of the value chain to identify critical entry points.

While technology is important to increase productivity and marketable surplus, critical constraints to develop a commodity may not necessarily be technological. In some cases, constraints related to input supply and services, the institutional environment or output marketing can be more important. The traditional technology development or transfer approach, on the other hand, usually mainly focuses on production technology interventions. This approach ignores the important fact that adoption of and benefits from improved technologies critically depend on input supply systems, access to agricultural services, and access to and participation in profitable markets. Hence, a more comprehensive framework that includes technological and non-technological interventions is needed to develop a market-oriented commodity.

The IPMS approach to develop market-oriented commodities, therefore, started from the analysis of the 'value chain system' of a commodity in order to understand the constraints and opportunities to develop the commodity. Interventions are then identified and prioritized to address critical constraints.

ISP

The IPMS project also follows the ISP. Distinction is made between inventions and innovations. Inventions are new or improved knowledge that is created through research and development or indigenous sources. Innovations, on the other hand, are successful applications of inventions to economic, environmental or social benefits (Bacon and Butler, 1998). Experience throughout the world has shown that the conversion of inventions to innovations is not automatic, as evidenced

---

[2] Interventions can be technological, organizational or institutional.

by the many agricultural technologies that remained on shelves. Making the distinction between inventions and innovations helps researchers better analyze and understand the reasons for the lack or low level of adoption of improved technologies, thus the need to follow the ISP. Hence, the IPMS project identifies appropriate interventions from among available inventions to achieve innovations.

An innovation system is the set of organizations and individuals involved in the generation, diffusion, adaptation and use of new knowledge, the interactions among these actors, and the context that governs the way these interactions and processes take place. Hence, in its simplest form, an innovation system has three elements: the organizations and individuals involved in generating, diffusing, adapting and using new knowledge; the interactive learning that occurs when organizations engage in these processes; and the institutions (rules, norms, conventions, *etc.*) that govern how these interactions and processes take place.

The ISP, therefore, implies the use of the innovation lens in the design, implementation, and evaluation of the activities of the various actors involved in market-oriented commodity development. ISP sees that success in commodity development depends not only on the performance of individual actors, but on how they interact with each other as elements of a collective system and how they interplay with institutions.

Hence, the IPMS project makes deliberate efforts to improve the interactions of various actors involved in the development of market-oriented commodities. Organizing commodity platforms, improving communication and knowledge sharing among actors, better coordination among value chain actors, better coordination between value chain actors and service providers are some examples of activities undertaken by the project to improve the innovative performance of value chain actors.

Market-oriented extension

Although Ethiopia has adopted commercial transformation of smallholder agriculture as a strategy, its agricultural extension service still remains primarily production and technology oriented. Subject matter specialists and development agents are trained in the three technical disciplines of crop production, animal production and natural resource management, with little background in marketing, business and institutional issues. The main aim of the extension service remains improving productivity and production. Little attention is given to market-oriented production planning, and the input and output marketing services that are needed by smallholders to enhance their market orientation and market participation.

On the other hand, focus on commercial transformation of subsistence agriculture requires that the mandate of the extension officers be broadened to include support for rural households and their enterprises to earn better income from increased participation in markets. Facilitating market linkages and building marketing and agribusiness capacity of subsistence farmers should go hand-in-hand with the promotion of appropriate production technologies and practices.

Hence, the IPMS project focused on market-oriented extension service in order to help farmers link with and adapt to changing markets. Market-oriented agricultural extension refers to the total effort of (1) advising and supporting farmers to grow profitable market-oriented commodities and to adopt appropriate technologies and practices; (2) collecting and communicating market-related information; (3) identifying profitable markets and buyers, and linking of farmers to input suppliers and output buyers; (4) building the marketing capacity of farmers; (5) facilitating the organization of farmers to conduct collective marketing of their produce; and (6) building the capacity of specialized farmers in the production of agricultural inputs.

The market-oriented extension service that the IPMS project supports focuses on agricultural staff and farmers. An attempt was made to build the capacity of extension agents in market-oriented extension. Attention was also given to the training of farmer input producers.

Mainstreaming gender, HIV/AIDS and the environment

The role of women in agriculture has been recognized by many and it is assumed that a more gender balanced development will lead to an increased uptake of production technologies (Everts, 1999; Quisumbing and Pandolfelli, 2010). IPMS has used several mechanisms to achieve a more gender balanced development, including (1) increasing women's access to and control over assets, (2) increasing women's access to skills, knowledge and services, and (3) increasing women's participation in market-oriented agricultural production.

The increased movement of people in market-led agricultural growth may present additional risks of exposure to HIV infection in rural communities. The project strategy to combat the risk of the epidemic include (1) awareness-raising and understanding about HIV/AIDS, (2) reducing exposure to HIV infection, and (3) reducing vulnerability to impacts of AIDS. Market-led agricultural growth can potentially also result in negative environmental impacts (Pingali, 2001). Cognizant of this effect, the project includes an environmental assessment of the interventions in the planning process and proposes measures to mitigate the effects.

Results

Dairy

Developments[3] in market-oriented dairy production

Dairy production from improved dairy cows (Holstein/Friesian crosses; and a local dairy breed, Begait) was one of the key commodities the project and its partners tried to promote. Promoting adoption of improved dairy cows and associated feeding and management practices, and linkages with input and output markets were the major interventions. Community level survey results show that the number of households involved, the number of improved dairy cows owned and producing milk, and the total amount of milk produced and sold showed significant development between 2005/2006 and 2009/2010[4] (Figure 1).

---

[3] Developmental changes are for the period 2005/2006 to 2009/2010.

[4] Although project interventions and the survey focused on improved dairy animals and associated management and feeding practices, it is likely that interventions may have had spillover effects on dairy production from local cows. Moreover,

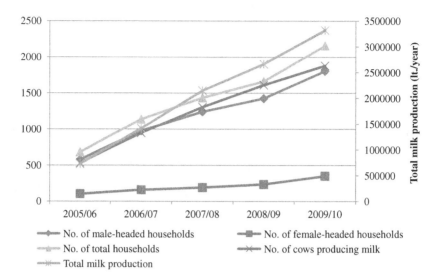

Figure 1.   Developments in market-oriented dairy (2005/2006–2009/2010) in five project districts (number of households involved, number of milk producing improved dairy cows, milk produced)

The number of households involved in market-oriented improved dairy production grew by 216% (from 682 in 2005/2006 to 2,156 in 2009/2010). The number of female-headed households involved also grew steadily by 238%. The proportion of female-headed households involved, however, fluctuated between 13.4% and 16.3%. The number of improved dairy cows owned and producing milk showed slightly higher growth rate of 253% (increasing from 532 to 1,879), indicating an increase in the number of dairy cows owned and producing milk per household.

Total milk production registered a growth rate of 356% (increasing from 726,924 L/year to about 3.32 million L/year), due to both the increase in the number of improved dairy cows producing milk and the increase in milk yield. Although still low relative to the attainable level, milk yield from improved cows also showed consistent

---

interventions were also made in urban dairy, but survey was limited to rural areas only. Hence, developmental changes reported here may be underestimated.

improvement from 4.48 L/day/cow to 5.79 L/day/cow. Price of milk increased consistently during the period. Controlling for price rise, total revenue from the sale of milk showed a growth rate of 200% in real terms (increasing from about 2.2 million to 6.5 million birr[5]). About 62% of milk produced was sold in 2009/2010. The proportion of households selling fluctuated between 50% and 52%.

Input supply and services

The project tried to promote private[6] artificial insemination (AI) services, animal health services, and forage seed and seedling supply, among others. Lessons on the introduction of private AI service in one of the pilot districts show that the private sector can take over the role of the public sector in providing AI services in urban, peri-urban and rural dairy systems. Private providers provided 98% of the about 825 inseminations in the district, contrasted with all the inseminations given by the public sector until 2008. Currently, the project is promoting AI with hormone assisted estrus synchronization with mobile teams.

The project promoted community animal health workers (CAHW) as an alternative to the public animal health delivery system. A study in one of the pilot districts shows that CAHWs were able to treat animals from about 43% of the sampled households in the study areas. A survey on the perceptions of the users also shows that 70% to 100% of the respondents who used the service provided by CAHWs express satisfaction with the effectiveness and timeliness of the service.

The multiplication and distribution of forage seeds, seedlings and cuttings grown on demonstration areas in the different pilot districts was well accepted. Customers included government/donor-funded projects. Multiplication of seeds/cuttings by private farmers for distribution to neighboring farmers is also reportedly working in several of the districts. Commercial production of seeds by farmers, however, has not reached commercially viable stage.

---

[5] The exchange rate between the US$ and Birr was 16.50 in 2010/2011.
[6] Private sector in this chapter includes farmer cooperatives.

Animal feed

Analysis of the dairy value chain revealed that animal feed, in terms of both quality and quantity, is the main constraint of dairy development in the pilot districts. Interventions to increase feed availability include development of grazing land enclosures and promotion of stall feeding through cut and carry system, enrichment plantations of improved forage species, development of irrigated and backyard fodder, processing of crop residues to increase their feed value, and improved awareness of and access of farmers to processed feed. Results show that biomass yield of grazing lands increased from 3 metric tons/ha to 5 metric tons/ha in the free grazing lands to about 10 metric tons/ha in the enclosures. Moreover, the species composition in the grazing lands showed significant change toward more palatable grass and legume species. Legumes covered about 25% to 30% of the standing herbage biomass in the enclosures. Farmers started to harvest green forage three times per year, as opposed to just once annually before enclosure. Survey data indicate that this fodder resource was used primarily for dairy animals.

Improved breed and management, and household income

A household survey conducted with project farmers in 2008/2009 also found differences in milk production and value of dairy products sold between farmers who adopt improved breeds and/or feeding and management practices (adopters) and those who do not (nonadopters) (Table 1). Results indicate that the adoption of grade animals plus associated practices had the most significant effect on household milk production, sale of dairy products and butter. Although not statistically significant, results also indicate that adoption of practices other than improved cows may also contribute to increased household milk production and sale of dairy products and butter.

Dairy marketing and processing

Collective marketing and processing of milk was one of the major interventions IPMS promoted to increase households access to milk

Table 1: Average volume of fluid milk produced, dairy products sold and value of butter sold per household (adopters *versus* non-adopters)

District	Farmer Type	Animal Type	Obs.	Average Milk Production (L/year)[a]	Obs.	Dairy Products Sold (birr/HH/yr)[a]	Obs.	Value of Butter Sold (birr/HH/yr)[a]
Atsbi	Adopters	Improved	20	2051.4***‡‡‡	20	3701.65***‡‡‡	18	1048.78*‡‡
		Local	31	666.0‡‡	31	688.00‡‡	30	638.93
	Non-adopters	Local	25	355.8	25	414.48	22	446.46
Alamata	Adopters	Improved	21	1137.4‡	21	2014.76*‡‡	21	1778.57
		Local	41	897.7	41	1234.34	38	1069.68
	Non-adopters	Local	41	748.1	41	979.05	31	1200.68
Fogera	Adopters	Improved	8	2210.0***‡‡‡	8	3614.13**‡‡	4	1706.25
		Local	35	677.1	35	489.80	13	1249.46
	Non-adopters	Local	38	714.3	38	243.00	13	710.31
Bure	Adopters	Improved	0		0		0	
		Local	25	407.4‡	25	234.20‡	11	532.27‡
	Non-adopters	Local	30	223.6	30	78.17	13	180.38
Ada'a	Adopters	Improved	13	4139.2***‡‡‡	13	14566.38*‡‡	4	505.00
		Local	19	524.6	19	483.63‡	14	586.79
	Non-adopters	Local	31	436.2	31	282.13	12	666.67

(*Continued*)

Table 1: (Continued)

District	Farmer Type	Animal Type	Obs.	Average Milk Production (L/year)[a]	Obs.	Dairy Products Sold (birr/HH/yr)[a]	Obs.	Value of Butter Sold (birr/HH/yr)[a]
Mieso	Adopters	Improved	0		0		0	
		Local	51	1011.4	51	2332.10	32	671.91‡‡
	Non-adopters	Local	50	777.7	50	1792.58	27	505.22
Dale	Adopters	Improved	12	1779.3*; ‡‡‡	12	2860.58*; ‡‡	3	1342.67
		Local	52	1085.2‡‡‡	52	642.35‡	32	565.13‡‡
	Non-adopters	Local	35	461.4	35	400.37	28	272.64

Notes: ***, **, and * are significantly different from the mean values of adopters with local cows at 1%, 5% and 10% level, respectively. ‡‡‡, ‡‡, and ‡ are significantly different from the mean values of non-adopters with local cows at 1%, 5% and 10% level, respectively.
[a] For those households who produced milk during the 2007/2008 production year.
[b] Adopters are HHs who adopted at least one of the project interventions.

markets. Collective action for milk marketing from rural to urban areas contributed to an expansion of the milk shed. Establishment of milk collection centers to facilitate delivery was also found to be useful. Milk processing in small local cooperatives worked well in one of the pilot districts, but was hindered by a lack of commercial orientation and managerial problems in all other pilot districts. At the same time, processing by some of the larger dairy producers in some of the district towns was observed.

Effect on gender

Women are heavily involved in dairy production in Ethiopia. The IPMS intervention in dairy development has benefited particularly women through efforts made in capacity development and knowledge management. It was observed, however, that empowering women is a gradual change process, especially in the rural and peri-urban fluid milk/butter systems. It was noted that women's participation in study tours was undermined if such events required an overnight stay. A significant impact on gender has been achieved in rural fluid milk/ local butter system in fodder and health interventions, since women handle the processing and marketing of dairy products. In general, women control the money thus earned for regular household expenses. Survey results on the effect of improved dairy development on women workload showed that 83% of surveyed women reported that their workload increased, and 72% reported that they were responsible for selling the product.

Actor linkages

Several actors have been involved directly or indirectly in market-oriented smallholder dairy development intervention. The key actors include producers, milk groups/cooperatives, private and public veterinary service providers, saving and credit institutions, concentrate feed suppliers, private processors, and milk and dairy product consumers (public/private institutions, restaurant, cafes and individuals).

The district offices of agriculture, cooperative promotion offices, development agents and farmer training centers, as well as local administration are key local actors.

Other important actors include agricultural research and education institutions, NGOs and development projects. The interaction and linkage among these actors to support dairy development was low prior to IPMS interventions. IPMS facilitated the establishment of Woreda (District) Advisory and Learning Committee (WALC) and in some cases, dairy platforms that coordinate actors and lead the innovation processes for sustainability. The establishment of WALC helped improve the interaction and linkage among actors to a considerable level.

Livestock fattening

Developments in market-oriented fattening of small ruminants

Interventions to promote this commodity include improved feeding, credit supply, improved use of crop residues, improved fodder production, and linkages with input and output markets. In one pilot district, innovative community-based insurance was also established and implemented. Developmental changes in small ruminant fattening as shown by several indicators confirmed significant developments (Figures 2 and 3).

The total number of households involved in market-oriented small ruminant fattening grew steadily by 98% (from 27,523 in 2005/2006 to 54,554 in 2009/2010). The number of female-headed households involved grew by 104% (from 4,657 to 9,519). The proportion of female-headed households, however, remained constant at about 17%.

The total number of shoats fattened grew by 91%. The number of fattened small ruminants per household was about 6, with only about 50% sold. There was no change in the number of fattened animals per household during the 2005/2006–2009/2010 period. The price of small ruminants increased significantly during the period. Controlling for price rise, total revenue registered a growth rate of

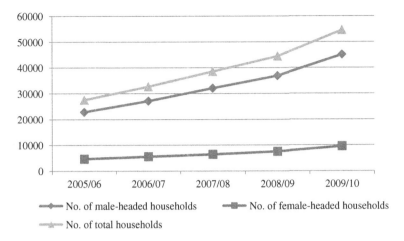

Figure 2. Developmental changes in market-oriented small-ruminant fattening (2005/2006–2009/2010) (number of households involved in fattening)

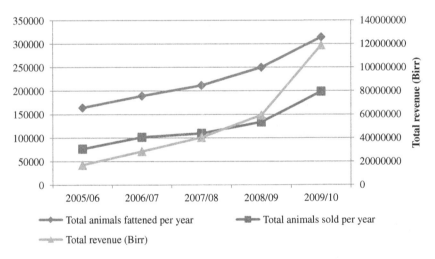

Figure 3. Developmental changes in market-oriented small-ruminant fattening (2005/2006–2009/2010) (number of animals fattened, sold and revenue)

159% in real terms (from about 46 million Birr[7] to 120 million Birr). Nearly all households involved in fattening small ruminants sell their fattened animals. On average, about two cycles of fattening per year are practiced.

---

[7] In 2009/2010, 1 US$ = 17 Ethiopian Birr.

Developmental changes in market-oriented cattle fattening

Most of the interventions on cattle fattening were based on improved feeding and housing, credit supply, improved forage production, improved use of crop residues, and linkages with input and output markets including establishment of marketing groups and cooperatives. The developmental change indicators all show that there have been significant developments in household involvement in cattle as business-oriented enterprise (Figures 4 and 5).

The number of households involved in cattle fattening grew by 296% (from 6,157 to 24,391). The number of female-headed households involved in the fattening business grew even faster at 587% (from 308 to 2,121). Thus the proportion of female-headed household in the cattle fattening business grew steadily, but slowly, from 5% to 9%. The total number of fattened animals grew by 380%. On average a household fattened two animals per year and sold both of them. There was no change in the number of fattened animals per household during the 2005/2006–2009/2010 period.

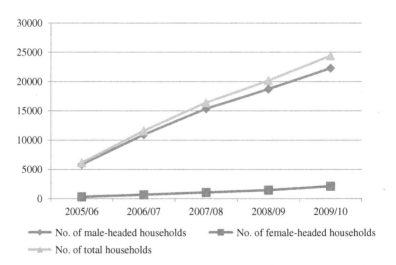

Figure 4. Developments in market-oriented cattle fattening (2005/2006–2009/2010) (number of households involved) in IPMS PLWs

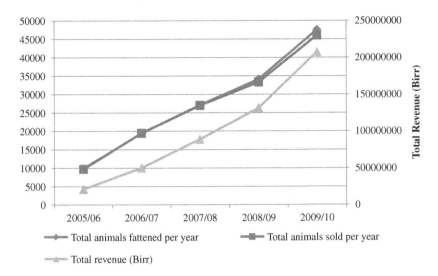

Figure 5.   Developments in market-oriented cattle fattening (2005/2006–2009/2010) (number of animals fattened, sold and revenue) in IPMS PLWs

As with many agricultural commodities, cattle price has also seen a significant increase due to the growing demand for meat both domestically and internationally. Controlling for prices, results show that revenue grew 867% in real terms (rising from about 44 million Birr to 208 million Birr). On average fattening cycle of 1.5 was recorded, which means on average a farm household completes fattening of a group of animals and offers for sell, and is in the middle of completing fattening the second group.

Input supply and services

The project and its partners tried to promote private bull stations, improved access to processed feed, the multiplication and supply of forage seeds, seedlings and cuttings, credit for fattening purposes, and community-based livestock insurance schemes. Mixed results were achieved on these interventions. Private bull stations in rural areas were not very successful due to lack of knowledge on heat detection, fear of the spread of reproductive diseases and prevailing cultural practices that make it unusual to allow payment for such services.

An attempt was made to supply locally selected sheep breeds for reproductive purposes. An example is the supply/placement of a meat type local sheep breed known as Washera in some pilot districts. Research results on the performance of the breed show that the breed was well accepted and managed by the community. Attention will have to be paid, however, to a follow-up breeding strategy with replacement rams to avoid inbreeding in the future.

Many of the linkages made between fatteners and suppliers of processed feed are still in the early stages of development and many changes took place during the project life. Because of increasing prices, several farmers decided to stop or reduce buying processed feed and use more home-produced feeds instead. So far, cooperatives have played a limited role in the supply of feed for fattening. This may change with the increase in business volume. It was interesting to note that some of the linkages created were established as a result of study tours organized for key actors.

The projects' intervention on the production and sale of urea molasses block (UMB) for fattening is used in one of the pilot districts, although on a limited scale, partly due to shortage in the availability of the basic ingredient, molasses. The UMB was used mainly as a kind of survival or emergency feed during feed shortage. The multiplication and distribution of cuttings and seeds, grown on demonstration areas in the different pilot districts is well accepted. Multiplication of seeds/cuttings by private farmers for distribution to neighboring farmers is also reportedly working in several pilot districts, notably the distribution of Napier grass cuttings in almost all districts. Commercial production of seeds by farmers has been initiated but has not resulted in a commercially viable business.

Credit used to promote commercial cattle fattening by smallholders had varying results. A loan offered for large ruminant fattening with experienced fatteners was repaid on time and showed that farmers can handle more than the traditional loan for fattening only one animal, showing credit is likely one key constraint of the development of fattening in Ethiopia. Most loans were provided to farmers who were relatively new to the fattening business. In some pilot districts, funds were successfully recycled two or three times. In other districts, poor attitude of fatteners and the lending institutes toward "project-funded" loans led to default and no recycling of funds took place.

Credit for sheep fattening was issued in 4 of the 10 pilot districts. Sheep fatteners in one pilot district repaid in full after the first cycle, but refused to use credit again. In one pilot district, several groups took credit and repayment was high, except for a few farmers. This affected the recycling of loan funds for a second cycle to the same group, since no consensus could be obtained on the repayment of defaulted loans by other group members. Loans provided to groups composed of female farmers had hardly any defaulters.

Community-based insurance scheme for sheep fattening was piloted in one of the pilot districts. Since the launch of the scheme, fatteners experienced loss of fattening sheep due to disease and wild animal attacks. Farmers reported the loss of their sheep through their fattening groups and development agents. About 87% of the losses were approved for insurance claims and the claimants were immediately compensated. Although the process of verifying and approving claims and effecting the compensation took about a month on average, claimants did not perceive this as a big problem. An assessment was made of the level of members' awareness of the community-based insurance scheme and their perceptions with regard to level of premiums, management of the common pool fund, claim application and compensation process, and overall importance of such a scheme. Results show overwhelming satisfaction with the scheme. Almost all of the scheme members expressed their satisfaction with the service. To scale out such schemes, an institutional support structure needs to be created.

Household level fattening practices and income

Household survey results show that on average farmers benefited from fattening of purchased oxen (Table 2). It was also noticed that most farmers have started using shorter fattening periods and stall feeding to fatten their animals. Several farmers also introduced shelters constructed from local materials. Most farmers de-wormed their animals at the beginning of the fattening period and sought treatment

Table 2:　Gross return analysis on cattle fattening (2007/2008 production year)

District	Obs. (HHs)	Average Buying Price (*birr/ox*)	Average Selling Price (*birr/ox*)	Average Cash Outlay[a] (*birr/ox*)	Average Return to Family Labor and Feed (*birr/ox*)	Average Number of Months Animals Stay on Farm	Average Gross Return Per Animal Per Month (*birr/ox/month*)
Metema	14	1791.58	2878.61	214.34	872.69	3.2	272.72
Bure	21	1291.17	2094.70	46.70	756.83	3.4	222.60
Ada'a	19	2055.90	3813.16	1116.05	641.21	4.2	152.67
Mieso	11	2139.00	5150.00	201.04	2608.00	7.0	372.57

Note: [a] Cash outlay is expenditure on purchased feed, drug, and veterinary services.
Source: Household survey data (2009).

from nearby veterinary services when animals were sick. Use of concentrates during the fattening period is commonly accepted, although farmers mostly use locally available protein- or energy-rich materials.

　　Use of crop residues, in particular sorghum and maize stovers and teff, wheat and rice straws, is widespread. Urea treatment of crop residues, however, has so far not been adopted widely, mainly because it is found to be too labor intensive. Also, new devices to chop the stover are not yet widely adopted, perhaps because of problems related to economies of scale. Crop residues from non-cereals such as stalks/halms from cow peas and beans are increasingly being used. Farmers in some districts also use green sorghum thinned from planted areas and fed during the rainy season. Sweet potato vines and poor quality tubers are also used as feed.

　　The production of fodder grasses and legumes from enclosed grazing areas and backyard planting is expanding *and* is increasingly used for fattening animals. Although as a result of the credit interventions multiple cycles of fattening have been introduced within a year, feed limitations have hampered the efforts of some farmers. Moreover, the project encouraged farmers to fatten several oxen within a cycle, but most farmers fattened one or two animals at a time, because of credit constraints and/or lack of experience.

Table 3:   Gross return analysis on sheep fattening (2007/2008 production year)

District	Obs. (HHs)	Average Buying Price (*birr/ sheep*)	Average Selling Price (*birr/ sheep*)	Average Cash Outlay[a] (*birr/ sheep*)	Average Return to Family Labor and Feed (*birr/ sheep*)	Average Number of Months Animals Stay on Farm	Average Gross Return Per Animal Per Month (*birr/sheep/ month*)
Atsbi	17	138.03	307.65	100.94	68.68	3.1	22.16
Bure	12	221.00	440.46	113.55	105.91	4.4	24.07
Gomma	17	179.12	426.82	165.60	82.10	4.8	17.10

Note: [a] Cash outlay is expenditure on purchased feed, drug, and veterinary services.
Source: Household survey data (2009).

Survey results show that, in general, small ruminant fattening has been a successful intervention in several of the pilot districts, in particular for women. Returns per animal, however, are relatively low (Table 3). Most farmers were therefore supported by the project to fatten several animals (five or more) at the same time to make it economically attractive.

In some of the districts, farmers initially fattened animals in a group, and distributed labor duties amongst members on a daily basis to reduce input cost per animal as well as to learn from each other. In a district where fattening by women groups was initiated in 2009, the women switched from fattening sheep after two cycles to other businesses, including fattening of oxen, cattle trade and dairy cows. Still they considered the initial startup in sheep fattening as a good strategy to get into market-oriented production.

Marketing

So far, the marketing of small and large ruminants has not encountered any major challenges. Most animals are sold in nearby local markets, through individual or collective action. One of the lead fatteners successfully organized a linkage between a group of cattle fatteners and an export opportunity to Sudan. Several market linkages that were created had mixed results, some becoming dysfunctional from time to time because of export restrictions imposed by importing countries. Overall, it is clear that the export market value chains are still developing, which may eventually lead to stable linkages with smallholder producers.

Effect on gender

Survey results show that none of the surveyed women had access to knowledge and skills on fattening before. Almost all "project" women received training on different aspects of market-oriented shoat's development. As a result, the survey showed that almost 83% of the interviewed women started using supplementary feeding, and 68% of them selected shoats especially for short-term fattening using new criteria on age, body size and sex.

The survey also showed that on average female farmers roughly doubled the sale of sheep from 4.6 animals/year to 9.4 animals/year, and women mainly control the income. Only 10% of the women reported that husbands controlled the income from the sale of sheep. Many women considered the fattening of small ruminants as a stepping-stone to other (more lucrative) business opportunities such as cattle fattening and dairy. Survey results on the impact of small ruminant fattening on women workload showed that 90% of the surveyed women had their workload increase.

Actor linkages

A number of actors have been directly or indirectly involved in different stages in the cattle and small ruminants fattening value chains. The key private actors included concentrate feed suppliers, private edible oil processors, cotton ginneries, and food processing plants as well as private, public and community-based veterinary service providers and micro-finance institutions. Key public actors encompass agricultural bureaus, Women Affairs Offices, saving and credit groups, community insurance groups, and local administrators. Prior to the intervention, interaction and linkages among these actors were negligible. The key actors were brought together in commodity platforms and their inter-action increased significantly. Moreover, establishment of the WALC helped improve the interaction and linkage among actors to a consid-erable level.

Conclusions and Implications

Smallholder-led agricultural transformation is vital for the social and economic development of Ethiopia. Farmers who move from a sub-sistence oriented to a more commercially oriented production system require a mindset change. Decision making needs to be based on market demands and farmers' comparative and competitive advan-tages. This transformative change should be nationally driven and the public sector has a critical role to play in the process. The private sec-tor is, however, expected to play an increasing role in the process of commercialization.

Commercial transformation of smallholders requires the devel-opment of institutional support services, provided by both the public and the private sectors. Market-oriented agricultural devel-opment is a continuous and dynamic process that requires different types of interventions at different stages of development. The IPMS project demonstrated such transformation in ten Ethiopian districts during 2004/2005–2009/2010. Project experiences show that market-oriented dairy and livestock fattening can be effective in increasing household income and achieve wider impact and eco-nomic growth. We present major conclusions and implications of this experience below.

Input supply and credit

In Ethiopia predominantly the public sector provides AI and veteri-nary services for dairy production. The project facilitated introduction of more privatized services such as private bull stations, privatized AI service, and paravets. The financial viability of these initiatives is, how-ever, constrained by the lack of economies of scale (low business vol-ume) and competition from government-subsidized service provision in the same location. Results imply that better attention will have to be paid to the development of private input supply and credit delivery system. The crowding out effect of the public input supply and service provision needs to be reconsidered. Moreover, the experience of the AI with hormone assisted estrus synchronization needs to be evaluated to draw lessons for scaling out.

Differences existed in the sources of animals fattened depending on the level of commercialization. At the early stages of commercialization households fattened their own animals, while at a more advanced stage farmers fatten purchased animals. To stimulate this development, credit for fattening is required. The project demonstrated successfully the use of credit for fattening purposes. Both farmers and credit institutions should, however, adopt a commercial attitude toward credit rather than the usual "project" attitude in which credit is considered a subsidy. Also, once the amount of credit required per farm increases, group collateral systems may need to be replaced by other flexible systems. The use of a community-based insurance scheme for small ruminants can be used to stimulate commercial fattening with credit, especially benefiting women. This insurance scheme may also be considered as collateral for individual and/ or group loans. Institutionalized support structure is also needed to scale out such schemes.

The awareness of farmers of processed feed is increasing, and is likely to increase faster with the level of market orientation. Hence, once the scale of the fattening businesses increases, feed agro dealerships should be further developed to ensure a regular quality supply of feeds. Project experiences show that different input supply systems including community-based, farmer-to-farmer, the private sector, cooperatives and the public sector can be appropriate and effective for different value chains.

Extension service

The development of market-oriented commodities is a continuous process, and requires new responses in knowledge, skills and interventions and different sets of actors depending on differences in the level of commercialization. Knowledge and skills in market-oriented extension service was non-existent when the project started operation. The traditional production and technology-focused extension service approach is inadequate for market-oriented agricultural development; market-oriented extension service is required. Although still at the initial stage, the project managed to successfully introduce market-oriented participatory extension approaches. However, sustained and continuous effort is needed to build capacity for market-oriented extension from federal to district levels. Market-oriented extension needs to be institutionalized in the structure of the Ministry of Agriculture. Moreover, with increased levels of commercialization, private advisory services may need to be considered. Project experiences confirmed that provision of market information in various forms, facilitating virtual or physical linkages of producers with buyers, and formal and informal collective action for produce marketing increase bargaining power of farmers.

Production

Farmers who applied improved production technologies have shown that dairy production is a good and dependable livelihood source. In the rural butter production systems, significant household income gains can be made, especially for women. Production interventions like backyard fodder production and grazing area improvements were successfully introduced by the project and showed a good synergy between natural resource conservation and utilization. Improved livestock husbandry/feeding practices with concentrates were successful in most locations, but hampered by inconsistency of quality and supply, and unpredictable price fluctuations. Linkages through agro business dealerships with emerging commercial feed companies should be explored in the future to improve economics of scale. Availability of improved dairy genetic material at affordable prices is still a critical limiting factor in the country.

Returns to labor of short-term commercial fattening of large and small ruminants with supplementary feeding, improved health care and appropriate shelter and other interventions were found to be profitable. These interventions can be scaled out. To contribute substantially to the family income, however, the number of animals fattened per farm should be increased once skills and knowledge have been gained. New production methods for fattening may be considered including fattening of young animals.

Marketing and processing

The project facilitated the processing/marketing of dairy products in several locations by introducing small cooperative dairy processing units in small urban centers. It has been observed, however, that almost all the cooperatives suffered from lack of economies of scale and inadequate agro business manpower. It is doubtful that such manpower can be gainfully employed at such low level of production/processing. A wider milk shed approach should be promoted and pursued in which small geographical locations will become collection centers. The involvement of medium to larger sized commercial dairy farms in processing of milk from small holders at the district level should also be explored. Marketing of small and large ruminants has so far not been a major problem and prices received have been increasing over time. Most sales are targeted at the domestic market. Market linkages/arrangements made for (collective) marketing require further development especially when volumes increase. For export market development regulatory bodies and quarantine services also need improvement.

Acknowledgments

We are grateful to the Canadian International Development Agency (CIDA) for the financial support for this work. We are also thankful to the many farmers and agricultural staff who patiently and willingly responded to our numerous survey and qualitative questions. We also thank the IPMS staff for their support.

References

Bacon F and Butler TW (1998) *Achieving Planned Innovation: A Proven System for Creating Successful New Products and Services.* New York: Free Press.

da Silva CA and de Souza Filho HM (2007) *Guidelines for Rapid Appraisal of Agrifood Chain Performance in Developing Countries.* Rome: Food and Agriculture Organization of the United Nations.

Everts S (1999) *Gender and Technology: Empowering Women, Engendering Development.* London and New York: Zed Books.

Gebremedhin B and Jaleta M (2012) Market orientation and market participation of smallholders in Ethiopia: Implications for commercial transformation. Selected paper presented at the IAAE Triennial Conference, Foz do Iguaçu, Brazil, 18–24 August 2012.

Gebremedhin B, Jaleta M and Hoekstra D (2009) Smallholders, institutional services and commercial transformation in Ethiopia. *Agricultural Economics* 40(S): 773–787.

Jaworski BJ and Kohli AK (1993) Market orientation: antecedents and consequences. *Journal of Marketing* 57(3): 53–70.

Jaworski BJ and Kohli AK (1996) Market orientation: review, refinement and roadmap. *Journal of Market-Focused Management* 1(2): 119–136.

Pingali P (1997) From subsistence to commercial production system: the transformation of Asian agriculture. *American Journal of Agricultural Economics* 79(2): 628–634.

Pingali LP and Rosegrant MW (1995) Agricultural commercialization and diversification: process and polices. *Food Policy* 20(3): 171–185.

Pingali LP (2001) Environmental consequences of agricultural commercialization in Asia. *Environment and Development Economics* 6: 483–502.

Quisumbing AR and Pandolfelli L (2010) Promising approaches to address the needs of poor female farmers: resources, constraints, and interventions. *World Development* 38(4): 581–592.

Romer P (1993) Idea gaps and object gaps in economic development. *Journal of Monetary Economics* 32(3): 543–573.

Romer P (1994) New goods, old theory and the welfare cost of trade restrictions. *Journal of Development Economics* 43(1): 5–38.

Selnes F, Jaworski BJ and Kohli AK (1996) Market orientation in United States and Scandinavian companies: a cross-cultural study. *Scandinavian Journal of Management* 12(2): 139–157.

SIDA (2006) *Addressing Food Crises in Africa: What Can Sub-Saharan Africa Learn from Asian Experiences in Addressing its Food Crises?* Department of Natural Resources and Environment, Division of Rural Development, Uppsala.

Timmer CP (1997) Farmers and markets: the political economy of new paradigms. *American Journal of Agricultural Economics* 79(2): 621–627.

Tsakok I (2011) *Successes in Agricultural Transformation: What It Means and What Makes It Happen.* Cambridge: Cambridge University Press.

von Braun J (1994) Introduction. In von Braun J and Kennedy E (eds.), *Agricultural Commercialization, Economic Development, and Nutrition.* Baltimore, MD: Johns Hopkins University Press, pp. 3–8.

World Bank (2008) *World Development Report 2008: Agriculture for Development.* Washington, DC: World Bank.

Chapter 11

THE ROLE OF GOVERNMENT IN ENSURING A LEVEL PLAYING FIELD: THE CASE OF SOUTH AFRICA'S COMPETITION COMMISSION AND THE MAIZE MILLING INDUSTRY

Lulama Ndibongo Traub

Bureau for Food and Agricultural Policy (BFAP)
Department of Agricultural Economics
University of Stellenbosch

In general, sustained agricultural productivity, growth and poverty reduction require an enabling policy environment that encourages private sector investments in input, output and financial markets. Using South Africa's maize milling industry as a case study, this chapter analyzes the impact of the Competition Commission's anti-trust ruling on the performance dimension of the maize sector; in particular on pricing efficiency. Using the Industrial-Organization Framework, the chapter explains the behavior of groups of firms within the context of the basic conditions (policy environment, demand characteristics, technology, *etc.*) and the market structure within which the firms exist. South Africa's utilization of an institution, such as the Competition Commission, demonstrates the ability of governments to create an enabling environment that stimulates private sector investment and minimizes market distortions within a staple food market.

Introduction

Meeting the challenges posed by high levels of poverty, unemployment, and food insecurity in Africa remains a major challenge to African governments, as well as to the regional and international development agencies. While various strategies and programs are being implemented across the continent, success has been limited to date. In general, sustained agricultural productivity growth and poverty reduction require not only increased public goods investment but an enabling policy environment that encourages private investments in input, output and financial markets (Jayne *et al.*, 2010).

To date, however, there is no consensus on the "right" mix of public investment and policy frameworks. Throughout most of the 1980s and 1990s the Southern African region underwent crucial structural adjustment programs where agricultural markets were liberalized. In step with ongoing structural adjustment programs Southern African Development Community (SADC) nations developed a number of policy and/or institutional structures with the aim of promoting agricultural growth and poverty reduction (BFAP, 2011). Despite these steps taken, sustained agricultural development within the region remains elusive. State interventions in food and input markets appear to be on the rise in Africa. Food and input markets in Africa continue to be hampered by unpredictable state operations, trade barriers and sudden entry and exit from markets (Jayne *et al.*, 2010). This high degree of policy uncertainty creates major market risks and impedes private investment from flowing into the agricultural sector. Policy environment will clearly influence the degree of private sector investment in both primary and agribusiness sectors.

Using South Africa's maize milling industry as a case study, this chapter utilizes the Industrial Organization (IO) Framework to examine the behavior or conduct of a group of firms within the context of their basic conditions and the market structure.

IO is the study of how productive activities are brought into harmony with society's demands for goods and services through some organizing mechanism such as the market, and how variations and imperfections in the organizing mechanism affect the degree of efficiency achieved by producers within the system (Bain, 1968; Scherer, 1980). The IO framework explains the behavior of firms within the context of the basic conditions (policy environment, demand characteristics, technology, *etc.*) and the market structure within which the

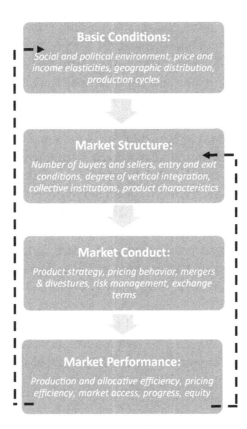

Figure 1.   IO framework

firms operate. The IO paradigm, illustrated in Figure 1, posits that market structure (S) strongly influences the competitive conduct (C) of firms, which in turns influences market performance (P).

In this study, IO framework is applied to the South African maize market in order to provide the context within which the Competition Commission ruled.

Basic Conditions of the Maize Sector

In general, basic conditions refer to the underlying characteristics of the product and of the environmental setting that shapes the type of market that evolves for the product. These include factors that influence the supply of and demand for the product (see Figure 1).

In the case of maize, cultivation can be divided into two geographic regions: major and minor growing areas. Included in the major growing areas are parts of the Free State, North West Province, and Mpumalanga. The minor growing areas include parts of the Free State, Northern Province, Kwazulu Natal, Gauteng and the northern-most parts of the Eastern and Northern Cape Provinces (Ntloedibe, 2001). Depending on the rainfall pattern of a particular geographical area, maize is usually planted between October and January, with harvesting taking place anywhere between the beginning of May and the end of June (Ntloedibe, 2001).

In general, maize production is divided fairly evenly between white and yellow maize. Rising global prices and lower domestic stock levels resulted in increased maize plantings from 2.37 million hectares in 2011 to 2.7 million hectares in 2012. White and yellow maize plantings increased by 15% and 11%, respectively, bringing the total area under white maize to 1.64 million hectares and yellow maize to 1.06 million hectares (see Figure 2) (BFAP, 2012). In terms of use,

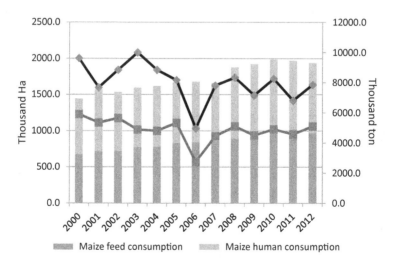

Figure 2.   Total maize area harvested and domestic consumption
Source: BFAP (2012).

approximately 75% of the domestic commercial requirement of white maize is used for human consumption, whereas 85% of yellow maize total production goes towards animal consumption or as input in the production of animal feed.

Over the past two decades, both domestic and trade policy interventions within the maize industry have occurred within the context of vast political and socioeconomic changes. Prior to 1996, the Marketing of Agriculture Product Act 59 of 1968 largely determined agricultural marketing policy (Bertelsman-Scott and Draper, 2004; Draper, 2003; Kirsten *et al.*, 2006; Robert *et al.*, 1994; Stern and Netshitomboni, 2004; Thirtle *et al.*, 2000; Traub and Meyer, 2010; van Dijck and Otto, 1995; van Rooyen *et al.*, 1997). For the maize industry, a single-channel fixed price scheme was established, which followed a cost-plus approach to commodity pricing and margin determinations. Under this structure, the maize board based its calculation of the maize grain prices for the next season on the current season's price while accounting for input costs. By the mid-1980s, due to internal pressure from domestic producers unsatisfied with the controlled marketing of many agricultural commodities coupled with macro-factors and international liberalization trends, a series of laws were enacted that reduced the role of government within the market and placed increasing reliance on market forces and the private sector.

Following the first free elections in 1994, the overall goal of government was to create an open and market-orientated economy while redressing the injustices of the past. It is the Marketing of Agricultural Products Act 47 of 1996 that currently shapes agricultural marketing policy in South Africa (Traub and Meyer, 2010). Under this act, the maize board was abolished in 1997, leaving prices within the industry to be based entirely on negotiation between market actors. As a result, new institutional arrangements, such as the South African Futures Exchange (SAFEX), emerged in order to facilitate trade and minimize transaction cost along the value chain. Ultimately, the change in the policy environment has had a direct impact on both the structure and conduct of the maize industry within South Africa as the maize industry moved away from a single-channel, fixed-price marketing system to a market structure where prices were now determined through negotiations between market actors.

Structure of the Maize Sector

In general, the structure of a market is underpinned by factors that shape the competitiveness. These include factors such as buyer and seller concentration, degree of product differentiation as well as ease of entry and exit.

South Africa's grain industry, one of the largest industries within South Africa's agricultural sector, contributed approximately 16% to the total gross value of agricultural production in 2011 (DAFF, 2011). It comprises all grain and oilseed industries, of which maize and wheat are considered primary staple commodities. In 2009/2010, maize contributed 10.5% to the total gross value of agricultural production, making it the third largest contributing agricultural commodity (after the poultry and beef industries), while wheat contributed approximately 2.5% (DAFF, 2011).

In general, the maize supply chain comprises six distinct activities namely production, storage, trading, processing, wholesaling/retailing, and consumption. Although the movement of grain from the farm level to the consumption level can be classified into six distinct activities, it is not quite so simple when trying to identify the key market participants involved within each activity. The reason for this is that many of the firms involved within the market are vertically integrated with either their upstream or downstream markets. Despite this degree of vertical integration in the maize value chains, the key value-addition activities along the supply chains include: primary production, storage commodity trading, processing (both animal and food processing), retailing, and consumption.

As a demonstration, the regional market of Soweto in Gauteng province is used to evaluate the degree of concentration along the maize value chain rather than an aggregated national value chain. The rational for this approach is multi-faceted. First, previous research shows evidence that the maize market was divided up between the major processors allowing for virtual monopolies within regional markets (Competition Commission, 2012; Traub and Jayne, 2004). Second, within Gauteng, four of the top five maize millers have mills located within the province. Third, Soweto Township is highly urbanized and densely populated with a wide range of household income levels, thereby allowing for examination of maize meal retailing across various retail-chains. The data presented here draw from research conducted under the Guiding Investments in Sustainable Agricultural Markets in Africa (GISAMA) project, headed by Michigan State University.

Figure 3 illustrates the flow of maize grain and meal within Gauteng,[1] focusing on Soweto as the output market. Gauteng is the smallest province in South Africa with a surface area that represents approximately 1.5% of the country's total land mass (Statistics South Africa, 2012). In terms of income, the province has the highest per capita income level and contributed approximately 34% to the national GDP in 2009 (Statistics South Africa, 2010). The township of Soweto is located within the City of Johannesburg Metropolitan Municipality. The most recent census data from 2001 estimate the total population as approximately 1.1 million living within 70 suburbs (Statistics South Africa, 2012). Subsequent studies, however, have estimated total population to have reached the 1.4 million mark (Market Decisions, 2012). The 70 suburbs, which constitute Soweto, can be classified into four geographic entities, namely Central, East, North, and South regions (Market Decisions, 2012).

For the purpose of this study the entire population of formal retailers within Soweto was interviewed, while a sample of *spaza* retailers[2] were selected from within each geographic entity. The methodology

---

[1] Gauteng is divided into three metropolitan municipalities (City of Johannesburg, City of Tshwane, and Ekurhuleni) and three district municipalities (West Rand, Sidiben, and Metsweding), which are further subdivided into eight local municipalities.

[2] *Spaza* is a term used to describe small, informal retail shops located in South African townships; *spazas* often operate out of a home.

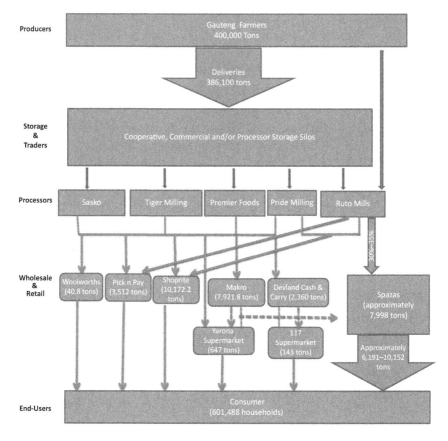

Figure 3. White maize and maize meal flow diagram 2008/2009: Soweto, Gauteng, South Africa

Source: GISIMA (2010)

involved in the sampling of *spazas* included randomly selecting three suburbs within each geographic region. The probability of selecting a particular suburb was weighted by income and population estimates. Within each suburb, the entire population of *spazas* was interviewed; the population size ranged from 12 to 20 *spazas* per suburb. Starting from the top we see that the maize supply chain within Soweto consists of five levels; production, storage/trading, processing, retailing/

wholesaling,[3] and consumption. The discussion that follows provides a brief description of the structure and conduct at each stage of the supply chain.

Producers

South African grain production comprises both commercial and subsistence producers. In 2005, there were approximately 18,000 commercial grain producers who accounted for 90% of all grains produced while approximately 3 million small-scale and/or subsistence farmers accounted for the remaining 10% (SAGIS, 2005). Of the 18,000 commercial grain producers, approximately 9,000 were maize farmers.

Grain farmers in Gauteng were responsible for approximately 5% of the total 7.5 million tons of white maize produced in the 2008/2009 marketing year. This amounted to a total of 400,000 tons of white maize grain (SAGIS, 2011). In general, commercially grown maize grain is delivered via rail and/or road transportation to either storage silos located near the production zone, or directly to processors, depending on the method of sale. It should be noted, however, that due to increasing storage costs, some producers are developing on-farm storage units in order to minimize costs (Hochfeld, 2007). In 2008/2009, of the 400,000 tons of grain produced, about 386,100 tons were delivered to storage silos.

Storage industry and traders

Currently there is approximately 17 million tons of bulk storage capacity within the country, 85% of which is owned by former

---

[3] For the purpose of this study the entire population of formal retailers within Soweto was interviewed; while a sample of Spaza retailers were selected from within each geographic entity. The methodology involved in the sampling of Spazas included randomly selecting three suburbs within each geographic region. The probability of selecting a particular suburb was weighted by income and population estimates. Within each suburb, the entire population of *spazas* was interviewed; the population size ranged from 12 to 20 *spazas* per suburb.

Table 1:   Relative share of bulk storage capacity and primary location: 2008

Silo Owners	Number of Storage Silos Owned	% of Total Silo	Primary Province of Location
Senwes (SWK)	55	23	Free State
Afgri (OTK)	55	23	Mpumalanga
Noordwes (NWK)	23	10	North West

Source: Farmwise http://www.farmwise.co.za/.

cooperatives (ITAC, 2007). Table 1 presents the concentration of ownership in the silo industry within the country where the top three co-operatives/companies own 56% of all the domestic storage facilities.

Following the Marketing of Agricultural Products Act 47 of 1996, the Agricultural Markets Division of the SAFEX was established. The objective of a commodity derivatives market is to provide an effective price determination mechanism in order to mitigate risk within a given market. In this regard, SAFEX is considered the benchmark for spot market prices of daily trade in maize and provides the platform for all maize grain trades within South Africa.

Two multinational companies, Cargill and Louis Dreyfuss, dominate the trading/brokering market within South Africa. In general, Cargill is involved in trading for the domestic market, whereas Dreyfuss is primarily focused on the import-export markets (Traub and Meyer, 2010). Cargill and Dreyfuss trade as much as two-thirds of the 70% of maize grain that passes through to the large domestic millers (Le Clus, 2004). The remaining firms involved in the market can be divided into three groups; independent traders with no affiliation to a bank or former cooperative; bank-associated traders linked to financial institutions that provide credit facilities; and silo-associated traders affiliated with one of the former cooperatives which were since converted into grain storage companies. For instance, currently there are 59 registered SAFEX brokers, four of whom are bank-associated traders, while nine are associated with grain storage companies (SAFEX, 2010). Currently the large domestic traders include Rand Merchant Bank, Senwes, Afgri, and Verus Farms. Smaller traders include Brisen, Bester Feed Exchanges, Farmwise, Unigrain and Free State Maize (DAFF, 2011).

Processors

Maize milling for human consumption consists of both wet and dry milling. Currently, there are at least 190 companies involved in maize milling with 22 of the large-scale millers accounting for approximately two-thirds of the maize meal produced within the country (NAMC, 2004). To date, the four largest millers are Pioneer Foods, Tiger Milling, Premier Foods and Pride Milling, which together account for nearly 40% of the market share (NAMC, 2004).

According to the survey results, within Soweto five millers are responsible for approximately 95% of the entire market (McConnelly, 2009). These include Sasko (owned by Pioneer Foods), Tiger Milling, Premier Foods, Pride Milling and Ruto Mills (owned by Foodcorp). Although other studies have looked at the impact of the informal bakkie-millers[4] within the South African maize subsector, there is no evidence that this informal sector exists within Soweto (Traub and Jayne, 2008). None of the retailers and households interviewed knew of such mills and there was no maize grain available for purchase at the retail level for milling purposes.

In terms of grain purchasing, millers either use grain brokers or work directly with the cooperatives to source maize grain (McConnelly, 2009). One miller interviewed indicated that at times they work directly with large-scale farmers. But typically these are farmers who have on-farm storage and are located closest to the mill. As for pricing the raw material inputs, SAFEX serves as a benchmark since millers use the commodity exchange for hedging. The SAFEX price, however, is not always an accurate measure of the true market price paid

---

[4] Informal maize milling in South Africa is divided into stationary and mobile *bakkie* millers. This sector provides maize-milling services to subsistence maize grain producers and/or rural and peri-urban consumers who source maize grain at the wholesale level.

Table 2: Frequency of brand occurrence on retail shelf: 11/2009

| Miller | Brand | Frequency of Occurrence | | Top Selling Brand | | |
		Formal ($N = 20$)	*Spazas* ($N = 153$)	Rank #1	Rank #2 ($N = 173$)	Rank #3
Tiger Milling	Ace	18	153	134	34	—
	Cream of Maize	2	8	—	—	5
Pioneer Foods–Sasko	White Star	18	146	39	117	1
Premier Foods	Iwisa	11	8	2	—	8
	Impala	8	3	1	—	1
	Super Sun	2	—	—	—	—
Foodcrop–Ruto Mills	5-star	7	—	—	—	—
	Tafelberg	9	—	—	—	—
	A1	9	1	1	—	1
	Safari	4	—	—	—	—
Pride Milling	Nation Pride	3	3	—	—	—
	Tops Everytime	5	—	—	—	—
Retail Own Brand	Woolworths	3	—	—	—	2
	Pick n Pay	2	—	—	—	1

Source: GISIMA (2010).

by millers for their raw material input, since all their prices are negotiated with the broker and/or cooperative (McConnelly, 2009).

In order to determine relative market share of each miller supplying the Soweto area, brand presence was tallied across both the formal and informal retail stores surveyed. Table 2 summarizes the findings.

The data indicate that Tiger Milling had the strongest presence within Soweto, followed by Sasko. In 2009, Ace maize meal was the most frequently occurring brand on Soweto retail shelves, closely followed by Sasko Milling's White Star. Of the 20 formal retailers surveyed, which represent the entire population, 18 carried both Ace and White Star. In the informal sector, of the 153 market stalls (*spazas*) sampled all outlets sold Ace, while 146 carried White Star. Although not an accurate measure of market share, the ranking of top selling brands by retail managers and/or owners substantiates these findings. Of the retailers who were able to rank their top selling brands, Ace was ranked number one more often than not, followed by White Star; 134 retail outlets ranked Ace as the number one seller while 39 ranked White Star as their top seller.

Retailers

Within South Africa, the channel of food distribution does not follow a traditional pattern of manufacture-to-wholesaler, wholesaler-to-retailer structure. Rather many of the larger retailers have internalized the role of wholesalers by creating their own distribution network, thereby dispensing with the need for wholesalers (Achterberg and Hartzenberg, 2002). Due to mergers and acquisitions the wholesale/retail sector has become highly concentrated (Achterberg and Hartzenberg, 2002; Ntloedibe, 2001). The consolidation within the market as well as the growing trend of franchising under the stipulation that franchisees purchase their products from or through their franchisers has led to the wholesale/retail sector having considerable bargaining power when negotiating buying terms with suppliers.

In terms of staple food retailing, national chains such as Woolworth and Pick n Pay, service medium-to-higher-income consumers, while Shoprite Checkers, Spar, and regional retail outlets and neighborhood *spazas* service middle-to-low-income consumers in rural, urban, and peri-urban areas. Within Soweto Township the formal national retailers include Woolworth, Pick n Pay, and Shoprite Checkers (see Figure 3). In terms of total volume of maize meal purchased both Woolworth and Pick n Pay have relatively low volumes (40.8 tons and 3,512 tons) compared to Shoprite Checkers, with 10,172 tons. Given the household demographics these retail outlets aim for, this discrepancy is not surprising.

Beside theses national retailers, two local supermarkets as well as *spazas* sell maize meal to households within Soweto. When the volume of maize meal purchased by the sample of *spazas* surveyed is extrapolated for the entire township, we estimate a total volume of nearly 8,000 tons of maize meal purchased by *spazas*. The combined purchasing volume is second to the largest maize meal purchaser, indicating that although individually small, *spazas* as a whole play an important role in maize meal retailing within Soweto.

In general, the flow of maize meal from millers to households within Soweto has a range of trade distribution channels. One possible channel involves the miller selling directly to large retail outlets, which in turn sell to households. Given the minimum volume purchase of at least 1 metric ton, this option is typically not viable for smaller-size retail concerns. In Soweto these retailers would include Woolworth, Pick n Pay, Shoprite, Yarona and 117 Supermarket. Together these retailers purchased approximately 14,515 tons of maize meal directly from the millers. A second channel involves millers selling to large cash and carries, which in turn sell to other smaller retail outlets. In 2008/2009, approximately 93% of all *spazas* surveyed sourced their maize meal from local cash and carries located outside of Soweto. A third distribution channel involves millers selling directly to *spazas*. Within Soweto only one miller, Ruto Mills, was involved in this arrangement whereby between 30% and 35% of total maize meal output was sold directly to *spazas* within Soweto.

Maize Sector Conduct

Market conduct encompasses the strategies that firms within a given industry utilize in order to compete. It includes pricing, advertising, mergers and acquisitions and can include both tacit and/or explicit collusion. In the case of the South African maize industry, earlier studies that examined the maize subsector found evidence of possible noncompetitive pricing behavior within the supply chain (Cutts and Kirsten, 2006; Traub and Jayne, 2008). Subsequent to these studies, the entire sector came under investigation by the Competition Commission of South Africa. The following section provides a brief overview of the institutional framework of the Competition Commission and a timeline on the legal actions taken against the industry.

Competition commission

Competition law

The Competition Commission is a statutory body empowered to control and evaluate restrictive business practices and to investigate abuse of dominant market positions as well as proposed mergers and acquisitions. The overarching aim is to balance economic efficiency with socio-economic equity and development within the South African economy (Competition Commission, 2012). Table 3 contains a chronological inventory of key domestic policy decisions that led to the establishment of the Competition Commission. Since many of these decisions were made within the context of reform, a brief discussion on the reform objective and specific policies and/or institutions established is presented.

The stated purpose of the Competition Act of 1998 is to promote and maintain competition within South Africa by

- Promoting efficiency, adaptability and development in the macro-economy;
- Ensuring competitive prices and product choice for consumers;
- Promoting employment as well as advancement of social and economic welfare;
- Expanding opportunities for South African participation in world markets while recognizing the role of foreign competition within the domestic market;
- Ensuring equitable and inclusive access to markets for small and medium-size enterprises;
- Promoting Black Economic Empowerment through increased ownership stakes of historically disadvantaged persons (Competition Commission, 2012).

Table 3: Chronology of South Africa's Competition Law, 1970–2012

Period	Policy/Institutions	Description
1955	Regulation of Monopolistic Conditions Act	Original competition law regime
1970	Review of 1955 Act	Found to be unsuccessful in preventing establishment of oligopolies.
1979	Maintenance and Promotion of Competition Act	Established as a result of the 1970 review process. The Competition Board was established and tasked with the administration of the Act.
1986	Amendment to the 1979 Act	This amendment gave the Competition board greater power and included the ability to act against existing monopolies and oligopolies. However, technical flaws constrained effective implementation both substantive and logistically.
1994	White Paper on Reconstruction and Development	Indicated the new government's intention to review competition law regime.
1997	Proposed Guidelines for Competition Policy	Outlined the proposed framework for a new competition policy framework compiled by the Department of Trade and Industry. Formed the basis for negotiations with the National Economic Development and Labour Council (NEDLAC). Objective of this process was to reach agreement between the private sector, government and labour on policy principles and competition legislation.
1998	Competition Act	After a 14-week public consultation process, the Act was passed by Parliament in September 1998.

Source: Competition Commission (2012).

Institutional framework

In order to achieve the stated objectives, three separate and independent institutions were established under the Competition Act of 1998. These include Competition Commission, Competition Tribunal, and Competition Appeal Court. Figure 4 illustrates the institutional framework.

The Competition Commission is made up of seven divisions. These include:

- Office of the Commissioner: its mandate is to coordinate the division and liaise with stakeholders, which include government, international organizations, and private sector.
- Enforcement and Exemptions: its mandate is to investigate and evaluate claims of noncompetitive behavior with a given industry.
- Mergers & Acquisitions: its mandate is to investigate and analyze proposed mergers and acquisitions.
- Cartels: the primary function of this division is to investigate potential cartels as well as to oversee the corporate leniency policy (CLP).
- Advocacy & Stakeholder Relations: its core responsibility includes communication and public relations with both international and domestic stakeholders.
- Legal services.
- Policy & Research: this unit undertakes economic analysis of complex cases and proposed mergers.
- Corporate Services: this unit provides administrative services.

The Competition Tribunal is the branch of the Competition Commission that is empowered to grant exemptions, authorize or prohibit large mergers (with or without conditions), as well as determine rulings in connection with market conduct prohibited under the Competition Act (Competition Commission, 2012).

The Competition Appeal Court is granted with national jurisdiction and in this way is similar to the High Court. Its primary function is to serve as a court of appeals in matters arising from opposition to a particular ruling of the Competition Tribunal. It is empowered to

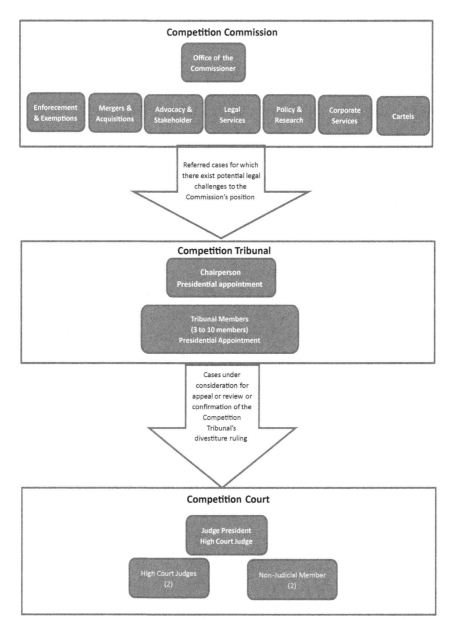

Figure 4.   Institutional structure of Competition Commission

Source: Competition Commission Website (2012)

confirm, amend or set aside a decision or an order by the Competition Tribunal (Competition Commission, 2012).

Competition commission ruling

In terms of its mandate, the Commission has prioritized the following sectors:

1. Food, agro-processing and forestry
2. Infrastructure and construction
3. Intermediate industrial products
4. Financial services

The prioritization of these sectors is premised on two important considerations. First, resource efficiency; given the commission's broad mandate to investigate all complaints of anti-competitive practices within the economy, resources are largely devoted to sectors that have greater impact on consumers' welfare. Secondly, increased effectiveness; the Commission focuses on sectors which have the greatest economic impact in order to ensure effectiveness.

The South African agricultural sector is among the most liberalized in the global economy. Since 1996 several domestic and trade policy reforms were enacted in order to meet the objective of establishing a market-orientated economy (Traub and Meyer, 2010). A strong indicator of the extent of the reform policies' impact on the agricultural sector is a declining level of the producer support estimate (PSE) since 1994. The Organization for Economic Cooperation and Development (OECD) estimates that between 2000 and 2003, South Africa's PSE was approximately 5%, compared to the 31% average for OECD countries (OEDC, 2006). However, despite the structural change towards a more open economy, within domestic markets high levels of concentration were found in the trading, storage and processing of grain, in particular wheat and maize (see section on Basic Conditions of the Maize Sector). Given the degree of concentration and possible anti-competitive behavior, investigations were conducted and subsequent rulings enacted by the Commission. Table 4 contains the chronology of the investigation and subsequent rulings against the grain industry.

Table 4:　Chronology of Competition Commission's actions within the grain supply chain, 2005–2012

Period	Firms Involved	Action Taken
May 2005	Sasol Chemicals, Kynoch and Omnia Fertiliser	Referred to Tribunal for anti-competitive behavior in fertilizer industry. Complaints initiated by Nutri-Flo CC.
May 2005	Sasol Chemicals	Referred to Tribunal for anti-competitive behavior in the market for LAN, a nitrogen-based fertilizer. Complaints initiated by Profert (Pty) Ltd.
January 2007	Senwes Ltd.	Referred to Tribunal for alleged abuse of its dominant position in the market for commercial grain handling and storage. Complaints initiated by CTH Trading (Pty) Ltd.
February 2007	Pioneer Foods Ltd., Tiger Food Brands Ltd., Premier Foods Ltd.	Complaints of price-fixing by flour millers and bakeries initiated by bread distributors within the Western Cape. Conditional immunity was granted to Premier Foods Ltd. under CLP due to full cooperation.
November 2007	Tiger Brands Ltd	Tiger Brands admits to participating in flour milling and bread cartel, is fined R98,784,869.90, and applies for leniency in exchange for evidence against the cartel.
May 2008	Pioneer Foods (Pty) Ltd. and Foodcorp (Pty) Ltd.	Commission found the two firms had contravened Competition Act and proposed an administrative penalty of 10% of their annual turnover for the 2006/2007 financial year.

(*Continued*)

Table 4:   (*Continued*)

Period	Firms Involved	Action Taken
November 2008	American Natural Soda Ash Corporation (ANSAC)	Botswana (Botash) and Chemserve laid a complaint that ANSAC through its membership agreement eliminates price competition between its members in export sales of potash to South Africa. ANSAC agreed to pay an administrative penalty of R9,696,846.96 representing 8% of soda ash annual turnover in South Africa.
January 2009	Foodcorp (Pty) Ltd.	Settlement agreement with regards to Foodcorp's participation in the bread cartel referred to the Competition Tribunal. Foodcorp admitted to price-fixing within the bread market. Agreement included an administrative penalty of R45,406,359.82, representing 6.7% of Foodcorp's turnover from all its baking operations for the 2006 financial year.
May 2009	Sasol Chemicals	Admitted cartel behavior within the fertilizer industry. Sasol agreed to pay a penalty of R188,010,000. Due to lateness of full-disclosure, however, Sasol's fines were increased to R250,680,000.

(*Continued*)

Table 4:   (*Continued*)

Period	Firms Involved	Action Taken
May 2009	Masscash Holdings (Pty) Ltd. ("Masscash") and Finro Enterprises (Pty) Ltd.	Competition Commission recommended to Competition Tribunal that proposed merger be prohibited. Masscash, a wholly owned subsidiary of Massmart Group, and Finro compete in the market for the wholesaling of grocery products in the Port Elizabeth region and surrounding areas.
June 2009	Pick n Pay, Shoprite/ Checkers, Woolworths and Spar, Massmart, and Metcash	Commission initiates an investigation of alleged non-competitive behavior within the formal supermarket chains.
February 2010	Pioneer Foods	Competition Commission lodged appeal with Competition Appeal Court against Competition Tribunal's ruling on administrative penalty imposed on Pioneer. Commission asked appeal court to reverse Tribunal's finding on the penalty and impose a penalty of 10% of Pioneer's group turnover, which would amount to approximately R1.5 billion, an amount the Commission felt would be sufficient to deter cartel behavior.
March 2010	Pioneer Foods (Pty) Limited, Foodcorp (Pty) Limited trading as Ruto Mills, Godrich Milling (Pty) Limited, Premier Foods (Pty) Ltd. and Tiger Brands Ltd.	Competition Commission, subsequent to its investigation into collusion in the wheat milling market, has referred its findings to the Tribunal.

(*Continued*)

Table 4:   (*Continued*)

Period	Firms Involved	Action Taken
March 2010	Pioneer Foods, Foodcorp, Godrich Milling, Progress Milling, Pride Milling, Westra Milling, Brenner Mills, Blinkwater Mills, TWK Milling, NTK Milling, Carolina Mills, Kalel Foods, Bothaville Milling, Paramount Mills, Keystone Milling, Premier Foods and Tiger Brands	Competition Commission referred its findings of price fixing of milled white maize to Tribunal for prosecution. Commission has asked Tribunal to impose administrative penalty of 10% of annual turnover for the 2009 financial year on each of the firms involved, except Premier Foods and Tiger Brands, which were granted conditional immunity from prosecution by the Commission provided they fully cooperate in Commission's investigation and prosecution of this case.
June 2010	Maize milling industry	Competition Commission called on firms active in milling of white maize to approach it for possible settlement of their cases. This was a once-off offer for firms that may have been involved in cartel activity to cooperate. In return, firms would receive favorable settlement terms.
July 2010	Sasol Chemical Industries Limited ("SCI")	Competition Commission reached settlement agreement on the abuse aspect of the fertilizer case. This follows the settlement reached on the collusion part of the case. Settlement relates to SCI's abuse of dominance, exclusionary conduct and price discrimination in the supply of

(*Continued*)

Table 4:   (*Continued*)

Period	Firms Involved	Action Taken
		ammonia and derivative fertilizer products. In terms of the agreement, Sasol agreed to pricing and divestiture commitments aimed at removing SASOL's incentive and ability to exclude competitors in the fertilizer blending and retailing market.
November 2010	Pioneer Foods	Settlement agreement reached on bread collusion charges. Under the agreement Pioneer committed to pay R250 million as an administrative penalty to National Revenue Fund; pay R250 million to create an *Agro-processing Competitiveness Fund* to be administered by the Industrial Development Corporation (IDC); adjust its pricing of flour and bread (*i.e.*, 600 g and 700 g standard white and brown loaves) over a defined period so as to reduce its gross margin by R160 million when compared with similar period in 2009/2010; cooperate with Competition Commission in ongoing investigations; and stop anti-competitive conduct by implementing a competition compliance program. These commitments exclude the R195.7 million penalty imposed on Pioneer by the Competition Tribunal in February 2010.

(*Continued*)

Table 4:   (*Continued*)

Period	Firms Involved	Action Taken
December 2010	Pioneer Food	Pioneer Foods (Pty) Ltd. informed Competition Commission that it had begun to implement price reductions on bread and flour as per settlement agreement. The price of standard white and brown loaves of bread was reduced by an average of 30 cents. The price of flour was reduced by an average of R350 per ton.
December 2010	Pioneer Hi-Bred International and Pannar Seed	The Commission prohibited the proposed merger between Pioneer Hi-Bred International, a US based multinational seed producer, and the locally based seed company, Pannar Seed. Commission found that merger would substantially prevent or lessen competition in the maize seed market in South Africa.
January 2011	Grain South Africa	Commission rejected application for exemption from Competition Act lodged by Grain South Africa. Commission rejects application on the grounds that the surplus removal scheme would keep domestic prices of maize meal and inputs such as animal feed artificially high; would not be a viable mechanism to promote exports; and did not meet the requirement of the Competition Act as sector requiring economic stability as designated by the Minister of Economic Development.

(*Continued*)

Table 4:   (*Continued*)

Period	Firms Involved	Action Taken
January 2011	Pick n Pay, Shoprite/ Checkers, Woolworths, Spar, Massmart, and Metcash Retailers	Competition Commission concluded its investigation against major supermarkets and wholesalers for alleged contraventions of the Act. Investigation focused on retail of key staple foods, namely, poultry, bread, and maize meal, milk, fats and oils, and canned fish. Investigation revealed that there was insufficient evidence to show contraventions of Competition Act, in particular in the area of abuse of buyer power, category management and/or information exchange.
February 2011	WalMart and Massmart	Competition Commission submitted its recommendation on acquisition transaction between WalMart Stores, Inc. and Massmart Holdings Limited to Tribunal. Commission found that merger did not raise competition concerns. However, public interest concerns, in terms of labor rights and the effect of Wal-Mart's procurement practices on local manufacturers and suppliers, were raised. With respect to these issues, the merging parties assured the Commission that pre-existing union agreements would be honored, South African labor law would be upheld, and the majority of their products would be sourced locally.

(*Continued*)

Table 4: (*Continued*)

Period	Firms Involved	Action Taken
June 2011	Afgri Operations Limited (Afgri), Kaap Agri Bedryf Limited (Kaap Agri), MGK Bedryfmaatskappy (Pty) Limited (MGK) and Suidwes Agriculture (Pty) Limited (Suidwes)	Competition Commission reached a settlement agreement with the Grain Storage Industry, in which it admitted to fixing the daily grain storage tariff for SAFEX and for the physical grain storage market. All the respondents have committed to cooperating with the Commission, to cease and desist from engaging in anti-competitive conduct, and to develop and implement competition compliance programs. Furthermore, each firm paid an administrative penalty as follows: Suidwes, R1,529,726.63; MG R226,800; Kaap Agri, R1,199,075.36; Afgri, R15,600,000.
June 2011	Rand Merchant Bank (RMB) and NWK Limited (NWK)	The Commission reached a settlement with RMB and NWK over allegations of dividing the grain trade market by allocating territories and customers. This follows an agreement entered into by RMB and NWK in 2005 with respect to grain owned by RMB and stored in NWK silos. The settlement agreement amount to RMB — R2, 1 million; and NWK — R520 290.

Source: Competition Commission (2012) (www.compcom.co.za).

In general, the actions taken by the Competition Commission against the grain industry were comprehensive in that all levels of the supply chain came under scrutiny. As a result, rulings aimed at addressing non-competitive behavior in the input, trading, processing and, in some cases, retailing sectors were enacted. With respect to the maize milling industry the investigation was initiated as a result of Premier Foods'[5] disclosure during the bread cartel investigation that the existing cartel covered both the bread and maize milling operations of the accused firms. As a result of further investigation, the Commission found evidence of price fixing by Pioneer Foods, Foodcorp, Godrich Milling, Progress Milling, Pride Milling, Westra Milling, Brenner Mills, Blinkwater Mills, TWK Milling, NTK Milling, Carolina Mills, Kalel Foods, Bothaville Milling, Paramount Mills, Keystone Milling, Premier Foods and Tiger Brands. In particular, these firms agreed on the timing and degree of price increases. The agreements covered both regional and national markets and were mutually reinforcing.

Maize Sector Performance

The determination of a particular market's performance, given the structure and resulting conduct, can be measured by examining pricing, allocative efficiency, production efficiency, equity and/or profits. The analysis in this study considers the effect of the Competition Commission's investigation and subsequent ruling on marketing spreads without controlling for changes in other factors likely to affect marketing margins and prices. Therefore, it is impossible to use the data presented to determine precisely what portion of increased price variability may be attributed to government program and policy changes. These indications rather point to possible inefficiencies and would require further investigation where other factors such as

---

[5] Within the South African grain industry most mills are involved in both maize and wheat milling. As a result, what started as an investigation into the bread-flour sector broadened to include maize milling as it became evident over time that in both operations firms were engaged in non-competitive behavior.

production levels, seasonality, processing and distribution costs are controlled in the empirical analysis. The Law of One Price posits that under perfectly competitive market conditions, all prices within a market will be uniform after the costs of adding place, time, and form utility are taken into consideration. Prices within a decentralized economy guide and regulate production and consumption decisions. Under non-competitive conditions, however, prices fail to be efficient resulting in market distortions and welfare loss. Given the context of non-competitive behavior within the maize market and the subsequent actions taken by the Competition Commission the aim of this section is to analyze the impact on the pricing efficiency dimension of the market performance element of the IO framework. In order to accomplish this objective, pricing trends and variability are examined and the analysis draws from the approach followed by Traub and Jayne (2008). In this case, however, we are interested in distinguishing between the pre- and post-periods of the anti-trust rulings.

Monthly trends in price levels

Retail maize meal prices grew at an increasing rate, relative to maize grain prices over the sample period. Between 2000 and 2012, retail maize meal prices increased, on average, by approximately R0.70 per ton per month while SAFEX prices remained relatively constant with a slight upward trend of about R0.22 per MT per month. These relative growth rates imply an increasing spread between wholesale and retail prices within the industry. Figure 5 depicts the movement of inflation-adjusted monthly average SAFEX and sifted maize meal retail prices between January 2000 and March 2012.

With the initiation of investigations into the flour milling industry in February 2007, there is a sudden increase in maize meal prices up until September 2008. Although one could argue that rising global commodity prices underpin this sudden increase in retail prices, SAFEX prices remained relatively constant during the same period. Within the wheat sector, bread prices rose suddenly and simultaneously and as a result in January 2008 the Competition Commission noted the rise and requested an explanation from the milling industry.

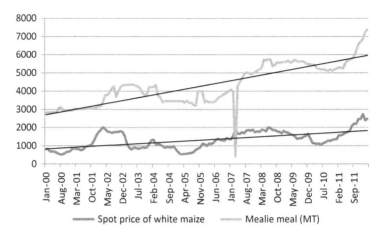

Figure 5. SAFEX and retail sifted maize meal price movements, South Africa: January 2000 to March 2012 (constant 2000 ZAR)

In the case of the maize sector, by 2010, when the Competition Commission began its investigation of the maize milling industry, retail prices for maize meal fell below their average trend line and remained relatively constant, despite the slight upward trend of maize grain prices.

Price variability

In general, government policies can directly or indirectly influence the level and volatility of agricultural prices (Krueger *et al.*, 1988; Lapp and Smith, 1992). In order to measure the level of price volatility facing different market participants within the maize industry, the standard deviation and coefficient of variation for SAFEX and retail prices were calculated for the periods 01/2000–01/2007 (price-fixing era), 02/2007–02/2010 (bread cartel investigation), and 03/2010–03/2012. Table 5 summarizes the unconditional means, standard deviation and coefficient of variations for maize prices during three time periods.

The actions on the part of the Competition Commission to reduce non-competitive behavior within the maize grain supply chain have

Table 5: Measures of maize grain and maize meal price variability in South Africa: 01/2000–03/2012

	Phase 1: Price-fixing Era 01/2000–01/ 2007 ($n = 85$)	Phase 2: Bread Cartel Investigation 02/2007– 02/2010 ($n = 44$)	Phase 3: Maize Cartel Investigation 03/2010– 03/2012 ($n = 25$)
SAFEX, maize grain (R/mt)			
Mean	1050	1694	1691
Standard deviation	392	187	534
Coefficient of variation (%)	37.3	11.1	31.6
Retail price, maize meal (R/mt)			
Mean	3546	5284	5707
Standard deviation	482	482	708
Coefficient of variation (%)	13.6	9.1	12.4

*Producer prices from 2000 onward are estimated as the SAFEX/Randfontein monthly spot price minus the median transport cost from various production points to Randfontein as published by SAFEX at http://www.safex.co.za minus an additional R43/MT representing commissions and storage charges.

resulted in reduction in retail price variability as well as slowing of the growth of the average retail price. The measures of variability for wholesale and retail prices have decreased in absolute terms as we move from Phase 1 to Phase 3 in the sample period. This indicates that the mean of the price spreads has increased to a greater degree than the absolute volatility of the spreads. This reduction in volatility implies decreasing price risk to producers, grain traders and consumers.

More importantly, however, as we move from Phase 1 to Phase 2, there is a slowing in the growth rate of the average retail price of maize meal. Between the price-fixing era and the initiation of the bread cartel investigation, average maize meal prices grew by approximately 39%, which was significantly higher than the 7.7% growth between Phase 2 and Phase 3. This slowing growth implies the increasing potential of consumer purchasing power.

Conclusion

In general, sustained agricultural productivity, growth and poverty reduction requires an enabling policy environment that encourages private sector investments in input, output, and financial markets. In the case of South Africa, following the 1994 free elections, the overall goal of government was to create an open and market-orientated economy while redressing the injustices of the past. Under the Marketing of Agricultural Products Act 47 of 1996 that currently shapes agricultural marketing policy in South Africa direct government involvement in the grain markets was suspended and prices within the industry were determined entirely on negotiation between market actors. Ultimately, the change in the policy environment has had a direct impact on both the structure and conduct of the maize industry within South Africa.

In terms of structure, given the parastatal system of the past, relatively high seller concentration occurs within the storage and processing levels of the maize value chain. As a result both of these sectors came under investigation by the Competition Commission for noncompetitive behavior and in both cases evidence of collusion was found. In the case of the milling, this chapter examined the impact of the Competition Commission's anti-trust ruling on one aspect of the performance dimension of the maize sector, in particular on pricing efficiency. The key findings include:

1. Maize meal prices fell below the long-term trend immediately following the start of the Commission's investigation into the maize milling industry.
2. The growth in the average retail price of maize meal slowed as the industry moved from the price-fixing era and the initiation of the sector investigation.

Although the analysis in this study considers the effect of the Competition Commission's investigation and subsequent ruling on marketing spreads without controlling for changes in other factors that are likely to affect marketing margins and prices, the findings do indicate possible inefficiencies.

South Africa's utilization of an institution, such as the Competition Commission, demonstrates the ability of governments to create an enabling environment that could stimulate private sector investment and minimize market distortions within a staple food market. Results of the empirical analysis indicate a reduction in the level of price volatility and a slowing in the growth of retail maize meal prices as a result of actions taken by the Commission. Such actions level the playing field and ensure a more competitive market structure, which can ultimately lend itself to addressing the government's goal of poverty reduction within the country.

It is important to note that the utilization of an institution such as the Competition Commission, in order to address the policy concerns within staple food markets, is not unique to South Africa. In March 2011 the African Competition Forum (ACF) was launched. The principal objective of the ACF is to

> ... promote the adoption of competition principles in the implementation of national and regional economic policies of African countries, in order to alleviate poverty and enhance inclusive economic growth, development and consumer welfare by fostering competition in markets, and thereby increasing investment, productivity, innovation and entrepreneurship. (Competition Commission, 2012)

Such actions, on the part of regional governments are a positive step in that they provide an institutional framework through which the public sector can ensure inclusive growth and development without distortions in staple food markets.

References

Achterberg R and Hartzenberg T (2002) Trade in distribution services in South Africa. Trade and Industrial Policy Strategies. Annual Forum. Muldersdrift, South Africa.

Bain JS (1968) *Industrial Organization*, 2nd edn. New York: Wiley.

Bertelsman-Scott T and Draper P (eds.) (2004) The TDCA: Impacts, lessons and perspectives for EU-South and Southern African relations. Report on the SAIIA Conference. Johannesburg, South Africa.

Bureau of Food and Agricultural Policy (2011) BFAP *Baseline 2011*. Pretoria: University of Pretoria.

Bureau of Food and Agricultural Policy (2012) BFAP *Baseline 2012*. Pretoria: University of Pretoria.

Competition Commission of South Africa (2012) *Annual Report of 2009/ 2010*. Available at www.compcom.co.za [accessed on February 2010].

Cutts, M and Kirsten JF (2006) Asymmetric price transmission and market concentration: an investigation into four South African agro-food industries. *South African Journal of Economics* 74(2): 323–333.

Department of Agriculture, Forestry and Fishery (DAFF) (2011) *Abstract of Agricultural Statistics, 2011*. Available at http://www.daff.gov.za/docs/statsinfo/Ab2012.pdf [accessed on February 2012].

Draper P (2003) To liberalise or not to liberalise? A review of the South African Government's trade policy. South African Institute of International Affairs, Report No. 1, Johannesburg.

Guiding Investments in Sustainable Agricultural Markets in Africa (GISAMA) (2010). Analysis in support of building agricultural markets in Africa: Report 3. Unpublished.

Hochfeld S (2007) Personal Interview. Managing Director, Hochfeld Grains (Pty) Limited. Johannesburg, South Africa.

International Trade Administration Commission (ITAC) of South Africa (2007) Report No. 235: Review of the Customs Tariff Dispensation on maize, maize flour and downstream products thereof. ITAC, Pretoria.

Jayne TS, Mason NM, Myers RJ, Ferris JN, Mather D, Beaver M, Lenski N, Chapoto A and Boughton D (2010) Patterns and trends in food staples markets in Eastern and Southern Africa: Toward the identification of priority investments and strategies for developing markets and promoting smallholder productivity. Food Security International Development Working Papers 62148. Michigan State University, Department of Agricultural, Food, and Resource Economics: East Lansing, Michigan.

Kirsten J, Edwards L and Vink N (2006) Distortions to agricultural incentives in South Africa. World Bank Agricultural Distortions Research Project Working Paper. Washington, DC: World Bank.

Krueger AO, Schiff M and Valdes A (1988) Agricultural incentives in developing countries: measuring the effects of sectoral and economy wide policies. *The World Bank Economic Review* 2: 255–271.

Lapp JS and Smith VH (1992) Aggregate sources of relative price variability among agricultural commodities. *American Journal of Agricultural Economics* 74: 1–9.

Le Clus K (2004) Personal Interview. Department of Agricultural Economics, University of the Free State, Bloemfontein, South Africa.

Market Decisions (2012) *Market Analysis: Dobsonville, Soweto.* Randburg, South Africa. Available at http://www.marketdecisions.co.za/includes/pdf/Desk%20Research%20Dobsonville.pdf [accessed on February 2012].

McConnelly J (2009) Personal Interview. Managing Director of Ruto Mills. Ruto Mills, Pretoria, South Africa.

National Agricultural Marketing Council (NAMC) (2004) *Final Report of the Food Pricing Monitoring Committee.* Pretoria, South Africa: NAMC.

Ntloedibe M (2001) Republic of South Africa Retail Food Sector Report. GAIN Report. Pretoria South Africa: USDA-FAS.

Organisation for Economic Co-operation and Development (OECD) (2006). African Economic Outlook: 2005–2006. OECD, Paris. Available at www.oecd.org/dev/publications/africanoutlook [accessed on July 2007].

Robert EC, Robert E and van de Brink R (1994) South African agriculture: structure, performance and options for the future. Discussion Paper. Washington, DC: World Bank.

Scherer FM (1980) *Industrial Market Structure and Economic Performance,* 2nd edn. New York: Rand-McNally.

South African Futures Exchange (SAFEX) (2010) Website accessed in January, 2011. Available at http://www.safex.co.za/.

South African Grain Information Services (SAGIS) (2005) *The Strategic Plan for the South Africa Grain Industry.* Available at www.agbiz.co.za/LinkClick.aspx?fileticket=iZ1SUghaXdo%3D&tabid=351.

South African Grain Information Services (SAGIS) (2011) Available at www.sagis.org.za.

Statistic South Africa (2010) *Statistics by Theme: Economy.* Available at http://beta2.statssa.gov.za/?page_id=735&id=1 [accessed on May 2010].

Statistics South Africa (2012) *Census 2001.* Available at http://www.statssa.gov.za/census01/html/.

Stern M and Netshitomboni N (2004) AGOA, Africa and agriculture: South Africa's experience. SAIIA Trade Report No. 3, Johannesburg.

Thirtle C, van Zyl J and Vink N (eds.) (2000) South African Agriculture at the Crossroads: An Empirical Analysis of Efficiency, Technology and Productivity. London: Macmillan.

Traub LN and Jayne TS (2004) The effects of market reform on maize marketing margins in South Africa. MSU International Development Working Paper, No. 83.

Traub LN and Jayne TS (2005) Opportunities to improve household food security through promoting informal maize marketing channels: experience from Eastern Cape Province, South Africa. International Development Working Paper, 85. East Lansing: Michigan State University, Department of Agricultural, Food and Resource Economics.

Traub LN and Jayne TS (2008) The effects of price deregulation on maize marketing margins in South Africa. *Food Policy* 33: 224–236.

Traub LN and Meyer F (2010) Alternative staple food trade and market policy interventions: country-level assessment of South Africa. In Sarris A and Morrison J (eds.), *Food Security in Africa: Market and Trade Policy for Staple Foods in Eastern and Southern Africa*. Massachusetts, USA: FAO and Edgar Elgar Publishing Inc.

Van Dijck G and Otto RJ (1995) Restructuring of agriculture marketing policy in South Africa. *Agrekon* 34(4): 205–210.

Van Rooyen CJ, Ngqangwenit S and Frost D (1997) Some considerations for a South African food policy. *Agrekon* 34(4): 301–308.

Chapter 12

THE QUIET REVOLUTION IN AGRI-FOOD VALUE CHAINS IN ASIA: UNDERSTANDING THE FAST EMERGENCE OF COLD STORAGES IN POOR DISTRICTS IN INDIA

Bart Minten,* Thomas Reardon,[†] K.M. Singh[‡] and Rajib Sutradhar[§]

*IFPRI, Addis Ababa, Ethiopia
[†]MSU, East Lansing, USA
[‡]ICAR, Patna, India
[§]JNU, New Delhi, India

In disadvantaged districts of Bihar, one of the poorest states in India and an area where smallholders dominate, we find that there have been dramatic increases and rapid up-scaling of modern cold storages, triggered by market reform, investment subsidies, and better overall public service provision and governance. Almost all potato farmers, small and large, participate in these cold storages. The availability of cold storages has seemingly led to improved efficiency in value chains because of lower wastages and some cold storages have become heavily involved in input, output, and especially credit markets. This emergence of cold storages thus leads to important changes in traditional potato value chains, with significant implications for smallholders.

Introduction

Technology changes and innovations at the farm level have been the driver for large productivity increases and real price decreases in agriculture. Most documented innovations have been linked to production technologies such as irrigation and improved seeds (*e.g.*, Evenson

313

and Gollin, 2003; Spielman and Pandy-Lorch, 2009). While innovations midstream and downstream in the value chain might also have significant impacts on agricultural performance, and might potentially benefit producers and consumers alike (Gardner, 1975), relatively little research has been done in this area.

However, the subject is receiving more attention in recent literature, *e.g.*, Swinnen (2007), Dries *et al.* (2009), Reardon *et al.* (2009). Most of the debate on changes of value chains in the literature has focused on the rise in the consumption of high-value crops (*e.g.*, Delgado *et al.*, 2008; Gulati *et al.*, 2007) but has not looked at the impact midstream or downstream. Others have shown the rapid emergence of modern retail outlets (*e.g.*, Reardon *et al.*, 2009; Reardon *et al.*, 2012) and their impact but have not looked at traditional value chains. Important changes are, however, occurring in traditional agricultural value chains in several developing countries (Reardon *et al.*, 2012; World Bank, 2007b). These changes are noted upstream at the farm level, midstream with traders and processors, and downstream in retail markets (Reardon and Timmer, 2007). Given that the changes are grassroots in nature, Reardon *et al.* (2012) call this a "quiet" revolution.

We present in this chapter the case of innovations and investments in post-harvest management and show how it is associated with important changes in traditional agricultural value chains. More in particular, we document in this study the case of the rapid emergence and up-scaling of cold storages in Bihar, one of the poorest states in India. The number of cold storages increased in Bihar overall by 67% in the last decade. In the two disadvantaged — as defined by India's Planning Commission — districts that were studied, an area characterized by a large number of smallholders, the number of cold storages in the last decade doubled in one district and tripled in the other. This rapid up-scaling of cold storages led to an even faster total capacity expansion, *i.e.*, a triple and five-fold increase over the same period. These cold storages are almost exclusively used for the storage of potato, the most important vegetable (in volume) in India and, more generally, in Asia.

The emergence of such large modern players mid-stream raises important questions and implications, which have not been studied to date. We address two questions in particular in this chapter. First, we study the factors that have contributed to the rise of the cold storages. Second, we look at the role of the cold storages in the value chain and how it contributes to increased efficiency of the marketing system. To document the role that cold storages play, we rely on different sources of information. First, we conducted key informant interviews with several stakeholders in the value chain. Then, we implemented a detailed structured questionnaire with the different agents in the value chain including cold storage owners, producers, local collectors, wholesalers, and retailers.

We find that the spread of the cold storages in these districts has seemingly been driven by a multitude of factors related to policy reform, the improved provision of public goods (road infrastructure and governance), by the availability and spread of new technologies within the cold storage sector, as well as by subsidies by the government. The increasing spread of these cold storages has led to a significant larger part of potato production going through it, *i.e.*, an increase from 39% in 1999 to 62% in 2009. Cold storages are also associated with improved efficiency of the marketing system because of lower wastages in the value chain. We further find that while almost all farmers use cold storages, relatively larger farmers participate more toward storage for sale as to benefit from higher prices in the off-season and they are then able to capture a higher share of the final consumer price. Smaller farmers benefit relatively more from the cheaper and more reliable storage of seed potatoes and possibly through the higher prices during the harvest period (because more potatoes are stored, *e.g.*, Fuglie, 1995).

The structure of the chapter is as follows. In the next section, we describe the area studied and the data collection methodology. The section that follows illustrates the expansion of cold storages over time. In the section on the role of cold storages, we look at cold storages in terms of not only storage behavior but also the other services delivered. In the penultimate section, we document storage behavior of farmers, the cost of storage in the value chain, and wastages. We finish with a section on conclusions and implications.

Case Study Area, Data and Methodology

Background

Bihar, the state where the study was done, is considered one of the lagging states in India. Its per capita income, at about US$160, is one of the lowest in India and its economic growth in the last decades has not kept pace with the rest of India (World Bank, 2005). Its performance seems to have improved in recent years, however, and between 2005 and 2010 Bihar has registered one of the highest economic growth rates among Indian states. Given its bad economic performance over a long period, poverty levels in Bihar are high and about 37 million of its 90 million people are estimated to be poor (World Bank, 2007a).

Potato is an important crop in India. India is ranked third in production in the world after China and Russia. The area under potato cultivation is estimated to be the largest among vegetable crops accounting for 23% of all area planted under vegetables (Kumar, 2009). Potato consumption is widespread in India and it is estimated that 92% of the people eat it (Das Gupta *et al.*, 2010). Faostat estimated annual consumption at 18 kg per person in 2007. Das Gupta *et al.* (2010) report that potato processing is limited: the share of fresh potatoes in potato consumption is about 95% and the importance of processed potatoes (for chips, French fries, *etc.*) is still minor (5%).

A major challenge in India is potato storage as potato production, which takes generally place in the cold months of October to March, is followed by hot summer months, which makes refrigeration necessary for storage.[1] The number of cold storage facilities has grown: it is estimated that there were about 3,400 cold storage facilities in the beginning of the 2000s in India (CIP, 2006) and they had increased

---

[1] Also important is that potato is mainly grown in Indo-gangetic plains in the north so that there are no multi-season flows from different zones.

to 5,386 units in 2008, which could store over 18 million tons of crops (www.Indiastat.com).[2] Most of the cold storages in India are used for potatoes. CIP (2006) estimates that approximately three-fifths of potatoes in cold storages are table potatoes, intended for consumption, while the other two-fifths are used for seed. Using average storage charges from our survey and 80% of cold storage used by potatoes, it is estimated that traders and farmers spend about US$0.4 billion per year on potato storage, indicating the large size of this business.

Some characteristics of Bihar's potato economy differ from India's overall. Red potatoes are preferred and widely consumed in Bihar and a price premium is paid for them. In contrast, nationally it is estimated that 60% and 40% of the potato production are white- and red-skinned potatoes, respectively. Currently no formal potato processing sector is present in Bihar. Several varieties are being cultivated in Bihar and their adoption and dis-adoption seem related to different factors.[3]

---

[2] Cold storage is usually referred to as a refrigerated warehouse space as to preserve food products. Storage conditions and length of time in storage influence the quality of the products and their consequent susceptibility to handling. By lowering the temperature during storage of food products, they can be stored for longer periods and can then be marketed during periods of the year when no production is possible. Cold storage of table and seed potatoes is usually done at a temperature of 2–4°C. This temperature, however, induces the conversion of starch to sugar, leading to the sweetening of potatoes that are less desired in the market place. Customers are thus usually willing to pay a premium for 'fresh' potatoes, potatoes that have not gone through cold storage.

[3] First, the lack of resistance against the *late blight* disease is leading to the increasing disadoption of the *Kufri Senduri* variety. Second, varieties that grow for shorter periods (90 days instead of 120 days) can be better intercropped with maize, which matures after the potato crop, after 6 months on average, and thus the land can be more intensively used. Shorter-duration varieties can also be sold earlier on the market and might thus fetch a premium because of that. On the other hand, shorter-duration varieties contain less dry matter, making it more prone to rotting. Third, there is a trade-off between yields and dry matter for the choice of varieties. Lower yield varieties are often associated with higher dry matter, making it better suited for storage. The higher the dry matter, the lower the likelihood of rotting becomes (personal communication with Dr. R. P. Rai, Central Potato Research Station).

Data collection

Surveys were conducted in the two disadvantaged[4] districts of Vaishali and Samastipur, where potato production, as measured by total quantities produced, is significant. Several surveys were developed at the end of 2009 to understand the role of cold storages, storage behavior of farmers, and the role of storage in potato marketing in Bihar. They included surveys with potato producers and a village survey, wholesale and retail trader surveys, and a cold storage survey.

The trader survey and cold storage surveys were set up as follows. First, two village trader/collectors were randomly selected from those that were active in the selected villages and were then interviewed. Second, 30 traders were interviewed from the local wholesale market in the district. Third, 20 urban wholesale traders and 164 retailers in Patna were randomly selected and interviewed.[5] To implement the cold storage survey, a list of all the cold storages in Samastipur and Vaishali districts was obtained from the Horticulture Department (all cold storages have to be registered). Twenty-seven of these were randomly selected and detailed surveys were conducted with them. For all cold storages that were not visited for a detailed survey, the date of establishment was collected through key informant interviews. We also collected data on cold storages that had ceased operations. This information allowed us to analyze their net growth over time.

The village-level household survey was set up as follows. For potato farming households, the most important potato producing *tehsil* (commune) — in terms of quantities produced — in Vaishali and Samastipur were selected. Given that Samastipur is a bigger potato producing area than Vaishali, more villages were selected in the former.[6] In each selected village, a village questionnaire was

---

[4] Based on several indicators (agricultural productivity per worker, agricultural wage rates, and share of the scheduled caste/tribe in total population), 150 districts were assigned 'disadvantaged district' status by the Planning Commission of India.

[5] Ten retailers were interviewed additionally on pricing specifically in May 2009.

[6] The sample in Samastipur was done as follows. In a *tehsil*, Gram Panchyats (GPs) were ranked from big to medium to low producing GPs (three terciles). Three GPs were randomly selected from the big producing GPs, one from the medium producing GP, and one from the low producing GPs. In each selected GP, two villages were

implemented. In each selected village, a census of households was conducted to enumerate the potato producers. Using the census questionnaire, a list of all the potato producing households in the village was made. Each household was asked questions on its total land cultivation, and potato cultivation in particular, and if it was a seller of potato. Eighteen potato producing households in 14 villages were then randomly selected, half from the largest and half from the smallest farm group so as to reflect their importance in the potato value chain. In all, 254 potato farm households were thus interviewed.

Descriptive statistics

We first present some descriptive statistics on the different surveys implemented (Tables 1 and 2). The potato farmers in the survey are on average 55 years old (Table 1). They have a household of about 7.4 family members and 98% of the heads of households are reported to be male. About 10% of the potato farming households are illiterate, significantly lower than the average at state level as 53% of the population was estimated to be illiterate in the national census of 2001. The value of the land of these farmers — their most important asset — is estimated at Rs 2.6 million, or US$59,000. The value of land assets owned by larger farmers is almost three times as high for the larger farmers as for the smaller ones.

Potato farmers selected in these two districts are in general small, as they only cultivated 2.23 acres on average, of which on average 0.95 acres are allocated to potatoes. An average potato farmer cultivates 3.2 potato plots. Farmers own 90% of the cultivated potato land and 10% of the land is leased. Farmers sold an average of 5.3 tons of potatoes in the year prior to the survey. About two-thirds of the

---

selected at random. For the GP of the lowest producing tercile, only one village was selected. In Vaishali, the following strategy was used. GPs were ranked from big to medium to low producing GPs (three terciles). One GP was randomly selected from the big producing GPs, one from the medium producing GPs, and one from the low producing GPs. In each selected GP, two villages were selected at random. For the GP of the lowest producing tercile, only one village was selected.

Table 1: Characteristics of potato farmers

| | Unit | Statistics | |
		Mean	Median
Number of observations	Number	256	
Background information household			
Age head of household	Years	53	55
Household size	Number	7.4	7.0
Gender of head of households	% Male	98	
Illiterate heads of household	%	10	
Land and assets			
Land owned and cultivated	Acres	2.02	1.29
Land owned but cultivated by another household	Acres	0.10	0.00
Rented in land or received for free	Acres	0.21	0.00
Number of plots cultivated	Number	9.5	7.00
Value of land owned	Rs 1,000	2,660	1,592
Value of livestock assets	Rs 1,000	40	21
Value of farm assets	Rs 1,000	47	13
Potato activities			
Potato land:			
Land owned and cultivated with potato	Acres	0.85	0.55
Rented in land or received for free cultivated with potato	Acres	0.10	0.00
Total potato land cultivated	Acres	0.95	0.55
Number of potato plots cultivated	Number	3.2	3.0
Was growing potatoes 10 years ago	%	87.3	
Use of potato production:			
— own consumption/seed use	%	30	
— wasted	%	5	
— sales	%	65	
— total	%	100	
Total potato sales in 2009	Ton	5.3	1.7

Table 2: Descriptive statistics agents value chain surveys

	Unit	Mean	Median
Cold storage:			
Number of observations	Number	27	
Capacity of cold storage	Tons	6,288	6,000
Value of cold storage	US$1,000	1,140	1,064
Wholesalers:			
Number of observations	Number	65	
Quantities procured daily	kgs/day	635	170
Value of assets	US$1,000	1.25	0.24
Working capital	US$1,000	3.39	1.94
Traditional retailers:			
Number of observations	Number	164	
Quantities procured daily	kgs/day	130	
Value of assets	Rs 1,000	8.6	1.3
Value of assets	US$1,000	0.19	0.03
Working capital	Rs 1,000	19.3	10.0
Working capital	US$1,000	0.43	0.22

potatoes produced are sold as a cash crop, while 30% is kept as seed and for own consumption. Households estimate that 5% of the production is wasted before, during, or after storage.

Table 2 shows information about the other value chain agents who were interviewed. In total, 27 cold storage owners, 65 wholesalers, and 164 retailers were interviewed. The results show the significantly larger capital that cold storages have at their disposal. The value of a cold storage in the surveyed region amounts to about US$1 million. This compares to average values of assets (and working capital) of US$1,250 (US$3,390) for wholesalers and US$190 (US$430) for retailers. Of all agents in the value chain, retailers have the least capital at their disposal for their business. The turnover of wholesalers is estimated to be almost five times as much as that of retailers, *i.e.*, 635 kg and 130 kg per day, respectively.

Table 3:   Changes in the potato economy, as reported by village focus groups

		% of Answers	
		1999	2009
% of households growing potatoes	Mean	71	83
	Median	70	90
Of the potato grown in the village,			
— % white potato	Mean	49	62
	Median	35	60
— % red potato	Mean	55	38
	Median	70	40
Number of village traders that buy up potato in the village itself	Mean	10	14
	Median	2	6
% of potatoes produced in village that is stored in cold storage	Mean	39	62
	Median	27	67

Data from the village surveys show how the value chain of potatoes has changed in the last 10 years. Village leaders were asked to evaluate different indicators related to potato production and marketing (Table 3). The number of households that are involved in potato production has increased significantly over the last year. The percentage of producers increased from 71% 10 years ago to 83% in 2009. We also see a switch from red potato (55% and 38% of the total production 10 years ago and now, respectively) to white potato. The number of village traders also increased significantly over that period. While the median number of village traders was 2 in 1999, it increased to more than 5 in 2009. Finally and most importantly, the estimated percentage of potato production going through cold storages increased from 39% in 1999 to 62% in 2009, illustrating their rapidly increasing importance in these districts. In the next section, we look in more detail at this rapid change at the district level and at the factors that triggered their rise.

The Emergence of Cold Storages

Building on a list of cold storages distributed by the National Horticultural Board, we evaluated through key informant interviews, as well as formal surveys, the evolution in number and capacity of cold storages. It is estimated that the number of cold storages in Bihar overall increased between 2000 and 2009 from 195 to 320, an increase of 64%.[7] Figure 1 shows the expansion of such cold storages in the two districts in particular. It shows that there were 20 cold storages in each of the districts at the time of the survey. The graph shows how the growth of cold storages has mostly happened in the last decade, or even more recently. The district of Samastipur had only 10 cold storages in 2005 but the number has doubled since then. Before 1998, there were only four cold storages in the district as a whole. The growth in Vaishali was much smoother as cold storages 'only' doubled in the last decade.

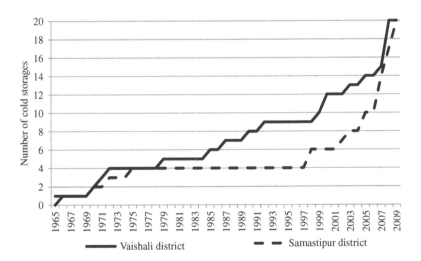

Figure 1.   Expansion in number of cold storages in two disadvantaged districts in Bihar, 1965–2009

Source: Authors' calculations.

---

[7] Indiastat and personal communication, Bihar Horticultural Department.

    While the number of cold storages increased dramatically, the
graph does not take into consideration the increase in expansion of
existing cold storages. As we implemented a survey with the cold storages and questions were asked on their capacity expansion over time,
this allows us to calculate complete capacity expansion in these two
districts. The average capacity per cold storage was between 1,000
tons and 2,000 tons in the beginning of the 1970s but at the time of
the survey, this figure was as high as 5,142 tons in the district of
Vaishali and 8,350 tons in the district of Samastipur. Combining the
growth of capacity per cold storage with the total number of cold
storages gives the total cold storage capacity expansion in the two
districts. As expected, the results (Figure 2) show an even more dramatic increase than in the previous graph. In the last decade, total
cold storage capacity expanded almost three-fold in the case of
Vaishali, while it expanded more than five times in the case of
Samastipur. Total cold storage capacity in 2009 was just over 100,000
tons in Vaishali and about 170,000 tons in Samastipur. If all the
capacity of the cold storages were used, this would result in an

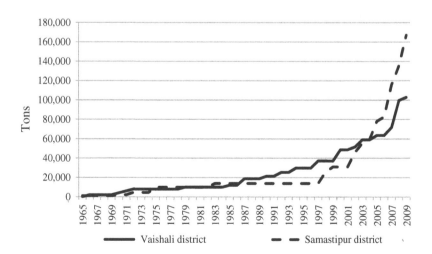

Figure 2.   Capacity expansion of cold storages in two disadvantaged districts in
Bihar, 1965–2009

Source: Authors' calculations.

approximate yearly business or revenue of just below US$10 million in the two districts combined.[8]

Based on in-depth discussions with cold storage owners, several factors were identified that contributed to the boom of cold storages in these two disadvantaged districts. The triggers relate to the provision of public goods by the state government, policy reform, subsidies for cold storage investments by national and state governments, and the availability and spread of new technologies.

The first trigger was a series of improvements in Bihar in the last decade in public good provision and in policy reform that created a better business environment. Three factors were crucial. First, deregulation of the sector seems to have given an important impetus. Key informants indicated that there were but few cold storages in the two districts in the 1960s through 1980s, hardly sufficient to meet demand, which often led to a scramble among farmers for space in the cold storages.[9] During the regulatory period, cold storages were supposed to be used only for seed potatoes. The district horticulture department assigned each cold storage a certain number of blocks determined by the capacity of the cold storage. Getting quota in the cold storage was an onerous task for a farmer in those days as he had to submit his land documents to the block officer who would verify his area of potato cultivation and then assign a certain quota, based on the seed requirement of the farmer.[10]

---

[8] The average cost in these two districts of US$33.2 per ton, *i.e.*, Rs 75 per bag of 50 kg, would amount to US$8.9 million of storage costs.

[9] Though Bihar was not regulated by the Cold Storage Order 1964 promulgated by the Ministry of Agriculture under Section 3 of the Essential Commodities Act (1955), the state had its own regulation with which it has persisted even after the central government repealed the Cold Storage Order in 1997.

[10] Before the deregulation period, Bihar had a separate Cold Storage Order, which was not governed by Central Cold Storage Order. However, one of the requirements to benefit from the national subsidy scheme provided by the NHB was to abolish the state Cold Storage Order. The state issued a new Cold Storage Act in the year 2003, but it had several flawed regulations including the fixing of cold storage fees by state government. The government of Nitish Kumar removed that clause from the act in the year 2007 and left it to the cold storage association of each district to set the storage fees before the beginning of each harvesting season.

Second, Bihar has suffered from the lack of public infrastructure provision and has ranked poorly compared with the rest of India on this item. The government that came to power at the end of 2005 in Bihar, however, has made — and is further planning — significant investments in road infrastructure, improving the marketing of agricultural products from the more remote and disadvantaged districts. Making improved road infrastructure one of its key priorities, the state government planned to spend more than US$3 billion on road construction in three years (Government of Bihar, 2006). It has been estimated that between 2005 and 2009, 6,800 km of roads and 1,600 bridges have been constructed (Kumar, 2010).

Third, Bihar has been known for a lack of law and order in the state, discouraging businesses from locating in Bihar, especially in the rural areas (World Bank, 2005). This seemed to have changed in recent years. For example, the number of reported kidnappings for ransom dropped to 317 for the period 2006 to 2009, a significant decrease from the 1,393 cases reported in the previous four years (Kumar, 2010).

The second trigger was the doling out of subsidies by the Indian government in an effort to stimulate innovation in the horticultural sector. In its 1999–2000 budget, the central government proposed a subsidy scheme for the construction of cold storages. It is estimated that between 1999/2000 and January 2005 the NHB provided financial support amounting to Rs 3.1 billion for the establishment of 1,242 cold storages in the country, covering 23 states (Patnaik, 2005). This expanded cold storage capacity by 4.9 million mt nationally. Uttar Pradesh accounted for the largest share in terms of additional capacity created (2.2 million mt), number of facilities (464 cold storages), and subsidies (Rs 1.4 billion). Maharashtra (216,000 mt) came second and Bihar (225,000 mt) third in additional capacity created. The cold storages in Bihar started receiving the subsidies late compared with the rest of the country, due to the reluctance of the state government to change its Cold Storage Order. On top of the subsidies from the central government, the new state government gave additional incentives that seemingly stimulated the rapid diffusion of cold storages. In addition to the 25% subsidy given by the

NHB, the state government reportedly gave another 15% subsidy, including 10% by the State Industrial Promotion Board.

The third trigger was the availability and spread of new technologies. First, the introduction of high speed compressors in the cold storage operations around 2000 meant that less time was required to bring down the temperature and that electricity consumption was significantly reduced, which, according to some of the interviewed owners, led to a reduction of operational costs of about 20–30%. Second, the research and extension system made investments to improve the spread of potato varieties that were apt for storage since the red potato commonly grown and preferred in Bihar was more difficult to store for longer periods than most varieties of white potato.

Role of Cold Storages

Storage behavior

Cold storage owners were questioned about the type of people that stored potatoes in cold storage (Table 4). About 2,245 people store potatoes in the average cold storage. Interestingly, 91% of the users of cold storages are farmers. The average cold storage contained in the last year almost 100,000 50 kg bags. Two-thirds of the stored bags belonged to farmers. Of the bags 31% belonged to traders, indicating that the average quantity stored by traders is significantly higher than that stored by farmers: the average farmer stores 33 bags compared with 144 bags on average per trader. The number of bags stored by the cold storage owner himself is estimated to be significantly less important in total (0.3% of all the bags stored).[11]

Storage behavior is changing quickly over time. First, we see an important process of up-scaling of these cold storages (Table 4). While a cold storage was holding 4,200 tons at startup on average in 1996, this figure had increased to 6,300 tons at the time of

---

[11] The trader would still be considered a big trader as he sells double the quantity of an average trader.

Table 4: Characteristics of cold storages

	Mean	Median
Number of observations	27	
Overall information		
Year of start-up	1996	1998
Storage capacity (in tons)	6,288	6,000
Storage capacity (in tons) at start-up	4,272	3,500
Storage capacity at start-up (in tons), if started up before 2000	3,672	3,000
Storage capacity at start-up (in tons), if started up after 2000	5,145	6,000
Current value of the cold storage		
— millions of Rs	54	50
— millions of $	1.1	1.1
People that store in cold storage		
Number of farmers	2,034	1,600
Number of traders	211	50
Total number of people	2,245	1,800
Quantity of potatoes stored		
Number of bags stored by farmers	66,308	54,000
Number of bags stored by traders	30,368	19,000
Number of bags stored by cold storage owner	326	0
Total number of bags stored	97,003	93,000

the survey. If a cold storage was started up before 2000, its storage capacity was on average only 3,600 tons. If started after 2000, capacity was as high as 5,100 tons. Second, the type of potatoes stored has changed. While more than two-thirds of all potato storage 10 years ago was seed potatoes, this share has now been halved (Table 5). The other half of potatoes now stored is table varieties, indicating the increasing commercialization of potato in these districts. This increase seems to lead to an increasing importance of the role of traders and cold storage owners over time in potato storage, *e.g.*, while traders

Table 5:   Evolution in storage behavior over the last decade

	Simple Average % of Answers		Weighed Average* % of Answers	
	1999	2009	1999	2009
Use of potato				
Seed potatoes (%)	67	52	70	53
Table varieties for sale on market (%)	33	47	30	46
Processing varieties (%)	0	0	0	0
Ownership of potatoes in cold storage				
Owned by farmers (%)	89	73	90	74
Owned by traders (%)	9	19	8	16
Owned by cold storage owners (%)	2	9	2	11

*Weighed by size of the cold storage.

owned 8% of all stored potatoes in 1999, this share had increased to 16% in 2009.

Farmers' Participation in Cold Storages

Detailed information was asked about farmers' storage behavior in the year prior to the survey (Table 6). About 92% of the farmers reported that they had stored potatoes in 2009. Most of those who did not store potatoes reported that they could not store because they needed money urgently after the harvest. Those who did store reported to have done so because they expected the price of potatoes to rise (35%) or because they were storing for seed potatoes (62%). All the farmers who stored potatoes in 2009 used cold storages to do so and it thus seems that traditional storage schemes had disappeared over time.

To understand the role of cold storages for farmers, questions were asked on the importance of reasons for choosing a particular cold storage. Farmers' distance to cold storage and the quality of cold storage were the most important reasons given. Access to input markets and financial services were judged to be less important. At the bottom

Table 6:   Storage by potato farmers

	Unit	Small	Large	Total
Storage behavior				
If no storage, why not?				
— I need the money urgently after harvest	%	88	82	87
— I expected the price of potatoes to fall	%	9	9	9
— Storing is costly	%	2	9	4
— Total	%	100	100	100
If storage, why?				
— I need the money later in the year	%	3	3	3
— I expect the price of potatoes to rise	%	31	46	35
— I store for seed potatoes	%	66	51	62
— Total		100	100	100
% of farmers that stored and that used cold storages in 2009	%	99	100	99
If use of cold storage				
"Very important" or "A bit important" reason for choosing a cold storage				
— Low cost storage	%	48	38	44
— Quality of storage	%	92	90	91
— Distance to cold storage	%	92	90	91
— Access to quality seeds	%	44	43	43
— Access to extension advice	%	26	14	22
— Access to chemicals	%	20	18	19
— Access to input advances before storage	%	15	10	14
— Credit given at time of storage	%	24	21	23
— Finding a buyer	%	27	22	26
Cold storage transactions in 2009				
Quantity stored	Bags	40	251	111
Month of deposit (% of farmers that deposited in March)	%	71	82	75

(Continued)

Table 6: (*Continued*)

	Unit	Small	Large	Total
Received input advances from cold storage	%	1	4	2
Bought potato seeds through the cold storage	%	1	3	2
Cold storage extended loan	%	1	4	2
Month taken out (% of farmers that took bags out in October)	%	58	66	60
Potatoes that were wasted during storage	%	5.7	5.6	5.6
Major use of potatoes				
— Own seeds	%	36	25	32
— Own consumption	%	0	0	0
— Sales	%	6	8	7
— Combination	%	58	67	61
Amount paid for storage	Rs/bag	77	78	77
Cold storage put farmer in touch with buyer	%	4	8	5

of Table 6, statistics are presented on storage transactions in the year 2009. The average farmer stored 111 bags in cold storage. This would mostly be done in the month of March while the majority of the stored crop would be taken out in the month of October. Only a small minority of farmers reported that they received inputs from the cold storage or that the cold storage owner put them in contact with a buyer. Most of the farmers stored for the combined reason of having access to seeds for the next harvest and sales in the off-season.

We further discuss the different timings of sales and their relationship with prices obtained. Figure 3 shows cumulative density functions for sales prices in the harvest period and after cold storage. They show that the prices after cold storage dominate the harvest period prices by a significant margin over the whole domain. Of the reported prices at the harvest period 96% were below Rs 7/kg, while 99% of the sales prices after cold storage were above that level in the off-season period. This shows the extent to which farmers were able to

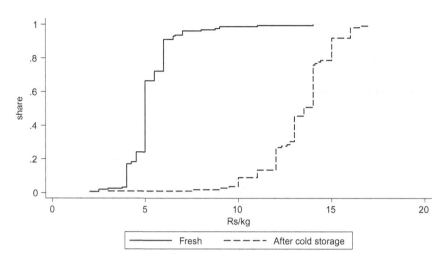

Figure 3.   Cumulative density functions of farmers' potato price

postpone sales benefited from doing so, and that the benefit of post-
poning sales far outweighs the costs (the monetary cost of cold storage is about Rs 1.5/kg).

   To illustrate how farmers spread their sales over time and who
benefits from these higher prices in the off-season, we present a graph
on the importance of sales for small and large farmers over the course
of the year, simply aggregating sales over the (un-weighted) sample
(Figure 4). About 55% of the potatoes are sold fresh (defined as during the period from February until June) and 45% of the sold potatoes
have gone through cold storage (from July until November). Small
and large farmers sell significant portions of their potatoes fresh as
well as after cold storage. The importance of off-season sales is, however, relatively bigger for larger farmers. While the quantities sold in
fresh and cold period are the same for large households, small farmers
sell only half the quantity of the fresh period in the off-season.

Cost of storage in the value chain

Questions were asked on the price evolution over the last year at different points in the value chain (producers, cold storage owners,

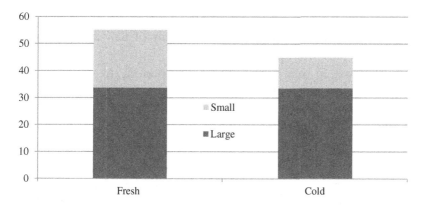

Figure 4.   Importance of timing of sales for small and large farmers (100% = total sales over the year)

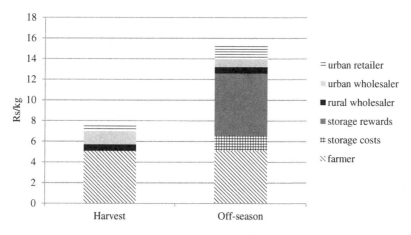

Figure 5.   Potato retail price composition

wholesalers in urban and rural areas, and urban retailers in Patna). This information allows us to decompose the final retail price and to evaluate the size of the margins in the value chain. Figure 5 shows the (red) potato price evolution in the 12 months prior to the survey at each level of the value chain as calculated from recall questions from a representative number of interviews at each level. The date show that prices tend to rise after the harvest period due to storage costs and the opportunity costs of money. In the 2008–2009 season, potato retail prices in Patna rose from a low of Rs 7.5/kg in March to a high of Rs 15.3/kg in September.

It is estimated that during the harvest period, the producer share of the final consumer price in Patna was 68%. The cost of marketing potatoes from producer to urban consumer was about Rs 2.4/kg during that period. The share of the final consumer price of producers willing and able to store potatoes for sale increased to 82% by September, when most of the potatoes held in cold storages are taken out. This share is significantly higher than those conventionally found in horticultural value chains in India. This fact may reflect the better options potato producers have than producers of more perishable crops, as the former are not obliged to sell immediately.

The results further show that storage accounts for only a minor share of costs in the potato value chain. The costs accounted for less than 10% of the final retail price that consumers in Patna paid for potatoes in the off-season. A big share in the final retail price is explained by the rewards from storage, which account for 40% of the final retail price. It is important to note, however, that 2009 was an exceptional year in that potato prices were significantly higher than normal and thus the rewards are significantly inflated compared with regular years.[12]

Wastage in the value chain

Conventional wisdom is that the traditional supply chain for staples in India is necessarily mired in high rates of wastage. For example, Mattoo *et al.* (2007) find that the average losses in horticulture overall and potato value chains are as high as 12% and 11%, respectively. They also mention, "According to one study, India wastes more fruits and vegetables than those consumed in the UK" (Mattoo *et al.*, 2007, p. 43). Others put wastage of horticulture crops between 20% and

---

[12] In a period of low prices, the high producer share in the final retail price observed in the survey period would also decline and the relative share of marketing costs would obviously increase.

40% (CII/McKinsey, 1997; Mittal, 2007). In Bihar, the World Bank (2007a) estimates the wastage in the potato value chain at 24%.

Several questions were included on wastage. First, farmers were asked about the responsibility for losses that might occur during storage. The majority of farmers reported that they alone were responsible, even when losses during storage exceeded 10%. In the latter case, however, 31% of farmers believe that the owner of the cold storage would somehow compensate them. In some cases the cold storage may thus provide an insurance scheme that puts a floor under the losses that some farmers would have to bear.

Second, to get at the level of total wastage in potato value chains, we asked the different agents how much product was wasted in storage, during the process of obtaining and selling potatoes, and during their last transaction when potatoes may have to be transported. This gives us a reasonable approximation of the total waste in the value chain. We find that the total quantities of potatoes wasted, and not used for consumption, are equal to 8.0% in the harvest period and 9.3% in the off-season of all the quantities that enter the value chain (Table 7). This performance may even be better than that in developed countries, where quality and cosmetic criteria are more severe (Kader, 2005; Parfitt *et al.*, 2010). While some have argued that the cuts in electricity in Bihar lead to major losses for potato cold storage, all cold storages in our surveys have diesel generators that keep the storages cool at times of electricity cuts, at admittedly higher costs. Because of the availability of cold storages, wastage levels seem to have come down, as these wastage numbers are significantly lower than those in previous estimates (World Bank, 2007a).[13]

---

[13] Transport costs of about Rs 100/ton from producer to wholesale market in Patna are of minor importance in the final retail price and account for only about 1% of the final retail price. While the relatively low cost of transport is known to some, the problem that is argued to exist is that the quality of trucks and services is poor and slow, leading to high wastages (Mattoo *et al.*, 2007). The relatively low importance of wastage and transport costs we found may be due to the development of better infrastructure (cold storage and road infrastructure), but may also reflect lack of evidence in other studies of the actual situation on the ground given lack of primary data.

Table 7:   Wastages in the potato value chain

	Unit	Harvest	Off-season
Wastages during marketing and storage			
Producer before storage*	%	2.4	2.4
Cold storage**	%	0.0	1.3
Producer after storage*	%	2.1	2.1
Rural wholesaler***,#	%	0.7	0.7
Urban wholesaler***	%	0.4	0.4
Urban retailer***	%	2.4	2.4
Total wastage post-harvest	%	8.0	9.3
If potatoes damaged, who bears losses? If losses less than 10%?			
— Myself	%		97
— The owner of the cold storage	%		2
— Joint responsibility	%		1
If potatoes damaged, who bears losses? If losses more than 10%?			
— Myself	%		68
— The owner of the cold storage	%		29
— Joint responsibility	%		3

*wastage reported during marketing in last transaction; **from farmer surveys; cold storage only; ***based on last transaction information; #average of off-market and on-market rural wholesaler

Conclusions and Policy Implications

We present here the case of innovations and investments in post-harvest management and show how it is associated with important changes in traditional value chains. More in particular, we document in this study the rapid emergence of cold storages in poor disadvantaged districts in Bihar, an area characterized by a large number of smallholders. In the two disadvantaged districts studied, the number of cold storages in the last decade doubled in one district and tripled in the other one and rapid up-scaling of cold storages led to an even faster total capacity expansion, *i.e.*, a triple and five-fold increase over the same period.

The spread of cold storages in these districts has seemingly been driven by the improved provision of public goods (road infrastructure and better governance), by policy reform, by the availability and diffusion of new technologies, as well as by government subsidies. The increasing spread of cold storages is associated with lower wastages and changes in market factors. We thus show that market innovations, even in poor settings, can be important drivers for better agricultural performance.

The analysis illustrates how improvements in post-harvest management technologies can have large impacts on value chains. However, high capacity use during a year when potato production was bad, relatively high prices charged for storage, and the high profitability of investment in cold storage all point to the need for further investment in this area in Bihar so as to ensure a more competitive environment that would further drive down prices. While government subsidies have helped stimulate the setting up of cold storages in Bihar, they have not (yet) led to the lower storage costs one would expect.

Finally, the results of our study point to several important policy implications. First, the study has shown the importance of appropriate policies to stimulate the takeoff of agricultural businesses in Bihar. These policies should focus foremost on the provision of public goods such as reliable electricity, road infrastructure, and good governance. Given the still existing large deficiencies, Bihar should make further investments in this area so as to allow private business to further flourish and to allow farmers in disadvantaged districts to become better integrated in the market economy. Second, policymakers should further stimulate increased investments in the cold storage sector, but not necessarily through subsidies. More competition in the cold storage sector is desirable so as to drive down the cost of storage. The further spread of cold storages as intermediaries in the potato value chains might also open some important opportunities toward upgrading the potato value chains as cold storages can serve as focal points for the distribution of better seed varieties, extension advice, marketing advice, *etc.* This development could especially benefit smaller farmers who, because of liquidity constraints, are less willing to sell after storage and benefit from the higher off-season prices.

Acknowledgments

We acknowledge funding of the project by IFAD and by the NAIP-India and we would like to thank Thelma Paris and Prakash Thakur for their support in the implementation of the project, Sudhansu Behera and the (late) Sri Raman for the supervision of the survey.

References

CII (Confederation of Indian Industry)/McKinsey (1997) *Modernizing the Indian Food Chain.* New Delhi: Confederation of Indian Industry.

CIP (International Potato Center) (2006) *India, World Potato Atlas.* Available at https://research.cip.cgiar.org/confluence/display/wpa/India.

Das Gupta S, Reardon T, Minten B and Singh S (2010) The transforming potato value chain in India: potato pathways from a commercialized-agriculture zone (Agra) to Delhi. IFPRI-ADB, mimeo.

Delgado CL, Narrod CA and Tiongco M (2008) Determinants and implications of the growing scale of livestock farms in four fast-growing developing countries. Research Report 157. Washington, DC: International Food Policy Research Institute.

Dries L, Germenji E, Noev N and Swinnen J (2009) Farmers, vertical coordination, and the restructuring of dairy supply chains in Central and Eastern Europe. *World Development* 37(11): 1742–1758.

Evenson RE and Gollin D (2003) *Crop Variety Improvement and Its Effect on Productivity: The Impact of International Agricultural Research.* Wallingford, UK: CAB International.

Fuglie KO (1995) Measuring welfare benefits from improvements in storage technology with an application to Tunisian potatoes. *American Journal of Agricultural Economics* 77: 162–173.

Gardner BL (1975) The farm–retail price spread in a competitive food industry. *American Journal of Agricultural Economics* 57(3): 399–409.

Government of Bihar (2006) Bihar: Approach to the 11th Five Year Plan: Vision for Accelerated Inclusive Growth, Planning and Development Department. Patna: Government of Bihar.

Gulati A, Minot N, Delgado C and Bora S (2007) Growth in high-value agriculture in Asia and the emergence of vertical links with farmers. In Swinnen JFM (ed.), *Global Supply Chains, Standards and the Poor.* Oxford: CABI.

Kader AA (2005) Increasing food availability by reducing postharvest losses of fresh produce. *Acta Horticultura* 682: 2169–2175.

Kumar B (2009) *Indian Horticulture Database 2008.* New Delhi: National Horticulture Board.

Kumar R (2010) Bihar, a growth story. Times of India, January 10, 2010. Available at http://articles.timesofindia.indiatimes.com/2010-01-10/special-report/28139867_1_gdp-growth-sq-km-biharis [accessed on 1 June 2012].

Mattoo A, Mishra D and Narain A (2007) *From Competition at Home to Competing Abroad.* Washington, DC: World Bank.

Mittal S (2007) Strengthening backward and forward linkages in horticulture: some successful initiatives. *Agricultural Economics Research Review* 20: 457–469.

Parfitt J, Barthel M and MacNaughton S (2010) Food waste within food supply chains: quantification and potential for change to 2050. *Philosophical Transactions of the Royal Society* 365: 3065–3081.

Patnaik G (2005) Review of Government of India agricultural marketing/processing policies and programs. Mimeo. New Delhi: Global AgriSystems.

Reardon T and Timmer P (2007) Transformation of markets for agricultural output in developing countries since 1950: How has thinking changed? In Evenson RE and Pingali P (eds.), *Handbook of Agricultural Economics,* Vol. 3: *Agricultural Development: Farmers, Farm Production and Farm Markets.* Amsterdam: Elsevier, pp. 2808–2855.

Reardon T, Barrett CB, Berdegué JA and Swinnen JFM (2009) Agrifood industry transformation and small farmers in developing countries. *World Development* 37(11): 1717–1727.

Reardon T, Minten B and Chen K (2012) The Quiet Revolution in Staple Food Value Chains: Enter the Dragon, the Elephant, and the Tiger. Manila: IFPRI/ADB.

Reardon T, Timmer P and Minten B (2012) The supermarket revolution in Asia and emerging development strategies to include small farmers. *Proceedings of the National Academy of Science*, 109(31): 12332–12337.

Spielman DJ and Pandy-Lorch R (2009) *Millions Fed: Proven Successes in Agricultural Development.* Washington DC: IFPRI.

Swinnen J (ed.) (2007) *Global Supply Chains, Standards and the Poor.* Wallingford: CABI.

World Bank (2005) *Bihar: Towards a Development Strategy.* Washington, DC: World Bank.

World Bank (2007a) Bihar agriculture: Building on emerging models of "success." Agriculture and Rural Development Sector Unit, South Asian Region, Discussion Paper Series, Report No. 4, Washington, DC: World Bank.

World Bank (2007b) *World Development Report 2008: Agriculture for Development.* Washington, DC: World Bank.

Printed in the United States
By Bookmasters